Sex-Driven People

Books on Sexual Behavior
by R. E. L. Masters:

THE ANTI SEX
  (*with Eduard Lea*)
THE CRADLE OF EROTICA
  (*with Allen Edwardes*)
EROS AND EVIL
FORBIDDEN SEXUAL BEHAVIOR AND MORALITY
THE HOMOSEXUAL REVOLUTION
PATTERNS OF INCEST
PROSTITUTION AND MORALITY
  (*with Harry Benjamin*)
SEX CRIMES IN HISTORY
  (*with Eduard Lea*)
SEX-DRIVEN PEOPLE
VIOLATION OF TABOO
  (*with Donald Webster Cory*)

Sex-Driven People

An Autobiographical Approach
to the Problem of the
Sex-Dominated Personality

by R. E. L. Masters

Introduction by Allen Edwardes

Sherbourne Press, Inc.
Los Angeles, Calif.

Contents

Sex-Driven People

Introduction

Upon determining to write *The Jewel in the Lotus,** I was em-
boldened by the dearth of modern books on sexual customs
and saw a further challenge in the fact that most of these works
were either scientifically or literally "suggestive." Hence, the
time was ripe for a thoroughgoing treatment of a subject once
deemed too controversial to more than hint at.

When my esteemed friend, R. E. L. Masters, informed me
that *The Jewel in the Lotus* had influenced him to seek publication of his own sexological studies, I was gratified to associate
myself with one who felt as I did that superstition and hypocrisy must at last bow to scientific sensibility in the light of
human experience; thus our collaboration on *The Cradle of
Erotica,*** which remains the most detailed study of Afro-
Asian sexual expression heretofore published.

With rare insight, and with a penetration of wit that
strikes at the heart of truth, Masters has again produced a
unique and in many ways decisive contribution to our better
understanding of human (and animal) sexuality. No field of
erotic activity has been left untrodden, unexplored by him; and
his boldly conscientious scholarship puts to the blush those

* *The Jewel in the Lotus: A Historical Survey of the Sexual
Culture of the East,* New York: Julian Press, 1959.
** New York: Julian Press, 1962.

who think but little and know less. I know of precious few, dedicated to such endeavor, who make as much good sense as does R. E. L. Masters—simply because he has no arbitrary self-interest to serve, no authoritarian axe to grind, in the popular cause of pseudo-science.

Masters has hit upon a choice expression in "sex-driven-ness," or active obsession with erotic release. Such extravagant behavior may appear to be an appeasement of emotional lone-liness, the inability to identify with and gain lasting or mean-ingful satisfaction from one particular sex partner. It may also be an alternative to suicide, the impulse to which often arises out of emotional frustration indirectly connected with physical drives. But perhaps it is partially genetic in some instances, and a psychophysiological imbalance is aggravated by environ-mental influences. The common concept of one being "over-sexed" may therefore be a myth in many cases, as opportunity and inclination are apt to make one extremely potent who is not so otherwise; i.e., his or her ordinarily dormant sexual energy may become activated by a highly stimulating "love object." In any case, generalizations should never be struck. There are those who seek venereal outlets compulsively; yet their potential may be equalled by those who do not, but who become so situated (e.g., in a substantial love relationship) as to give free rein to their dormant or sublimated amorosity.

Masters' motives in revealing the detailed sexual history of a Roman Catholic priest are indeed laudatory; for we must never forget that men of the cloth are also men of flesh, that men of God are endowed with the same psychophysiological functions as other men. Nor is it consistently proper that the "sins" of such special mortals should be the vicious butts of anti-Catholic jokes.

Certainly it has been set forth in most popular periodicals that clergymen *do* have sexual problems, just like the rest of us, but somehow the Pauline (i.e., asexual) mystique still clouds serious thought of ecclesiastic carnality in the minds of countless Catholics. These problems are therefore left to other priests, or perhaps psychiatrists, to solve; which often leaves little hope for salvation on the basis of hieratic or sophistical dogma. Any unrealistic or arbitrary approach to sexuality in general, and therefore in particular, is bound to generate and feed those guilt and persecution complexes which make the inherent conflict of life more unendurable, thus producing such self-tormented souls as were the Christian martyrs of antiquity.

Susceptibility to "temptation," and therefore to compulsiveness, may stem from those mental complications aroused by the unconditional enforcement of certain taboos in one's early development. Such as are not exposed to such irrational prohibitions may not become slaves to temptation, blown about by every gust of impulse. Emotional discipline and stability being best instilled by force of Reason, which may be determined by weighing and gauging the sum total of human experience (i.e., objective–subjective truth), it stands to such reason that we should be happier and healthier to accept and enact our natural instincts without having to be whipped and spurred by the Serpent of Evil, whose venom is anxiety and whose hiss is the artificiality of all unreasoned existence. But the travesty is as old as the instructive fable of forbidden fruit in the garden of innocence, giving rise to the priest's attitude (*re* his erotic urge) of "Needs must when the Devil drives!"

One momentous point in the priest's testimony is his confession that, by the innocence of "uninformed" youth, he never questioned the "naturalness" of his homosexual activity—that it seemed quite normal to use anus rather than cunnus—a truly Oriental attitude; which opens the much-debated argument of "polysexuality."

Despite the apparent reproductive instinct native to all creatures—an instinct whose creative impulses may be expressed (i.e., "sublimated") in many nonsexual manners, as in the processes of art and platonic love—does homoeroticism (and other forms of "deviation") have a genetic basis, or is it merely an acquired phenomenon? It may be either or both, depending upon the individual! Certain theorists are almost fanatic in their denial of man's polysexual capacity, but the voice of practical experience cries them down. Perhaps they protest too much, to allay fears of their own potential—a potential, not in keeping with pet dogma, that has rarely known free expression in the so-called "democratic" West. And as Sir

Richard Burton wisely advised, one ought to "make the experiment" before offering an opinion upon a sexual subject—and even then, only as a matter of personal taste. This is, after all, the very essence of "truth," which is predominantly a purely personal matter. Therefore, we need only concern ourselves with the destructive or "antisocial" (uncivilized) aspects of deviant behavior, their origins and aspects and antidotes.

St. Paul's condemnation of homosexuality, a thorn in every "gay" Catholic's side, is an obvious throwback to the old utilitarian Yahvist-Mosaic injunction to increase and multiply —for the greater glory (i.e., numerical strength) of Church and State.

Self-admittedly, here is a man unhappy as a priest but happy doing priestly work; which says little for a society that will not allow the likes of Jesus to walk in its midst without fear of institutionalized tyrants telling him how to be charitable.

Masters notes the overconcern, even obsession, of homophiles with phallic proportions; and others have observed that those who are most enamored of large penises, and delight in damning small ones, are not so lavishly endowed themselves. This is not to be wondered at, since we often condemn in others those psychophysiological shortcomings that muddy the waters of self-image.

The sooner this nonsense about genital size is made amenable to reason, the better many a psyche will be for it. It is a form of depersonalization, reducing the individual to a walking phallus; and the promiscuous attitude and activities of exclusive homosexuals, who view each other in terms of penis rather than personality, is tragicomic if man is ever to become reasonably civilized through mutual empathy. (In a heterosexual sense, the male who views the female almost exclusively in terms of breasts, buttocks, and genitalia—who is emotionally riveted to some faddish physical image, unable or unwilling to appreciate those more meaningful aspects of character and the quality of "inner beauty"—often comes to a rude awakening when he himself is accepted or rejected on grounds of arbitrary objectivity!)

In the case (here presented) of the woman who acts out her sexual life in imagination, we are reminded of the curious fact that anticipation of an erotic act and the concomitant phantasies are often more potent and satisfying than performance itself. Indeed, without compulsion, but with empathetic feelings for one's partner, the sex act can be very rewarding psychically, perhaps resulting in stronger and more relaxing sensations.

In the case of nymphophilia and incest, it is noted that the subject was not behaviorally reoriented but was released from guilt in relation to his propensities as a result of psychiatric treatment. But release of guilt can only be achieved through some form of sophistry or rationalization which may be inconsistent with the so-called reality of circumstances. It is well that psychotherapy should help us to deal with or accept the conflicts inherent in all existence, but not with such a weapon as *Lust-ohne-Schuld* (pleasure without responsibility, license to lust). And it seems the height of presumption that "science" should claim to eliminate all inner conflict, thus reducing us to the level of idiots. Perhaps our "depressions" are merely cooling-off periods, a regeneration of exhausted psychic energy, and if we view them as a mental clearing of the air, in relation to nature's storms and lulls, we may take heart to bear with them and await the sun to break through those depressing clouds.

What is most typically striking is the nymphophile's "object" compulsion—that the age and type of "nymphet" are preeminently important to his libido—hence his lack of reasonable compassion. Though he would like a meaningful long-term relationship—the common urge for a settled and secure emotional life—he is incapable of it. And so he becomes objective rather than subjective in his interpersonal affairs.

It would seem that the nymphophile's desire for his adult daughter proves that he grew to view her as a whole being, not just a sex object—a stereotype nymphet. His need for her then becomes self-defeating, since she is unable or unwilling to respond; hence the tragedy of contradictory personalities.

In his rationalization of incest, the nymphophile bases his behavior on the premise that paternal initiation under favorable conditions is not likely to prove so traumatic to one's virgin daughter as defloration by another hand. But he fails to take into account the emotional (i.e., asexual) aspects of such a relationship; being a sex-driven person, he cannot conceive of a platonic or psychic love life. He reduces all to an incestuous *jus-primae-noctis* (right-of-the-first-night) level, which is selfishly primitive in the extreme. His eventual rejection of each nymphet, once the desired age or aspects are past, is indicative of irrational thinking and a lack of that very empathy he boasts of having.

Many little girls, especially the precocious ones, are indeed demonstrative in their affections; but to reason (like the Arabs) that this is an erotic approach, or that they desire amorous exercise, is wishful thinking. One can certainly lead them in such a direction, but one must be predisposed so to lead.

What appears to be the height of hypocrisy, but is in fact a mere part of an overall inconsistency of thought and behavior, is that though the nymphophile is freely nymphophilic with his own daughters, he cannot conceive of allowing another man to touch them, or of other parents being so permissive with or exploitative of their offspring—though he wishes he knew of some who were! So his drives (impulses) overset his reason.

Masters' case histories of zoophilia are unparalleled in sexological literature, considering that precious little has been written on this bizarre subject. The demonstrated willingness of animals to receive human approaches is noteworthy, serving to prove the forethoughtfulness of Moses in forbidding the mixing of beasts for fear that man might be so tempted. And the comment of one correspondent, that animal contacts make men out of boys, is an old Arab idea; for Moroccan lads are encouraged to mount donkeys, to make their members grow.

What is noble if not praiseworthy of the zooerast, as in the nymphophilic case, is that he never forces an animal; that his greatest pleasure lies in the beast's willingness and receptivity, which he of course may help provoke by means of suitable injections and suchlike expedients.

The apparent tragedy of the homoerotically oriented zoophile is that though he once seemed capable of sustaining a relationship with one woman, all such relationships ended in his disfavor, driving him into that loneliness and despair which were spurs to obsessive deviation.

In addition to what Masters says about a new race of hybrids throwing jurists and clergymen into confusion, what dire effects must such a creation have upon psychology and psychiatry!

Since the matter is mentioned in this book, one cannot help but comment on how the circumcision mania dominates homosexual predilections—as indeed the desires of many females, who refuse to marry uncircumcised males simply because they are now branded as potential cancer producers. This irrational obsession, doubtless rooted in man's sexual guilt and explained away in pseudo-scientific terms of "hygiene," has taken the "civilized" world by storm in a manner once worthy of primitive cultures; and those who wish to gain some insight into how far this circumcisiomania may develop should consult my forthcoming book, *The Rape of India.**

The abysmal loneliness and struggle for identity of the transsexualist is truly moving, and her very testimony makes it maddening to think that we are ruled by knaves and fools who will not tolerate or assist such individuals in their quest for a place in the sun. The extraordinary history of this tortured soul should be read and reread by every thinking man and woman in America—the better that they may understand the workings of their own psyche and of the male–female relationship, its improvement and perfection.

Masters rightly observes that a pattern of promiscuity *before* a sex-change operation is likely to diminish or disappear *after*, because the subject assumes a more positive self-image and is no longer obsessed with the expending of erotic energy. It often happens that promiscuous people have a poor opinion of themselves, physically and/or intellectually, and therefore cannot sublimate raw erotic energy as creative individuals.

The social acceptance of "perverts" in Eastern countries, as contrasted with the "democratic" West, is worthy of note, as is the recent adoption (for politico–economic motives) of psy-

* A Biography of Robert Clive and A Sexual History of the Conquest of Hindustan. New York: Julian Press, 1966.

choanalytically oriented moral codes (a scientized Judeo–Christian ethos) by certain Orientals, who must now appear ludicrous in the light of their age-old liberal attitude of "no accounting for taste."

The childlike attitude of the Syrian transvestite-homosexual is characteristically Arabesque, unburdened by Judeo–Christian dogma, and therefore all the more impressive and even startling. He does not question or judge his activities in the typical manner of Occidental deviates, for the patterns of his culture and faith have been those of acceptance rather than rejection. What is most distressing about reading Western case histories is the repetition of recited guilt, shame, religiosity, contemporary community standards, etc. It sounds hypocritical, but sadly enough it isn't; for the brainwashing one suffers in early youth is extremely onerous to reason out of one's intellect in adulthood. Certain ravages almost always remain in the form of noticeable scars.

Loneliness, emotional desperation, feelings of inferiority and persecution: such phenomena do strange things to our powers of reason and can reduce many of us to sex-driven people. The sex-driven person may think that his or her body is the one identifying and identifiable asset, offering a *raison d'être,* as one seemingly rational and intelligent female informed me: "I can't be accepted merely for my intellect; my body is more important to me." However, a pattern of promiscuity had been established simply because she felt that men only wanted her for her body—that such was all she had to offer—and now that she was striving to develop intellect, the thought of sharing it in a sex–love relationship was alien to her old manner of being.

In presenting and commenting upon these cases, R. E. L. Masters is offering an inestimable service to humanity; and we trust that he will continue his pursuit of justice and common sense, so long as free and responsible men and women may express their thoughts without fear and without penalty.

Allen Edwardes
Kansas City, Missouri
APRIL, 1966

The Premise of Sex-Drivenness

The cases (autobiographies) to be presented in this volume are among the most unusual and interesting that I have encountered in more than two decades of research into the many and curious anomalies of human behavior, including the sexual. Even as recently as several years ago, it would not have been possible to publish documents so thoroughly detailed and otherwise revealing as the ones to be offered in these pages. But now, with so many old barriers swept away, it is possible to speak about sex with a freedom that has not been equalled in the Western World in almost two centuries. This situation is not, I think, without its dangers; and whether the results will be mainly good or bad remains to be seen. Meanwhile, the opportunity *is* present to make available for the first time accounts of human sexual behavior which make plain what formerly was only hinted at and, by so doing, enlarge and deepen the dimensions of our understanding. The cases in this book cannot fail, I believe, to increase our understanding of some of the crass realities of sex. A picture may be worth ten thousand words, and these autobiographies, I am convinced, tell us more about certain aspects of existence than have scores of volumes purporting to deal with similar materials but retreating, instead, into jargon and pallid evasion.

In selecting the various autobiographical statements to be included in this book—and for which I am indebted to authors who, for obvious reasons, must remain anonymous—I have chosen, as a unifying theme, the notion of sex-drivenness. And the sex-driven person is defined as one for whom the gratification of his or her sexual desires is a need that is not to be denied—and a value which, by the criterion of behavior, often proves itself transcendent to all others. As preliminary illustrations of what is meant by sex-drivenness we here might examine two rather brief statements from two very different, but equally sex-driven, individuals. The first is a homosexual priest, who wrote to me:

"Allow me to introduce myself. I am the Reverend Father Howard Barton, an assistant pastor at ——— Church here in New Orleans.* I was ordained on January 16, 1951, and since that time I have been a member of the ——— Order, and am presently in the Diocese of New Orleans. If after three years, the Bishop is pleased with me, he will incardinate me into the Diocese. Otherwise, I must return back to the ——— (name of his Order).

"Last night I read, at a single sitting (!), your book, *The Homosexual Revolution*. Maybe I shouldn't be writing to you, but I am—possibly so that others in similar trouble can learn of my case (and trusting that you will find a way to guarantee protecting my good name).

"You see, I am in deep crisis. However, it is only one of a long series of crises I have had in almost fourteen years of priesthood. Things only get worse instead of better, despite all my efforts. I will try to be as honest as you were in your book, although it is difficult to write down such painful facts. I am a homosexual priest. I am forty-three years old. I have had terrible difficulty in my priesthood—from my tendencies, but also from the priests I live with. Once, I would have placed the blame upon the latter. But now I believe that the real basic source of all my difficulties is unending sex frustration. Yet, I

* In this volume all names, places, and other items which might serve to identify the writer have, of course, been altered. However, I have tried to make all essential changes in such a way that the significant facts of the case remain accessible to the reader.

realize, perhaps more than you do since religion is my vocation, at least temporarily, that homosexuality is a sin against the Sixth Commandment of God (which you failed to mention in your book—also St. Paul's denunciation of it in his First Chapter to the Romans, although you do mention St. Paul, for which I was happy.)

"My dilemma is this: I love doing priestly work, but have never been able to adjust myself to avoid the difficulties with my fellow priests, particularly, and above all those in authority, those who can make me feel the sting of the whip, and my great desire to love and be loved has never found a realization in the holy priesthood. My difficulties became so great that I left the priesthood at one point last year, but I returned a week later after receiving all sorts of promises from the Provincial.* After I came back, he applied the full rigor of the law.

"I can only beg your pardon and indulgence if I seem to meander in this presentation of my story. It is, undoubtedly, of the greatest difficulty to write a letter of this kind, and things just will not 'flow.' But I had my first homosexual experience at the age of six years with the 'gang'—a neighborhood group of boys ages fourteen down to six. Although 'it never affected me,' I assuredly never forgot it. When I was thirteen, someone perhaps around eighteen years old approached me in a movie theater, which I attended alone, and asked if I would let him 'play' with me. I consented. Just before or after this, I cannot remember for sure, I was introduced into the facts of life by the gang—in the form of exhibitionism. That definitely led me on to masturbation and to a 'natural' desire which I attempted to put into practice and sometimes succeeded with— the touching of other boys of the gang on their genitals and especially putting the penis into the 'rear.' It would appear that I always thought of this as being most natural; it really never did occur to me that 'it would be better' to put it into a vagina.

"From the eighth grade on (I was at the time fourteen

* Member of a religious order presiding over his order in a particular district or province. Among other things he handles matters of discipline.

years of age), I was 'satisfied' with masturbation, but always in a more violent form than any to be considered within the range of the normal. I masturbated throughout high school. However, I did not do so excessively in terms of the frequency of the act. Not long after finishing high school I became engaged to a girl with whom I had been having dates. But a few months later I broke off the engagement, on the advice of a priest who told me that I had a vocation for the priesthood. Having decided to be a priest, I gave up masturbating without any difficulty.

"Shortly after being introduced to the (homosexual) facts of life, I got a number of very weird dreams—particularly as to the size of my penis, so that sometimes it went even to the length of a vine! I began to straddle the bathtub. Somehow, I became convinced (and for over twenty-five years remained so) that by doing this straddling I had made my penis 'go back in' (retract into the lower abdomen). I had at least a six-incher at the time, but, to my mind, by reason of such rough play with myself, I 'induced' it to 'go back in' me and then it was hardly more than 'mere skin.'* That has been a great, great cross of my life. Yet, despite this cross, or perhaps because of it, I became a priest. I had no difficulty refraining from masturbation during my seminary days, nor during the first year of my priesthood. Then, fourteen or fifteen months after my ordination, I

* This disturbance of the body image with the penis being thought of and even perceived by the senses as smaller than it actually is, I have encountered repeatedly among homosexuals. Sometimes the 'abnormally small' penis then is advanced as a justification for the homosexual practices, the individual stating that because of his genital inadequacy, he would be ashamed to try to have relations with a girl. Most often, as with this priest, the person does not actually perceive (visually and by touch) his penis as small, but has an idea of it as being small—and, at the same time, he may rationally know that his penis is not small. However, although it may be a 'six-incher' when he measures it, still he clings to his feeling, which can generate considerable emotion, that the organ is small. Hypnosis and psychedelic drugs, such as LSD and mescaline, can be extremely effective in giving such persons a realistic body image, which can have the further effect of eliminating the homosexual behavior by giving a capacity for heterosexual intercourse.

went to a Boys' Club where they swam in the nude, and like an atomic explosion my inferiority feelings about the size of my penis erupted, and I have never been the same since.

"I began once again to masturbate and this practice I have never ceased since. And always, I have done it with a definite 'touch' of sadism. In other words, 'ordinary' masturbation was not enough for me. I cannot bring myself to tell about this and will have to leave the rest to your imagination.

"Several years ago, I am sorry to say, a young man of twenty-one years came to see me for advice. He had been a 'professional' homosexual (male prostitute) since the age of fourteen. Telling me of the many details of his life, he got me all excited, with a raging fire in my bosom. It resulted in at least twelve homosexual acts, with every kind of activity involved, if you understand what I mean.

"I was later sent to Cleveland and there the superior was hard on me, but only five per cent so hard as the Provincial had been before him. The Provincial had claimed that I was harming the priesthood and souls, etc., etc., etc. Finally, I requested laicization.* He refused me this. After quite a few weeks, with nothing to do, because the superior would give me nothing to do, I called the Provincial and asked him please, please to take some action, that I could not stand it any longer. So I got sent out to Denver. There I attempted to make 'contact' (with homosexuals) but never succeeded, mostly because of the hour when I had to return back to the rectory. From Denver, I was sent to still another place, to replace a priest who had gotten into some difficulty and had to be removed. I wrote to several Bishops to accept me, but none did. So I just left. I was taken in by a male hustler in Philadelphia, even though I was miserably poor and without any kind of job. I note in your book a listing of organizations ready to help a homosexual find a job. Thanks. My brothers and sisters would not help too much. I just couldn't go on. So they promised me a fare back to Cleveland. I returned. I returned by way of Columbus, Ohio, where I visited with a college buddy of mine who was always the picture of a devout, even perhaps fanatic,

* That is, to no longer be a clergyman.

Catholic. And I discovered to my total amazement that he was a 'gay' (homosexual) person! A meeting was arranged with the Provincial and he talked me into returning. How I was tormented for months afterward! When I had experienced his kind of mercy, I wrote to the Bishop and was accepted for a three-year trial in the New Orleans Diocese.

"But my present pastor, an Italian-born priest, is most difficult to live with. In fact, and indeed, he ordered me to leave the priesthood only this night before last. It was an incredible, nightmarish scene, to say the very least. He wanted me OUT that very night! I bawled and cried and pleaded and called upon God's name. After fifteen or more minutes of what was for me the most excruciating agony, I must have been able to touch his heart. He sobered up in an instant and his wrath was gone. Now he has been away for a day and I have talked to my priest friends about it. (Although my pastor told me that the priests in New Orleans do not want me around. That really HURTS. They, of course, deny it.) I talked on the telephone long distance with another priest friend of mine and he talked me out of laicizing, although it was all but certain that I would quickly take that step. In a few quick strokes, that brings me up to the present.

"Is there no one who can advise me what to do while giving me advice I can accept? I am unhappy as a priest, although I *am* happy doing priestly work. I am perhaps above average in piety, even though full of so many 'gay' desires.* (Indeed, the flesh wars against the spirit!) My own personal belief is that I should laicize, which would mean becoming a layman with the right to attend Mass and to receive all the Sacraments, though with no right to marry. In your book you mention many of the difficulties and unpleasant things of the 'gay' life. Mine could not be any worse than it is now, and I mean including the loneliness. I went swimming at the YMCA this past Tuesday and swam alone for a whole forty-five minutes.

* The inappropriateness of the term "gay," as a synonym for homosexual, has been frequently pointed out to me by homosexuals. In the present case, we have an example well calculated to make the point.

"If only someone could supply a proper explanation of St. Paul's condemnation of homosexuality in Romans, Chapter One! That, in my opinion, is the knife in every 'gay' person's back.

"I am far from being financially well off. Please believe that! After all, as a Religious priest, I was not allowed to keep a penny ! ! ! I face the prospect of grave financial woes, should I decide on leaving the priesthood. I hear there are 'many' priests, who have left the priesthood, and live as homosexuals, in New Orleans. But although I have heard of this I have never been able to confirm the fact.

"Again, I am at such a loss to try to decide what God would have me do? I do not have any aversion to being homosexual. I am not ashamed of being 'gay,' believe it or not. But, ultimately, my concern is to do the will of God. Can I ever reconcile that with the 'gay' life? Am I only deceiving myself? Would I die in poverty and abandonment? Am I simply reaching for the stars, for the impossible? Am I asking God to condemn me to hell?

"May God's mercy touch your heart and urge you to answer me. You can do it in just a few lines if you have time for no more—that is, simply yes or no. May God inspire you to say the right thing to me.

<blockquote>
"Hopefully, a homosexual priest,
in Christ our Lord,
(*Rev.*) *Howard Barton*"
</blockquote>

In a subsequent letter, in which he announced that he had definitely decided to laicize, this unhappy priest commented again upon his feeling of sex-drivenness—here, a largely situational sex-drivenness since, as a priest, he could not legitimately appease his desires in any way. It is doubtful, in this case, that there is any abnormally powerful libido; but *some* satisfaction is required and, also, and perhaps more importantly, some emotional relationship with a sexual component. Had it not been for his religious "calling," this individual might possibly have lived out his life as a homosexual without his homosexuality coming to so dominate his life. He writes:

"I do not propose to leave the Church in order to obtain the satisfactions of the 'gay' life, but because I feel the great need for relief—my body craves for sexual release to the extent that it is almost beyond all control. To my mind, considering all I have read and heard—and that has been plenty, needless to say—there is really no answer for this kind of problem short of fulfilling the craving.

"All too many psychiatrists contradict themselves again and again. Perhaps, the average reader will be able to swallow their line; but I do not, and neither do those whose attention I call to their statements.

"I am hanging on by a thread. This is perhaps my worst day yet. For at least two weeks all matters are going from bad to worse. But I will hang on until laicization if it kills me. If it does, then perhaps you can call me a saint! God's ways are not our ways!

"No one I have ever been able to talk to can really solve this problem of homosexuality or even explain it. For this reason I can only rely and trust in the mercy of God.

"It is strange to say, yet I repeat that I accept myself for what I am, and moreover, I am glad I am such. If God made me homosexual, either directly or indirectly, why should I condemn myself? I can't see it. It may be I accept myself for what I am far too easily. My personal impression is that I'll be the 'gayest of the gay,' a breath of fresh air for them (the homosexuals). Yet I sense that God has a 'secret' mission for me among them. But that may be nothing but wishful thinking, a way of justifying my intention to sin boldly and recklessly yet not without regard for civil law. I am making myself clear, I do hope.

"If God wants to take me to eternity now, then He may. He is the boss. The pottery cannot say to the potter—Oh, why did you make me thus?

"So I hope that I will leave the priesthood with honor instead of with disgrace. This is most important to me, since then I will be able to live with myself. I enclose for you, finally, my letter to the Holy Father in Rome, which I think you may find to have some interest."

In this letter, to Pope Paul VI, he recounts his losing day-to-day battle with his homosexual desires, expresses the fear that he will bring disgrace on the priesthood, and asks for laicization—noting that he is aware that if this is granted he will continue to be bound by his vow of celibacy!

There are, of course, many ways in which sex can dominate the life of an individual, make existence a torment, and lead to self-destructive patterns of behavior. The following case is that of a woman who, in her early thirties, still has never had sexual intercourse, although she wants nothing more. (Or says that she wants nothing more.) However, she masturbates "three to ten times a day," employing elaborate masturbation phantasies and, more recently, letters and photographs she receives from persons with whom she corresponds "from the safety" of a post office box she has rented under an assumed name. She states (and I condense her statement):

"As you can see from what I already have told you about my secret sex life, I am not exactly a sexually indifferent person or one who is aware of being opposed to sex in any way. I have been had in every way possible, but only in my own imagination. The problem, as I explained, is that I am not able to enter into intimate relationship with any other person. Lord knows I have tried, and with women as well as with men, so evidently I am not a lesbian either. I simply freeze up completely whenever anyone touches me or seems ready to do it, and in such a situation I am terrified that at any instant I will start shaking all over and become hysterical. I have had enough such experiences to convince me that my response is not going to change. Apart from this, I am not a cold person and get along well with my friends and business associates. I have a pretty good social life, with girl friends, although I often do not have the time since, odd to relate, I seem to have to give more time to my imaginary sex life than they have to give to their real ones.

"Because I am the way I am, I have had to live sexually inside of my own imagination for most of my life. While I have been lonely sometimes, I managed rather early in my life to reconcile myself more or less to the fact that marriage and love just would never be possible for me. I learned to satisfy my strong desires by masturbating and except in the beginning have not felt guilty about that practice. But now, since I gave in to my impulse to correspond with these people who put sex ads in the weekly newspapers, I am in a nervous and depressed state of mind a lot of the time. I am feeling guilty and kind of dirty all over, but that is not the worst of it. Even though I have covered my tracks very well, taking the post office box under a fictitious name and in a city some miles from here, I know that I am running the risk of being arrested and exposed for writing as I do, and also of being blackmailed should one of these characters I write to manage to find out who I am. I have enough income to make blackmail tempting, and I tell you with complete sincerity that if my letters ever become known to my family and friends I would have no choice but to kill myself, since I would be totally shamed and dishonored. That would be no good solution either, since the hell my parents would undergo because of the obscene letters would just be made worse by my death.

"Why, then, don't I stop writing these letters? I find I just can't! Please don't believe I haven't tried! This correspondence is a disease, and I need no psychiatrist to tell me that. But please don't, as I am sure you will want to do, recommend I have psychotherapy. I could no more submit to psychotherapy than I could submit to someone sexually, however much I might sometimes want to do both. I try to stop writing these sexy letters, and I do stop it for a few weeks, but then I can't resist starting up all over again. The problem is that, with these letters, I can, in a way, have sexual relations with another person. It is the closest thing to a fulfilling sexual relationship I have ever known, and that is a satisfaction beyond my power to relinquish at this time.

"I am giving you numerous letters (copies) I have written and received, and also photographs, drawings, stories, etc. Sometimes I wonder if the people who run these ads, and who exchange all these things, ever really get together and do all they talk about? Or are they writers only, vicarious livers, like myself? But I am sure they do get together and do things, and that means to me that some of them are capable of destroying my life just for their own amusement or sexual kicks. Believe me, I would like more than anything to be able to have normal and even fairly experimental sex, but some of the things in these letters, even some of the things in some of my own letters, are things I think I'd rather die than actually do. My imagination may be thoroughly depraved, and I suppose I would have to say it is, but I still feel that imagining and doing are far from being one and the same thing, although the *Bible* says that to sin in the imagination is as bad as to sin in the flesh.

"I can never go to sleep without masturbating at least once, and I also often have to masturbate before I can go off to work, go out to a party, or receive company, because not only does this give me much pleasure, it frees me from nervous tension that builds up when I don't do it. (I also can get rid of almost any ache or pain in this way.) I definitely would not want to be deprived of this (masturbatory) pleasure, which is the only sexual pleasure I am able to have. But I do wish I had never, never become involved with these letters and been turned into a compulsive sex correspondent, or whatever you want to call me. Now all pleasure I get from my imaginings is very second-rate as compared to the pleasure I get from imagining I am doing the things people write to me about, and doing those things with *them,* with *real people,* not just with the people conjured up by my own mind.

"I would think I am a serious mental case, but I do get along quite well, except for my sex life, which so far has never hurt anybody. I know most of the scientific sex terms, from my reading, and would like you to use them in discussing this problem with me. Maybe then I will not use our discussion as just more fodder for mental sex, and I would rather not do that in this relationship."

The letters supplied to me by this woman, both those written by her and those she has received, are not much different from a great deal of similar correspondence I have seen, and which has been exchanged by other total strangers who have made contact through advertisements. A specimen or two of these letters will be well worth reproducing. In reading them, it should be remembered that what she writes about her own activities is pure fabrication. In answering the ad of one man "who sounded as if he would be able to write a very sexy reply," she began the correspondence as follows:

"Dear 'Sophisticated Linguist',

"Somehow your ad has really gotten to me. I haven't ever answered one of these before, but my boyfriend got a copy of the paper and has been trying to talk me into meeting with another couple . . . but somehow your ad sounds like more what I need.

"It's funny, with him and with my other dates, I am extremely proper—not prudish, but proper—and almost never use an improper word. But your ad . . . WOW! Somehow when you mentioned exotic pleasures . . . I just flipped! Have you ever felt that you wanted to be just as sexy as possible, and talk real dirty and filthy? I guess this is my only sex problem, that I just can't let myself go all the way in speaking with the guys I go with. Even now, though I'm going to do it, my tummy is just doing flips at the thought of what I am going to say . . . but you did say you would do whatever a silly gal wanted to do, didn't you?

"My most secret kick is that I love to think about talking sex with a man. (But, damn it, I almost always act cold and reserved and can't do it.) Can I say these things to you? I just love to *fuck* . . . and the most wonderful thing is to have a man go down on me and lick my tits . . . and then my belly . . . and my thighs till he comes to the cunt hair and then to feel his tongue licking and sucking all over my naked cunt. It doesn't take but a minute till I want his . . . your . . . prick too in my mouth. I do that, and love it, with my boyfriend, but it's funny I still can't talk to him like this. If we do get together will you promise me you will use all the words? I am embarrassed about it, but still I want it. The hottest I have ever been was when a boyfriend I had two years ago kept telling me while he was kissing my tits that my tits made him hot. He'd kiss and suck my cunt and while he was doing that I'd play with his balls and suck his prick, but again the thing that really got me hot was his talking about how my mouth and tongue felt on his prick and how my cunt felt in his mouth. He would always whisper to me about how my cunt felt around his prick while he was fucking me, and again that was better than the fuck itself. Now tell me honestly, do you think I'm nuts?

"Despite the way I have been talking, I'm afraid I am not too experienced . . . will you teach a willing beginner a little bit, or a lot? You said you were an expert at French and on that I *do* know what I like and just where I want your tongue and lips. But I think you can probably teach me a lot, even when it comes to frenching. I only have done it with three men, and only went the whole way with my present boyfriend. But I do like it . . . here I go again . . . I want to find out if the come from your balls tastes the same as his does. I hope you meant what you said . . . that you'd do anything at all to please a gal. I couldn't talk like this except for the fact that right now I don't know you. I'll probably drop dead when I meet you face to face . . . but please *promise* . . . talk the same way to me the minute we first meet . . . talk about cunt and prick and fucking and cocksucking and cuntlapping . . . and don't let me be cold and reserved like I usually am. God, if my boy-friend could read this, he'd drop dead! Isn't that funny?

"I've put my address in . . . please don't fail to write to me. If you write a good letter, next time I'll be more daring and send you a photo of my cunt . . . I'll do that IF you send me one of your prick . . . real naked and *hard,* please?

"P.S. I get to Topeka at regular intervals, so the question of your having to travel isn't involved. And don't worry, I'll be sure to make my trip at the right time of the month ! ! ! I'll let you know a few days before I come, so that you can save up your strength for me. Not that I'm greedy, or not much. I just want you to have the time of your life, and so write to the gal who is prepared to give it to you."

The response to this letter was an expression of interest in a meeting and a willingness to "try out anything and everything." However, the writer was cautious with his language, mentioned that he wanted to take no chances on getting into trouble with the postal authorities, and begged the lady's pardon for not being as outspoken as he surmised she would like him to be. He said he would make up for that when they met. Meanwhile, he was sending a (clothed) photograph, and he hoped she would send him the photo she had mentioned, "also one of all of you."

To receive so restrained a letter was, of course, disappointing. Therefore, as was usually done in such cases, another effort was made to elicit a response that would provide adequate material for masturbation phantasies. As this woman put it, she "dangled a carrot in front of his nose" in the form of some additional promises, but with the condition that he first write her a more candid letter. She also sent him a "teasing" photo (very vague and with face unrecognizable) of herself in the nude. These Polaroid photos, which she took of herself, ranged from the sharply contrasted to the intentionally overexposed and were of the entire body, the genital area only, etc. When sending a clear photo including the upper body, she always cut out the face to prevent recognition. Her second letter, to this same correspondent, follows:

"Ted dearest,

"I was so thrilled when your letter came today and so excited and trembling that I could hardly open the letter.

"And I am pleased that you do want to meet me and indulge all my desires. But I am so disappointed that your letter was so cold and formal and that you didn't enclose the kind of snapshot I asked you to (although the one you did send was nice, and you are very good looking.) I know you will understand that before meeting you I would like to know just a bit more about you, especially about your likes and dislikes in the matter we have under discussion. I'm afraid I was *quite* frank about mine in my last letter! As I'm sure you guessed, I am not too experienced at this type of meeting and I was hoping that in addition to the things I suggested that I like, that you might suggest some things that you like or that you have learned from the other girls you have met through your ad.

"I feel rather funny now about writing very frankly to you after the coolness of your letter, but I guess I can understand your feeling that the letter I wrote was not really from me. Now that you do know I'm real, can I expect more frankness from you and the kind of talk that I mentioned gave me such a wonderful, unforgettable thrill?

"I would love to hear of the experiences you have had with the other girls you have met through your ad. Particularly, if some of them are a bit out of the ordinary . . . I'm eager to learn all about how to experience new thrills. I hope you have had lots of experience and have met and have fucked lots of different women. Won't you please tell me all about them and about all the details while you have the prick in me that you had in them?

"I do so hope that you have a large prick. I had hopes that you would enclose a snap that would show you all naked and *ready to go!*

"I would love to meet you this weekend, but I am just about due for my period and from the way I am feeling today . . . kind of headachy and funny . . . I would guess that it will probably start tomorrow, which would make it rather bad this weekend for what I want you to do to me. Would Saturday the twenty-third be okay? You didn't say, but the schedule you mention arranging . . . was that business? . . . or the schedule of all the many women you're fucking? ! ! ! I don't blame you one bit . . . there is no point in saving it . . . and somehow it just makes you more desirable to me when I know you are getting it with a lot of other women. Nothing like a bit of variety, and I feel the same way too.

"On the subject of variety, I would rather spend our first night together with just you and me, and maybe something nice to drink, but not too much of that . . . but if we satisfy each other and you would like me to stay over another day, I do have another little wish that you might like to indulge me in . . . something I didn't mention in my last letter but that I would like to try if it turns out that you don't object. I have never had the experience of having more than one man make love to me at the same time and of having two or three men fuck me one right after the other. Do you think maybe you would like to try that? Do you have one or two friends that you think might like to oblige?

"Have never done it the other way around either, sharing a man with another woman. Would you enjoy having two of us make love to you at the same time? Do you know another gal with a liking for variety that you think might want to try it? I have had only one experience, some years ago, with another girl, and I don't really have any strong lesbian tendencies . . . but I think in a threesome like that, that I might be tempted to participate with the other girl as well as with you to see what it would be like. Are you by this time kind of getting the idea that I'd like to try almost anything once?

"As a tease I have put in a faded full-length snapshot of me . . . and if you look hard enough you can see just the hint of my pussy. I promise much better ones IF I get a little (no, I mean *a lot!*) warmer letter from you and some sexy pictures in return. In fact, if I don't get something like that from you . . . a letter as candid as mine . . . and a photo of that big, hard prick of yours . . . I don't know if I'd feel able to come down and have that meeting with you. And I *do* want to have the meeting and do all of the things I've talked about!

"So write to me as frankly as I've written to you, and send me some nice photos. I'd love to see one of you with one of the other gals you've laid . . . maybe the one who will be with us when I see you . . . or how about one of you frenching? I'll be waiting anxiously to hear from you."

On the basis of correspondence such as this, which resulted in numerous responses in kind, this woman has been able to pursue an imaginary sex life rivalling in its extravagant abundance that of Messalina—while remaining physically a virgin. However, as she has made very clear, these activities yield much misery along with the pleasure and she feels that she is behaving compulsively— is a sex-driven person.

It is this feeling of *having to act* sexually in a way that conflicts with one's values, or that otherwise is opposed to one's best interests, that serves to identify in most instances the sex-driven individual. In what seem to be much less numerous cases, where neither the conflict of values nor the self-damage is admitted or perhaps even recognized by the person, it still may be possible to speak of sex-drivenness. But then we have to base the judgment upon factors exclusive of the person's own feelings, and upon those criteria which *we* accept—for example, whether the individual's conduct seems to us to be self-damaging, or whether his life, in terms of alleged norms, is so dominated by sex that he must be considered sex-driven even though he may see himself as a perfectly free agent and his conduct as altogether justified.

These are the kinds of sex-driven people—the self-diagnosed and the "obviously" sex-dominated—who will tell their own stories in the much more detailed and extensive autobiographical narratives to follow. Often their extremely intense values conflicts, and the rationalizations advanced to justify their conduct, will be just as interesting and instructive as is the unusual sex behavior they so candidly describe.

Whether sex-drivenness as exemplified here, with what seem to be its varying degrees of compulsiveness, can absolve the person of all responsibility, or of moral and legal responsibility in particular, are questions with which philosophy, psychology, and law, especially, are concerned. The present book does not attempt to answer such basic questions—ultimately, perhaps, an inquiry into the fundamental scientific and metaphysical issues of human freedom and responsibility—the purpose here is much less ambitious or grandiose. It is simply to provide some detailed first-person accounts and illustrations of sex-drivenness in a few of its myriad forms. At the same time, this book will exemplify, to an unusual and possibly unique extent, several of the sexual practices and aberrations of mankind.

In presenting the various autobiographies, I will provide some brief introductory remarks and then, at the conclusion of each case (or pair of cases), will offer more extended discussions of the behaviors involved. These may include something of the history, anthropology, and manifestations in our own and some similar societies today. I will also deal, as briefly as possible, with some of the prevailing psychological theories and conclusions—although most of these seem to me to say more about the psychologists and other investigators than they do about the behavior presumably being explained and described. Sexological psychology, after all, is not yet a science and is only rarely an art; for the most part, it is a jungle. Strange beasts prowl there, and not the least peculiar are those who, under one title or another, lay claim to being authorities on the region's phenomena.

Throughout the book, the footnotes will be my own unless otherwise indicated. Parentheses in the main text will be either the autobiographical writer's or will be obviously intended to define or clarify. Should I make an occasional parenthetic comment, it will be followed by my initials—R.M.

With these preliminary comments and examples, let us proceed to the data—remarkable sexological but, above and beyond that, *human* documents.

PART ONE

The Child-Lover

A Case of Nymphophilia and Incest

The following autobiographical fragments constitute what is, to my knowledge, the most complete first-hand account of a case of Nymphophilia,* or sexual desire for female children, and incest ever published. As such it is intended to be instructive and, therefore, useful. Such an intent, and the probability of its fulfillment, is needed to justify publication of a narrative as likely to distress and otherwise disturb some readers as this one.

The principal figure in this study, who soon will begin to speak for himself, is a man I will call Lawrence C. To repeat, and so minimize the chance of misunderstanding, not only his

* The most commonly used term for sexual desire for children is *pedophilia*. This then may be modified as heterosexual pedophilia, when a child of the opposite sex is the object, or homosexual pedophilia, when a child of the same sex is the object. Some authors have referred to a female pedophilia—in the case of adult women attracted to young girls. However, strictly speaking, the term pedophilia means a sexual desire for young boys; and where a male's desire for female children is concerned, I will stick to the term *nymphophilia*, which I first used in the discussion of this problem in my book, *Forbidden Sexual Behavior and Morality*, Julian Press, New York, 1962.

name, but places and other details that might serve to identify him and the other *dramatis personae* have, of course, been altered.

Lawrence C. first approached me subsequent to his reading of one of my books in which I dealt at some length with the problem of sex desire for children. He confided some important details of his life and these seemed to warrant my suggestion that he develop those details still further. Our relationship was defined from the start as that of two persons pooling their knowledge in a mutual exploration of a troublesome human problem that has resulted in many individual tragedies and continues to do so.

Lawrence C. has undergone lengthy and expensive psychiatric treatment in an effort to free himself of his aberration. But the treatment did not accomplish anything in the way of achieving that end; rather, it only liberated him from the guilt that in the past had resulted from his desires and practices. One supposes this was not the psychiatrist's aim; but it was the result of the therapy.

Lawrence C. is an intelligent, articulate man. In addition to knowledge and insight gained during treatment, he has read extensively in the psychiatric, psychoanalytic, sexological, and other relevant literature. Except where some of his own behavior is concerned, his thinking is rational and objective. As we will see, he loses objectivity most often and most drastically when he attempts to examine the emotion-charged area of his own incestuous relationships. In providing me with the materials to follow, Lawrence C. is conscious of several motives:

1. A desire to help others: by offering unusually detailed information that should prove of value to workers in a variety of fields.

2. Sexual pleasure: he is admittedly excited and to some extent sexually gratified by this literary "revivification" of his erotic "adventures."

To these I would tentatively add two other likely aspects of his motivation:

3. Exhibitionism: perhaps a sadomasochistic wish to shock

me by the recital of his doings, and a wish both to elicit condemnation from me and to enlist me as a confederate.

4. The need to confess: although very largely freed from his guilt, some residue still remains; I am, in a sense, his confessor.

Since becoming acquainted with Lawrence C., I have gained a further measure of respect for Vladimir Nabokov and his delineation of the character Humbert Humbert in *Lolita*. (Humbert is also, of course, a nymphophile, attracted to a type of little girl he terms a "nymphet.") Lawrence C. is a real-life Humbert Humbert: a well-intentioned but maimed man, driven by appetites with which he cannot cope. He makes all of the same rationalizations to justify conduct which, as he is fundamentally aware, cannot be justified by the rationalizations advanced. He likes, and wants to be liked by, his fellow men. The facts give every indication of bearing him out when he declares that his "whole life has been one of service to others." He "would not dream of hurting" the little girls who are the objects of his desires and, sometimes, of his sexual practices. He abhors violence. He has the same sense of the ludicrous and the same rather lacerating self-humor that is Humbert's.

Now middle-aged, Lawrence C. has had several successful careers in the world of business and industry. He is presently vice president of a Midwestern firm that employs him at a salary of over fifteen thousand dollars a year. He is the kind of man who is always active in civic organizations, who regularly turns up as the leader of the fund drive, and whose charitable activities are private as well as public. He enjoys the highest standing in his community. Never would his friends and neighbors associate him with the sort of activities revealed in his "confessions."

So far as I have been able to determine, never has Lawrence C. come under the slightest suspicion. He outlines for us the precautionary measures that he habitually takes, and they are enlightening. Yet, for all his awareness of the enormous risks involved in his behavior, and for all of the well thought-out precautions he has taken, there is a self-destructive component of his personality that sometimes drives him to behave rashly. Not only prudence and intelligence have protected him from exposure and consequent calamity; there also has been a considerable measure of "luck" involved. His participation in activities sternly proscribed by our society spans almost a full quarter of a century!*

* At first consideration, it may seem extraordinary that a man could engage, over so long a period of time, in practices so strongly condemned by society, and still escape detection. However, the authors of the most recent Kinsey report remark that "It is evident that a reasonably prudent pedophile can indulge in his predilection for years before the human law and the law of averages catch up with him. In fact, our most extensive pedophile, who had sexual contact with hundreds of little girls and boys, died in his sixties with never an arrest and only a few 'close calls' in his case history." (Gebhard, P., *et al, Sex Offenders,* Harper & Row, New York, 1965, p. 75.)

Confessions of a Nymphophile

"I have just finished reading your discussion of adult–child sex relationships and it was of very great interest to me—probably because of my own deep personal involvement.

"I am married, with five children, and am employed as a vice president of the ———— Company. My income is slightly more than $15,000 annually and my family's standards and habits of living conform rather closely to the norm—or at any rate the image—for a family in our income bracket whose salary comes from employment in the city: nice home on the outskirts, two automobiles, and a multiplicity of involvements in civic and social clubs and activities.

"Although I sincerely believe my marriage can be called a happy and successful one, I am—to use the word you have coined—a nymphophile, and have a history of the practice of nymphophilia that goes back some twenty-five years.

"Until very recently—eighteen months ago was about the turning point—I suffered tremendous guilt feelings because of the unorthodox nature of my sexual behavior as distinguished from what was expected of me—indeed, the behavior that was actually credited to me—as a responsible and highly respected member of the community. I struggled to rid myself of the intense desire that was a constant risk to the security and well-being of myself and my family. I searched for some kind of explanation, for an adequate understanding, of the roots of my desire. My suffering and groping were not altogether unproductive. I sought competent professional (psychiatric) help, and I have spent a good deal of money for it.

"The end result of all this is that it has become much easier for me to live with myself, to accept the way that I am in spite of the fact that I know that my particular preferences for sexual activities are entirely unacceptable from the standpoint of the morals and laws of our society. To be sure, the risks involved in my kind of sexual activity are great. But I have come to see that I can't really change myself, so I must accept those risks and compensate for them by the exercise of great care.*

"I am writing to you because I sincerely believe that I have an unusually interesting history of nymphophilia—one that would be of much interest to you as a sexologist. And I will be willing to make available to you in detail the history of my case, provided, of course, that there are adequate safeguards to insure that any communications from me of this nature will not expose me or my family to additional hazards. I also hope to learn from you something more about this kind of behavior.

June 14

"I fully understand and concur in the (research and nontherapeutic) conditions under which our relationship is at all times to be conducted.

"As background for the details of my sexual life as I will present them in this letter, it may be useful to you to know

* When, as happens in most cases, psychotherapy fails to alter the desires of sex deviates, society suggests that there are other alternatives besides continuing the practice while increasing precautions against getting caught—for instance, continence or masturbation. But the "sex-driven" person, who often has tried these, does not consider them realistic alternatives—thus, when therapy also fails him, he may feel more than ever justified in continuing his sexual practices.

that I was the only child of fairly wealthy parents. My mother and father were happily married and gave me a completely adequate and normal amount of affection. I have never had any reason to doubt that they loved me very much.

"I had very little early religious training but what there was of it was Protestant-oriented. Mother and Dad were not regular church-goers. They always seemed unable to find a church or denomination that suited their needs, and so they would go from one church to another. I believe that Dad's faith in God was profound, but he was never able to agree with the teachings of any of the particular churches that he and Mother tried. So they would keep on looking.

"I was born and raised in a Middle Western city of somewhat less than one hundred thousand population. Much of my education, up through high school, was received at a private school for boys several hundred miles distant from my home. I believe that my parents' reason for sending me off to a private boarding school at such a young age was mainly their strong dissatisfaction with the standards of the local public schools. Also, I think they believed that it would be better for me to be associated constantly with other boys of around my own age than to be raised in a household with no other children.

"So much for the family background.

"I don't recall that I had much interest in sex until I was around thirteen. Then I was introduced by my schoolmates to the practice of masturbation. I had my first orgasm at the age of fourteen and, finding the experience exceedingly pleasant, I masturbated daily from then on, sometimes by myself and sometimes in the company of other boys. There was always a great deal of shame and guilt associated with masturbation in those days. The penalty for it, at the school, was expulsion, and this, coupled with warnings I had received from my well-meaning father about its evils and dangers, must have provided a fertile ground for the development of severe guilt complexes and warped attitudes about sex. Believe me, I didn't realize until many years later that masturbation among boys was universal, and I honestly thought that I—and the few other boys I 'jerked off' with at school—were the odd balls or 'queers.' I was certain that I was a disgrace to my family on account of this practice.

"It was while I was still a university student that I met and married my present wife, Marilyn, who is about my own age and who has a background very much the same as my own. We were both uninitiated as far as heterosexual relations were concerned at the time of our marriage. We made a good sexual adjustment during the first month and throughout the years have continued to have intercourse about three times weekly. As I said before, I sincerely believe that ours is a happy and successful marriage. We get along well together, we both love our home, our children, etc., etc. However, my wife is not now, and seldom ever has been, my exclusive sex partner.

"Even from the beginning of our marriage, I continued to masturbate frequently—in addition to our marital relations.

"About two years after our marriage I became conscious of a strong desire to have relations with young girls. This desire was soon translated into action in the form of an almost continual watchfulness for opportunities for relationships with willing partners. (Force has no appeal for me whatsoever. Always, the girl must be willing.) Needless to say, I found the opportunities for actual, in the flesh, relationships of this kind extremely rare. No doubt I was restrained to some extent by my acute awareness of the risks involved, and was therefore unwilling to initiate a relationship with any one of a number of young girls who I knew and who knew and had confidence and trust in me. The result of this hesitancy was many acts of masturbation with a phantasy always of relations with a young girl.

"Finally, about twenty-five years ago, I saw the 'girl of my dreams' under conditions which seemed to me to be favorable for the real thing. It was summertime, and she was a dirty, barefoot street urchin, dressed in rags. She was eleven years old, her breasts just beginning to develop so that they could barely be noticed. As I passed her on the street she fairly exuded sex and seemed to be just waiting for someone to approach her. I passed her, then turned around and walked back to where she was standing in front of a store. I spoke to her casually—an ordinary greeting—and she responded. After a very few minutes of chit-chat, she agreed to go with me for a ride in my car. As soon as we were on a country road, I put my arm around her and began to feel her breast. At that time she put her left knee over toward me, partially on my right thigh, raised her skirt and with her right hand pulled her panties away from her vagina. (At this time I was still driving the car!) I placed my hand on her vagina and started to massage it gently, whereupon she said, 'Oh, that feels good!' Shortly I found a suitable place to park and we got in the back seat where we both removed our lower clothing. I was tremendously excited by this entire thing and especially by the girl's scant pubic hair which was just beginning to grow.* This girl was a virgin and my attempts to introduce my penis into her vagina were accompanied by pain. We did not, therefore, accomplish full union, but I sucked her and finally we performed mutual masturbation. I climaxed and I *think* she did too, although I can't be sure about this. In any event, the little girl was thoroughly aroused sexually and I believe she enjoyed the experience.

"After we were through I was terrified by what I had done and took her on back to town and got her out of the car just as quickly as I could. I never saw her again after that single experience. I was afraid to go looking for her, or for her to see me again, thinking that the possible serious consequences would be an unwarranted risk.

"This single experience with the girl described above has

* It has been suggested occasionally, following a case reported by Karpman, that the nymphophile has a "pubic hair phobia," hence his attraction to young girls who have no or scanty pubic hair. While I would be the last to deny that somewhere in this world of diversity there may be persons with pubic hair phobias, the typical nymphophile certainly appreciates the young girl's wispy pubes on a different basis from that one. The scanty pubic hair is, rather, one of several important signs indicating the immaturity of the girl. Like her immature body, her budding breasts, etc., the pubic hair is a symbol. These symbols, I have found, are very important to the nymphophile. So important, in fact, that a man who is perfectly potent with a girl so long as he believes she is eleven or twelve years of age, may be stricken with an irretrievable detumescence should he learn that, in fact, she is fourteen or fifteen.

provided me with phantasy material for countless acts of masturbation throughout the years.

"The next real experience I had with a nymphet occurred about six months later.* By design I convinced my wife that we should get a young girl from the county orphanage to come and stay with us to help with the housework in exchange for room and board and a small wage. Fourteen-year-old Susan then came to our home and promptly—within less than a month— Susan and I were "in love" with each other. Susan was a virgin but was quite willing to be seduced by me. We carried on this relationship for about two months under the nose of—and with the knowledge of—my wife. I realize now, but at that time I really don't think I understood fully, what a cruel thing this was to do to my wife. I honestly did not want then—and do not now—to in any way hurt her. I love my wife deeply, I want her for a lifetime partner. She has given me nothing but love, understanding, and forgiveness. But yet I have had this irresistible drive for extramarital relationships with young girls which she has never been able to—and naturally cannot be expected to—accept.

"Marilyn, my wife, was beside herself with anguish while the affair with Susan was going on, and she just didn't know what to do about it. She loved me and didn't want to leave me. At the same time, she was in an intolerable situation. The upshot of this was that she returned Susan to the orphanage one day while I was at work, telling the superintendent that the arrangement just wasn't working out.

"At about this same time, as it happened, I was sent by my company to England and various European countries on a rather lengthy business trip. By the time I returned, the episode

* Lawrence C. has a liking for Nabokov's term "nymphet," probably because it introduces a certain note of levity into discussion of a matter that usually is treated with some grimness. For Nabokov (in *Lolita*) the nymphet is a prepubescent girl between the ages of nine and fourteen. Her body is developing towards, but has not achieved, womanhood. Importantly, the nymphet's psychosexuality is precociously developed. She has about her something of the "child harlot" who captured the imagination of "decadent" French writers of the late Nineteenth Century.

had pretty much 'blown over' and my life at home went on about as before.

"After the unhappy experience with Susan in our household, I determined in the future to carry on my extramarital affairs with much more discretion, and in a manner that would not be likely to hurt or offend my wife. During the next several years—the latter half of the 1940s—I did have a number of very satisfying experiences with nymphets; the details of all these affairs, I think, are hardly necessary to recount. All of the experiences were about the same: a search, a quick pick-up, and a sexual union; guilt, fear, and no further contact with the girl. Ideally, the girls were from twelve to fifteen years old (but sometimes I had to, or was willing to, settle for a girl of sixteen, seventeen, or even eighteen). The girl had to be willing, and the relationship did not go beyond a one-time experience. I would have liked to establish a permanent or, rather, long-range relationship with a little girl, but fear of the consequences served as an effective deterrent to this.

"Then suddenly, one day, it dawned on me for the first time that my own little daughter, Cindy, then nine years of age, was about to become a nymphet herself. She had always been a very affectionate little girl, very close to me and, in fact, we had always adored each other.

"It was Cindy's habit to crawl in bed with me frequently —mornings, and sometimes in the evening if I went to bed early in order to do some reading. Sometimes I would lie down for a nap on a Sunday afternoon and she would crawl up on the bed and lie down beside me. At first, when I first found myself getting an erection when I would lie next to Cindy, I was horrified at the thought. Incest was completely unthinkable. But after a short while I was overcome by desire and began very gently to fondle her whenever she was in bed with me. She seemed to enjoy and respond to this. I would massage her clitoris and very gradually insert a finger into her vagina, probing the small perforation in her hymen. With just a suggestion from me that I would enjoy it, she began to reciprocate by fondling me. Before too long we had progressed to the point where I would place my erect penis between her legs and rub back and forth against her vagina until I ejaculated. After a very few minutes of gentle contact like this, there was sufficient lubrication to eliminate any painful friction—either for Cindy or for me.

"During one of these rubbing sessions, just before she was ten years old, my penis quite accidentally started to penetrate her vagina. I could feel this, of course, and she tensed slightly with the pain for just a minute. I didn't think that I had ruptured her hymen, and the sensation of having just the head of my penis in her vagina was so intensely pleasurable that I just left it there without any further movement. Very shortly, orgasm occurred and I withdrew.

"For two or three years after this Cindy bled very slightly —just a few drops. I should mention here that in this relationship I exercised extreme care to prevent Marilyn's discovery of me in a compromising position with Cindy. But, at the same time, I don't believe I ever warned her (Cindy) that we must be careful to keep the relationship a secret from her mother. Apparently, however, she understood or sensed the need for this secrecy and came to *me* with her blood-stained panties to rinse out. This episode frightened me very much, and I determined to be even more careful to prevent any further injury. I still thought that I had not ruptured her hymen—or perhaps that I had just partially torn it.

"About two months later—Cindy then was ten—she was just beginning to get the slightest amount of pubic and under-arm hair, and the breast nipples were just budding—Cindy and I were out in the car alone one day. I started to fondle her, slipping her panties off first. My penis was erect and out of my trousers. As I was seated she turned around, facing me, and straddled my legs with her knees on the car seat. She then, by gentle movements, worked my penis into her vagina to full penetration without apparent pain and no blood.

"Thereafter, and for the next four years, Cindy and I had a mutually enjoyable—intensely enjoyable—incestuous relationship. We had intercourse at every opportunity—as I recall, it was at least two or three times a week. The pleasure—or, at any rate, my pleasure—was marred by tremendous feelings of guilt. Frequently, when I was conscience-stricken about this relationship, I would explain to Cindy what a terrible thing we were doing, that we had to find a way to bring it to an end, that she *must not* let me ever touch her again, etc., etc.* None of this talk had any effect, and the next time I was ready to cohabit with her, she would join in happily. It got to the point where I was taking her to hotels, registering honestly as father and daughter, and cohabiting with her all day. As an explanation to my wife, I would say that we were going into town to do shopping. Another scheme was to take her along on some of my business trips, to which my wife always readily assented. (Marilyn could not come along on these trips, having to stay at home with the other children.) Then Cindy and I could spend the night together, of course with no one suspecting anything.

"But I was not, I think, entirely irresponsible as regards my duties as a father. As delightful as this relationship was— except for the agonizing pains of conscience—I knew as my daughter approached adolescence that it would have to stop. (I don't really think that it was because she was becoming a woman, and so had less appeal for me, that I determined to take the drastic action to terminate the relationship. Cindy has *never* ceased being attractive to me sexually. Today, although she is now a grown woman, I still long for sexual union with her. However, I cannot give expression to that longing. I burned my bridges thoroughly, and I'm sure that she would never permit the resumption of our former relationship.)

"It was some ten years ago that I came to realize that I was incapable of terminating the incestuous relationship with Cindy by my own unaided efforts. Or I could not do this so long as I was living in close proximity to her. So, the first thing I did was to isolate myself from her for a period of time. At that time, I had a position of sufficient importance in my company to arrange for myself a temporary position as head of one

* This imposition, by Lawrence C., of his own feelings of guilt upon his daughter is of course open to various interpretations. I was never successful in eliciting from him an explanation for this conduct which must certainly have been to some extent damaging to the child.

of our overseas offices. I chose a place where it would not be practical for me to have my family accompany me. I resolved, while there, to seek the help of God in overcoming my acknowledged sexual aberrations of the vilest kind. In the meantime, before leaving for this temporary overseas position, I arranged for my daughter to enter an excellent private girls' school in the Far West. A brief change of environment would be, I thought, a good thing for her too and might serve to erase or lessen the vividness of her memories of our relationship.

"My duties with this branch office were really negligible— a position actually had been created for me to give me 'a rest,' which I had said I sorely needed. This was just what I wanted and the spare time afforded me an opportunity to undertake an extensive study of religion and to meditate upon what I learned. My hope, of course, was to get closer to God and, thereby, to be infused with the grace and strength necessary to resist my sexual temptations which I had proved unable to withstand at home and by my own strength.

"The net result of all this spiritual endeavor, after a year, was that I was converted and my whole family and I embarked upon a phase of intense religiosity. I came on home, impregnated Marilyn, and we all were living a very pious, pure family life. For me it was a terrifically trying time—a very intense struggle. At first, I think I went for a period of possibly two or three months without ever masturbating. On two occasions, soon after my return home, Cindy and I had intercourse, but both experiences were terribly disturbing to our consciences and they were the last. The next time I was overcome by desire for her and attempted intercourse, she refused me, and after a couple more unwavering rebuffs, I was convinced that from then on I must not even approach her sexually. Otherwise, I would be running the risk of losing her affection completely.

"At this point I think it might be interesting to depart for a few minutes from my own experiences to outline briefly what has happened to Cindy since our incestuous relationship finally ended. She completed high school, but her academic record was such that she decided she would not attempt to go on to college. She is a very attractive girl, slim and shapely, but quite full-breasted, and with a face that is definitely pretty and might be considered beautiful by those who appreciate her type. She *says* that she is interested in marriage and in having children, but she has never taken any constructive steps in that direction. She has passed up all kinds of opportunities for dates with various eligible young men. She simply wasn't interested and I doubt that altogether she has had a dozen dates in her whole lifetime.

"This is not to say that she doesn't seem to be reasonably happy. She has a good job, which apparently she likes, and is active in several charitable organizations, doing volunteer work, etc. She has become quite a help to my wife, aiding us considerably in all sorts of ways. She and I have a fairly warm, apparently natural father–daughter relationship. We often see one another at my home, where she is a frequent visitor. We occasionally have lunch together when working, take in the theater now and then, etc. But there *is* a wall between us. If I put my arm around her or kiss her, she becomes very tense, physically as well as emotionally. Once, almost a year ago, after I had spent well over a year with a psychiatrist and had undergone something of a reorientation in my thinking and attitudes about sex in general, and incest in particular, I tried to talk to Cindy along these lines: 'Cindy, I'm sorry about what happened between us. I did not deliberately set out to seduce you —it just happened that way because we loved each other very much and were mutually attracted to each other in a sexual way. I have gone through a great deal of pain and have spent a great deal of money to discover that incest is not unnatural. It may be wrong. It is certainly condemned by the society in which you and I live. But is *isn't* unnatural for father and daughter to be attracted to each other sexually. Now let's be honest with each other. We can't deny that sex exists. I have the instinct and you have it too. These instincts brought us together in an incestuous relationship that extended over a period of years and which was, I believe, as enjoyable for you as it was for me. My only regret is that I took from you—or accepted from you —the fullness of your physical love before you were altogether competent to give it. Now you are a woman, and—if you will excuse the ego popping out—I think there is evidence in your life that you still want me as much as I want you—and have always wanted you since you were ten years old. So why don't we give it a try? We just might be able to make each other happy without any risk of hurting anyone else.'*

"Cindy's reaction to this was to smile a very far-away, wistful smile, shed a tear or two, and say to me: 'Dad, there's only one kind of relationship that can exist between us and that is a normal father–daughter relationship. As far as the past relationship is concerned, I would just prefer to put it out of my mind completely.' Cindy made it quite clear to me that she enjoyed maintaining close ties with her family, but that she could not or would not consider any change in our present relationship.

"I love Cindy very much and so it is natural, I think, for me to be deeply interested in the real effect on her life of the relationship we once had. The psychiatrist that I visited faithfully for close to two years seemed to think—or at least he gave me the idea—that Cindy very probably was repressing strong incestuous desires. At this point, it seems to me that there is not much to be gained by such repression. If she really does desire sexual union with me—as I do with her—what is there to lose?

"So much for Cindy, and back to me. To reorient our-

* This last is, of course, a highly implausible statement. Even granting Lawrence C.'s assumption that the new incest relationship could be kept secret, there remains the problem of his wife, whom he professes to love deeply. Conceivably, his own relationship with his wife could continue during the relationship with his daughter, although this is unlikely enough. But that his daughter then could continue to maintain the same relationship with her mother is probably outside the realm of possibility. There are also, of course, many other elements contained in this proposal which show it to be a product of distorted thinking. We will encounter further examples of such distortions in the mental processes of Lawrence C., and also in some of the other cases in this volume. Where the satisfaction of the powerful desire is concerned, clear thinking no longer occurs, and the most preposterous suggestions may seem entirely reasonable to the one who is making them.

selves chronologically, we are back shortly after my religious conversion, my return home, and the severance of the incestuous relationship—after two or three rebuffs from Cindy.

"During the following two or three years I struggled, I believe courageously, to confine my sexual activities to the standards of legitimacy laid down by my religion and by the customs of society. It was strictly a losing battle, however, and the harder I tried, the more often I fell. It was really ridiculous, as I see in retrospect. Every day or so I would masturbate—occasionally, I would look for a young girl, almost always without success—and then promptly I would run to confess what I had done to my minister and try to obtain his 'forgiveness.'

"About two and one-half years ago, while on my way to work one morning, I passed a little thirteen-year-old colored girl on the street who had the same look about her that my first eleven-year-old had—way back on that occasion I previously described. I went up to her and with no preliminary amenities asked her: 'Do you feel like doing anything?' She knew exactly what I meant and nodded her head affirmatively. I then asked her whether she knew of any place where we might go. (Mind you, this was right in the center of a respectable business district at nine o'clock in the morning.) She said 'No, but how about your house?' Well, that was out of the question. I wasn't about to let this opportunity pass, so I grabbed the first taxicab and directed the driver to take us to a cheap hotel where I registered us and we had our first in a series of several sexual experiences. She was also the street urchin type—very poor family, ragged clothes, etc. But she kept her body meticulously clean. I never detected the least body odor from that girl. She was really lovely looking—small for her age, slight pubic hair, small, erect breasts. But she was very experienced. She and I did just about everything in the book together without the least hesitation or embarrassment on her part. She told me that she had had her first intercourse when she was eleven years of age, and I imagine that she had been promiscuous from that time on. She didn't want any money from me—and apparently just fucked because she enjoyed it.

"Here again, after several meetings with this girl, I became conscience stricken and fearful of the consequences of continuing with the relationship, so it was terminated.

"At this point, I would like to say something more about my psychiatric treatment. This psychiatrist is eminent in his field. My period of almost two years of therapy with him has relieved me of most of the guilt feelings that used to be associated with my sexual acts, but has not in any way lessened my desire to engage in such acts. To the contrary, the psychiatric treatment has had the effect of considerably lessening any self-imposed restraint, has made me feel quite free to engage in any and all sexual activities that suit my fancy, with but one caution—watchfulness to prevent getting caught.

"The net result, today, is that I masturbate freely, without any guilt. My phantasy is exemplified by the girl in the attached picture clipped from a nudist magazine—which I buy in prodigious quantities.* I get a great deal of satisfaction from pornography dealing with the sexual experiences of young girls. But I have not yet been able to find a good, steady source for such material. I also derive considerable vicarious pleasure from reading certain case histories in technical books, such as Weinberg's *Incest Behavior* and Henry's *Sex Variants*.

"My 'real' experiences have become few and far between. This is not because I have not and do not continue a persistent search for willing nymphets. Very frequently, during the noon hour, I go over to a section of the city that is known to be a center of prostitution and other illegal activities. There I am always approached by assorted pimps who seem anxious and willing to satisfy my wants. However, when it comes right down to it, they are unable to produce. About the best they are able to come up with is whores eighteen years of age and up—mostly up. This has become most discouraging. So I would take issue with the statement in your book, *Forbidden Sexual Behavior and Morality*, that there is probably no large city where child prostitutes are unavailable. My not inconsiderable experience covers not merely my home city, but many other cities of the United States as well. I don't think I could be called stupid, and I know my search has been diligent. If these parents

* The full-page photo is of a slim, blonde-haired girl with breasts just beginning to develop and a few wisps of pubic hair.

and custodians you describe who are willing to provide their children as sex partners really do exist, then I wish someone would tell me how to establish contact with them!

"That about winds it up for the present. I agree heartily with the Marquis de Sade (although I am anything but a sadist) that 'there are few more delicious pleasures than sexual intercourse with one's own children.' In fact, I will go even further—in *my* experience, there has been *no* more delicious pleasure than the sexual intercourse I have had with my own loving daughter, Cindy.

"Now I will mention that my daughter, Sandra, presently five years of age, is very much like Cindy was at that same age. I can see a new incestuous relationship in the making. The experience with Cindy was traumatic for *me*—I am in doubt as to its real effect on her. Now, having undergone something of a reorientation in my attitudes about such things, I believe that a future incestuous relationship with Sandra and possibly my other, still younger daughters as they reach the age of ten, would not be hard on *me* at all. But I am still doubtful about the probable effect on them. I love them very much. They obviously love and trust me. I wonder: Under these circumstances, is it likely that a gentle, loving introduction of these girls to the natural pleasures of sexual intercourse by their father, will be injurious to them? I realize that's a big question. We do not live in a vacuum. We live in a highly organized society, and our lives and habits must necessarily be governed to a large extent by the existing laws and customs of that society. Unless we are able to adjust—or conform, if you will —we are bound to be unhappy misfits. If I introduce these little girls to sexual intercourse, regardless of how much they may enjoy it, as I am sure that Cindy enjoyed it, they are, very shortly, going to make the discovery that they—and I—have engaged in a practice that is abhorred by not only our own society but in virtually every society throughout the civilized world. What will be the probable effect of that discovery? Is there any preliminary orientation that one might be able to give them which might lessen or relieve the guilt feelings, or prevent them from occurring altogether? Is there anything that might lessen or prevent the child's condemnation of herself and her father which she might experience—if, indeed, such feelings within her are to be expected as a result of such a relationship?*

"As I mentioned in my introductory letter to you, I really do think that my history of nymphophilia and incest is an interesting one—and I have read a lot of case histories. I believe it is interesting because throughout the years of its practice, I have been able to maintain unity and happiness in our family and home; I have been able to maintain a position of leadership in the community in which I live; I am a highly respected citizen in our town, well known for active participation in all the worthwhile things; my record in business has always been outstanding; and, in my present position, I am very highly thought of and known for my ability to get things done.

"It does bother me somewhat—although less than it used to—to be constantly aware that my life is a lie—that if just the least of my sexual activities became known my reputation and my ability to provide for my family all at once would be ruined. But I have come to realize that I'm the way I am and nothing is going to change me, so I had better get used to it. After all, I have gotten away with this for almost twenty-five years and, with due care, I should be able to continue to do so.**

June 21

"I very much appreciate your comments and soon will read your book, *Patterns of Incest,* which you say will answer still more of my questions.

"You have asked me to describe for you the responses of

* At this point, I will only comment that beyond any doubt an incest relationship can be severely traumatic for a child. Frigidity, promiscuity, homosexuality, and prostitution are among the more frequently encountered consequences. Certainly, as he describes her, there are strong indications that Lawrence C.'s daughter, Cindy, was damaged by her relationship with him, although in assessing that particular case his constant expressions of guilt must be seen as a significant factor. I have explored these matters at length in my book, *Patterns of Incest,* Julian Press, New York, 1963.

** Following receipt of the above communications, I established beyond doubt the writer's identity and, in general, the authenticity of his narrative. Many subsequent communications followed, most of them given completely or in part below.

the young girls with whom I have had sexual relations; how they may have described and evaluated their own responses; their willingness or reluctance to engage in activities other than coitus; whether or not they claimed or appeared to experience orgasm, etc.

"As promised, I have given considerable thought to these various questions for the last several days.

"To begin with, I have never had much luck in eliciting from a young girl with whom I've had sexual relations an articulate description of her own feelings (either physical or mental) about the relationship. About the best I have been able to get from most of them have been direct answers to direct questions—e.g., 'Do you like it?' 'Yes.' 'Does it feel good?' 'Yes.' Little else save for that sort of thing.

"So I must rely pretty much on my own analysis of what I *believe* the girls' responses and feelings have been. As I have already told you, initial willingness on the girl's part is a condition of my own enjoyment of—in fact, my ability to consummate—the relationship. I recall one time in Mexico having a young girl out in my car and petting with her to the point where it seemed she was ready for intercourse. She was a virgin —fourteen or fifteen years old—and when I attempted to introduce my penis into her vagina, she experienced sharp pain and cried out in her broken English: 'I no like! I no like!' I immediately lost my erection and that was the end of my attempt to seduce her. This experience is typical, I think, of my own reaction to the girls' attitudes. So I believe it is safe to assume that in practically all of my relationships I have had the full cooperation of my girl partners.

"This is not to say that I have ever found any nymphets who seemed to me to be passionately aggressive. Only once have I ever had the experience of being asked by a girl to have intercourse before the idea ever occurred to me. That girl was Susan (mentioned earlier)—who asked for it within an hour or two after we had finished a previous copulation—and we were still lying in the bed together, so that probably doesn't count anyway. I had been the one to go to her bedroom and get into bed with her in the first place.

"My experience indicates that the young girls with whom

I have had intercourse are what I would call passively responsive. That is to say, they are quite willing—perhaps even
anxious—to engage in sexual activities, but at the same time
they want me—or they expect me—to take the initiative.
Countless times my daughter Cindy crawled in bed beside me,
but never did she make a sexual move before I did. And yet, as
soon as I would start to fondle her, begin to pull her pajama
pants down, or something of that nature, she would cooperate
fully.

"Early in the relationship with Cindy—after we had begun to have intercourse—when she was ten years old, we would
use vaseline as an aid to lubrication. It was my practice, when
intercourse was desired, to take her out in the car on some
pretense. Soon, it became standard procedure for her to go to
the bathroom and lubricate herself with vaseline just before
we went out alone in the car—*without the necessity for me to
say anything at all about it.*

"As for enjoyment, I really think most of the girls I've had
intercourse with have enjoyed it.* But believe me, with all of
the experience I have had, it still is difficult for me to tell
positively whether a girl has experienced an orgasm or not, but
I think that they usually do. I judge this by increased, heavy
breathing tempo, bodily movements, and what seems to be a
marked increase in vaginal lubrication. I have seldom experienced in young girls the moaning and groaning that is often
the indication of an orgasm in an older woman, and which I

* I would say that Lawrence C. is reasonably objective in evaluating matters of this kind. However, the usual nymphophile does
tend to exaggerate the responsiveness of the girl and, very often, her
part in initiating the proceedings. Especially when apprehended, he
will claim, even when there is much evidence to the contrary, that
the girl made the advances—and I think this often is done not so
much to enlist the sympathies of others as to diminish his own feelings of wrong-doing. This is not to say that even very young girls do
not sometimes behave seductively—there is abundant evidence that
they do. But the nymphophile wishes to think of himself as seduced
by the child and as having relations with children who respond with
passion, and this tends to color his statements. Again, Lawrence
C. is, for the most part, unusually objective in these matters.

suspect is very frequently feigned—practically always feigned by prostitutes. One reason that I am quite sure I usually bring the girls to climax is that my own staying power is great—probably due to the fact that I have such frequent orgasms myself. Normally, my length of intercourse is from ten to twenty minutes, and I am quite able to continue beyond that—that is, to delay my orgasm.

"My sexual activities with young girls, other than fondling and intercourse, have been quite rare—and when performed have been more in the nature of experimentation than fulfillment of any real desire. Cindy and I, for a long time, I would think from the time she was eleven or twelve and up until our relationship ended, engaged in mutual genital–oral contacts—using the '69' method. I *did* thoroughly enjoy this with her, and she was quite willing to participate. However, this was always preliminary to intercourse and never resulted in orgasm.

"If you will recall my mention of a series of several experiences with a thirteen-year-old colored girl, I guess it was with her that I went farthest in the way of experimentation. She was a very willing, *un*self-conscious partner to all of this—mutual sucking, urinating upon each other in bed, etc. But again, I didn't find any of these experiences as satisfying as actual intercourse and they merely served as an exciting prelude to intercourse.

"Pederasty (anal intercourse) does not appeal to me at all and I have never tried it.

"I have been able to detect very little, if any, difference in the actual physical sensation between the vaginas of a twelve-year-old and an eighteen-year-old.

"During the period when Cindy and I were having our incestuous relationship, she had two or three girl friends of her same age who came to our house frequently to spend the night. In those days I wasn't looking particularly hard for nymphets with whom I might establish a relationship because the one I had going with Cindy, plus the usual sexual relations with my wife, were about all I could—or wanted to—handle. However, one night when one of these little girls—a twelve- or thirteen-year-old—was sleeping at our house with Cindy, I went into Cindy's room to kiss her good night just after they had gone to bed. As was my usual practice when kissing her good night I knelt by her bed, put my hand up under the covers and fondled her lovingly for just a few minutes. As I got up to leave the room, the other girl said: 'Don't I get a kiss too?' Thereupon, I knelt beside her bed and handled her in the same manner. She received these caresses warmly without either of us saying a word, and after a few minutes I kissed her good night and left. I would guess that she and Cindy were engaging in the usual girlish sex play, and I have often wondered whether it is likely that they compared notes concerning my sexual advances, and, in particular, whether it is possible that Cindy told her, or, for that matter, others, of the full relationship that she and I were having. This girl continued to come to our house frequently and I continued to fondle her whenever the opportunity presented itself. I'm quite sure that I could have had intercourse with her, but at the time it just didn't seem to be worth the risk that was involved.

"A similar experience happened just a couple of years ago with the ten-year-old daughter of an attorney who lives in our neighborhood. Because these girls are sexually attractive to me, I pay attention to them, speak nicely to them, take an interest in what they are doing, etc. They like that attention and they like me because I give it to them. Well, it got to the point where this little girl would come over to our house to help me with any little chores I might be doing on a Saturday or Sunday. On the particular Saturday I have reference to, she spent nearly all day helping me with some carpentry work I was doing in my garage. It was a very hot day in summer and in the mid-afternoon we decided to take a 'coke break' in the living room, where it was cooler. We were alone in the house at the time. So inside we went and I invited her to sit on my lap in an overstuffed chair, which she did. I embraced and kissed her, she responded, and soon I had a hand up the loose-fitting leg of her shorts and was fondling her genitals. Her breathing was heavy, there were marked movements of her hips, and I suspect that she may have had an orgasm. She did not touch me nor did I suggest that she should do so. After a while we hugged, kissed, she told me that she was my 'girl' and we went back out to the garage where I finished up my work. From that point on, I am sure that she avoided being alone with me —and we never had another experience.

"Absolutely, I *do* know *now* that little girls are able to engage in and very much enjoy sexual intercourse. I only wish that I had known what I know now twenty years ago—because it would have saved me much worry and many lost opportunities that resulted from my ignorance. Several questions come to mind at this point, and these are matters I often have wondered about: To what extent, if any, can a little girl around ten years of age be depended upon to protect the older sex partner by using discretion in her talk and actions? Does she—or can she be expected to—realize the possible consequences to her sex partner if the relationship is discovered? And is it likely that she cares? On first consideration, I would think the answers to all these questions would be negative. On the other hand, it seems to me that there are indications, some indications anyhow, that the girls are quite conscious of the need to be discreet and that there is, at least to some degree, a desire to protect the partner. For example, never once in all the years of our relationship did Cindy ever say a word or make any move that would reveal to anyone in authority the relationship that existed. Remember how, at nine years of age, without anything in the nature of a warning from me, she gave *me* her blood-stained panties to rinse out after I had ruptured her hymen?*

* Concerning the question he raises, there can be no doubt that a great many children will keep silent about a sexual relationship they have had. We know this because some long-standing relationships are disclosed only after the couple has been apprehended—caught *flagrante delicto,* or when the child eventually attains adolescence and becomes pregnant. Also, adults may disclose that they were seduced when children but kept silent about it for one reason or another—probably, in most cases, because the child is fearful of being punished for engaging in what she knows is a prohibited activity. But human, and especially childish, behavior is erratic and no nymphophile or pedophile can ever have any certainty that the child will not expose him. It would seem that

"As I mentioned in my previous letter, I clearly see another incestuous relationship in the making. At this point I honestly don't fear this new relationship—as I did the previous one with Cindy. I love my little girl very much, I will be gentle and patient with her, and I am looking forward to the experience, to be quite frank. Of course, should it turn out that *she* desires no part of this I shall then abandon my attempt to introduce her to sexual activities. However, if her present actions and attitudes at five years of age are any valid indication, there will be no problem in this regard.

"My only concern about my own intentions with regard to Sandra—and probably my other daughters—is the question about the residual effect of early incest on these girls. I wonder, as I remarked before, if regardless of how gentle, loving, and pleasant this relationship is for the girls, they may ultimately be filled with guilt and remorse upon becoming aware of the powerful barriers society has erected against such relationships? Is it likely that an incestuous relationship could jeopardize the ability and the desire of a normal, healthy girl to marry and to have a happy, well-adjusted family life? Is the incest likely to result in promiscuity later on?

"I have often wondered to what extent, if any, the incestuous relationship between Cindy and me has determined her lack of interest in boys, her apparent satisfaction at maintaining close relationships only with her family?* Today, Cindy

---

girls are especially likely to keep silent about an incest relationship with their father—because of guilt, because of fear of the father, because they recognize the potential threat to the family upon which they depend for their security, or because they do not wish to be deprived of a pleasurable experience, etc. There may be a combination of these and still other motives. But again, it is seldom if ever possible to predict what a child's reaction will be, and a daughter may expose her father, for example, not because she wishes to harm him, but because she wants to boast of her "exploits" to a friend—who then tells the story to some adult, leading to exposure and punishment.

   * If Lawrence C. were not personally involved, he would have no difficulty reaching the conclusion that his daughter was damaged by their incest relationship. This is probably clear on the basis of

and I have a pleasant, sexless relationship. It by now has been many years since we last had intercourse. We never discuss the relationship we previously had because every time I have raised the subject, it has been obvious to me that she was uncomfortable. She is a lovely looking, refined type of girl, well oriented to the accepted patterns of sexual behavior cut out by our society. There is an iron wall between us as far as communication on this subject is concerned. I love her so much that I value greatly the relationship we *do* have and I don't want to risk alienating the affection she now has for me. On the other hand, sex *is* one of our primary instincts, and I'm sure she has sexual urges now just as she had them as a hot little girl ten years ago—probably her urges are even stronger now than they were then. I would love to find a way to break through the communication barrier which now exists between us and get from *her* a thoughtful analysis of our previous relationship—as she remembers her reactions at that time, and how she evaluates the residual effects that it may have had on her life to date.

"Under the circumstances I believe that a considerable amount of mental conditioning would be necessary before she would be able to make and express such an analysis. It is my feeling that if this were possible of accomplishment it would be of great help to me by way of guiding my future course of action.

"And, as I have said before, I still find the idea of sexual intercourse with Cindy very attractive. I would welcome an opportunity to reestablish an incestuous relationship with her . . . I really believe that, as far as I am concerned, I have made the break, have rejected the customs of our society with respect to sexual behavior, and have substituted my own code by which I can live without qualms of conscience. If (and I think it is a big *if*) Cindy is frustrated by a conscious or subconscious desire for an incestuous relationship with me, it seems to me that a

information provided to the reader; it seems certain in the light of some additional information provided me, but which I am not able to divulge.

reorientation of her own attitudes toward incest, matching my own, would be all that is required to pave the way for what might be a really fulfilling interpersonal relationship between us. Today, unfortunately, she considers incest unnatural and terribly sinful. I have learned, of course, that it definitely *isn't* unnatural and that, at least for me, it is not sinful. Condemned by our own society—yes; but so what? If this is something that we both really want, if no one else will be hurt as a result of it, if we don't cause a public scandal, why should we care what the customs are?

June 31

"About a week ago I wrote Cindy a long letter explaining the evolution of my thinking and attitudes about our particular relationship—former, present, and future. The points I made in that letter were generally as follows:

"1. We entered the relationship through what seemed to be a mutual desire, and for the years during which it existed it seemed to be mutually enjoyed *except* for the fact that *I* became progressively more tormented by feelings of guilt to the point that I took drastic steps to sever the relationship.

"2. In recent years I have, with the help of others, undergone a complete reorientation of thinking on the subject and I can now look back on the relationship which we had years ago without any sense of guilt and see it as a really lovely experience flowing out of a father–daughter love—with nothing in any way sordid about it.

"3. There is a real question in my mind about the nature of our *present* relationship. While it seems to be warm, friendly, and all of that, nonetheless each time I touch you, kiss you casually, etc., you seem to tense up or freeze. Is that because you are afraid of yourself and of me and the intimate relationship which you think might result if you were to relax —a relationship which you are horrified to face up to because of the strict bans against it? Or is it simply because you have by now outgrown that kind of love for me and the idea of a physical intimacy with me has no appeal for you at all?

"4. If your reason is the former—if you do love me in a way that would make physical union with me attractive to you, provided that you saw nothing basically wrong in it—I wish you would give me an opportunity to convince you, as I have come to believe, that, for us, under existing circumstances, it could be a very satisfying relationship about which we need have no guilt feelings at all. I don't expect you to accept this philosophy all at once—because it has taken *me* years to reach this point in the development of my own thinking on the subject. At the same time, I would like to ask you to keep an open mind about this matter, and to let me present, in a leisurely way over an adequate period of time, the step-by-step logic that has enabled me to reach my conclusions.

"The above is a very abbreviated version of the thoughts I expressed in my letter to Cindy. Her reply to me is enclosed, and I think you may find it to be of considerable interest.* As for myself, I now can only conclude that she has absolutely closed the door to me as far as any further attempts to influence her thinking on the subject are concerned. Possibly others might influence her to revise her attitudes, but not me. I believe that were I to make any further attempts to do so, I would risk alienating whatever affection she does now have for me.

"Cindy has told me recently that *in her opinion* our incestuous relationship had no effect upon my ability to exercise paternal authority—a point you discussed in one of your letters —and I *did* exercise it effectively. This was in direct response to a question I put to her, since this has been and continues to be one of the doubts in my mind concerning the advisability of establishing an incestuous relationship with Sandra.**

* His daughter's reply is a strongly worded rejection of his appeal to resume the incest relationship. It does seem to disclose, however, some ambivalence, and includes an appeal to him not to enter into similar relationships with his other daughters. Unfortunately, since in fact it is of very great interest, I cannot reproduce this letter.
** Breakdown of the paternal authority has often been mentioned as one of the more frequently occurring problems resulting from father–daughter incest. The daughter's relations with her mother may be a still more serious problem when there is incest with the father. The incest relationship places the daughter in an extremely difficult position *vis à vis* her mother. The girl can scarcely avoid, for example, the conclusion that she is trespassing

"It is clear from Cindy's response that she has thought about the possible involvement of her sisters in the same kind of experience that she had and she makes a strong plea that this should not happen. (Incidentally, the statement in her reply to the effect that she was afraid during our relationship that others in the family might be hurt by it, seems to me doubtful. I am quite certain that she was never frightened by our relationship *except* in the respect that I, *myself,* in my more conscience-stricken moments and in a state of near-panic, explained to her what a terrible thing we were doing and repeatedly urged that she should never let me touch her again.)

"I honestly believe that I am as strongly motivated by concern for the welfare of my children as I am by the anticipation of the pleasure of sexual intercourse with my daughters. However, at the same time I know that I must guard against a selfish desire giving birth to the logic that justifies the act. With that reservation, let me outline my thinking and see whether the logic will stand up under close scrutiny.

"Today, children in America seem to be in a full-scale revolt against the sexual standards of our society. It is a safe bet that a large percentage, if not the majority, of girls will have lost their virginity by the time they are half-way through high school. The conditions under which the girl loses it will probably be unfavorable for the formation of good, healthy attitudes about sexual behavior. The initiation to sex will probably take place in the back seat of a dark car with an inexperienced boy who is just experimenting himself, who really cares nothing about satisfying *her,* and who, besides everything else, will, or may very easily, hurt her physically. It seems to me that this is enough to really frighten a nice little girl.

"Now contrast this picture with the leisurely, gentle, lov-

---

on her mother's preserves. The daughter's position in relation to the mother is one of bad faith. Both father and daughter are placed in the position of coconspirators against the mother. When the daughter loves her mother, but must repeatedly deceive—and, as she is likely to regard it, betray—her, great guilt is customarily generated. Since this guilt is so painful, the daughter is likely to come to dislike or despise the mother—since one does not feel so guilty about deceiving someone one dislikes or despises.

ing introduction of a little girl to sexual experience by an experienced man—her father—whom she knows best of all in the world, whom she loves and trusts, and, above all, who cares for her. I do not believe that under any circumstances should a father force this upon his daughter. But, on the other hand, when she begins to awaken of her own accord, and if she starts making up to her father in an innocent, groping, but definitely sexual way, I am not at all sure that it wouldn't be much better for the father to help her along—to show her the way. Of course, this would have to be accompanied by the right kind of mental conditioning—and this is where I think I failed Cindy the most. I panicked, and I believe that my own mental attitude of that time was transmitted to Cindy, as should never have happened.

"What form might this mental conditioning take? I am not at all sure, and I don't really know whether *any* orientation that a father might give to his ten- to twelve-year-old daughter would 'take' and would effectively offset or preclude the possible psychological damage resulting from the experience. But suppose it went something like this—and this comes right off the top of my head, with no forethought at all: 'What we are doing together and enjoying is strictly forbidden by the laws and the customs of our society and our religion. Nevertheless, it is a very natural thing that comes to people who love each other—and it has been done openly by daddys and their little girls in other parts of the world ever since men have been living on this earth. So when you grow up and learn all about such things you are going to find out that almost everybody around us will say how awful the thing is that you and daddy are doing. Listen to them if you want to, but don't pay any attention to what they say. *We know* it's not wrong. God gave us our bodies and made them so that when two people love each other very much their bodies just naturally want to come together. It is only when people don't love each other, and are just looking for a thrill, that sex becomes cheap and dirty. No, what we are doing is nothing for us ever to be ashamed of, but because in our country our customs don't allow it, it's something that we have to keep all to ourselves—a very wonderful private thing.'

"I wonder if this, or something along similar lines, could be understood by a ten- to twelve-year-old girl? I wonder if she could be spared the guilt feelings that otherwise might result? I wonder if a girl's confidence and trust in her father could extend so far that she would accept his philosophy even though she would find out later that such a philosophy is contrary to the standards of the society she must live in and adjust to? As I told you, having arrived at a completely unorthodox attitude about this whole thing has many advantages insofar as freedom from guilt is concerned. But, on the other hand, it is lonesome in the respect that I have not yet found any kindred souls who agree or are in accord with my unconventional attitudes.*

* Repeatedly, in my exchanges with him, I brought to the attention of Lawrence C. a variety of scientific, and also moral, objections to the further incest relationships he was contemplating. As regards some of the points he has raised in the last half dozen or so paragraphs, I wrote to him (in part):

"I would think that the odds against a father's being able to so indoctrinate his daughter that she would entirely accept his permissive approach to incest are very great. Probably his chances of accomplishing this would be better if the mother were not in the home; but, even so, the father is pitted against the whole society. Remember, too, that the effectiveness of such persuasion in sparing the daughter psychological damage quite possibly cannot be assessed at the time. Perhaps not until she is a young woman will it be possible to say whether she was damaged. And by then, if it turns out that she has been harmed, it may be too late to undo what has been done . . . Since serious neurosis is always a possible outcome of an incest experience, the father, at the very least, is gambling with his daughter's future. Let us even suppose that his daughter might, as you believe, stand to gain from the incest. You still would be a bit like the man who, knowing that it is useful to be able to swim, throws his son into the river. The boy may learn to swim; but, also, he may drown . . .

"Because of the limited experience of a girl of ten, responsibility rests upon the shoulders of the mature parent who should be aware, as the girl is not, of the full range of possible consequences . . . One should not pretend to oneself that one is acting in the best interests of the child—for instance, sparing her an unfortunate defloration in the back seat of an automobile by some inept youth. If it is really a satisfactory sexual experience you desire for your daughter, then you could arrange for some competent person to

"Please forgive me if the suggestion I am now about to make is in any way inappropriate or out of order. However, it has occurred to me that in the course of your work you must be in communication with others whose attitudes and ideas are akin to mine and who would enjoy the acquaintance of like-minded persons just as much as I would. (This is beginning to sound like I'm suggesting that you serve as a focal point for a pen-pal or lonely hearts club, which I don't mean at all!) Do you, though, have any idea where a person like me can turn to find others with similar tastes and interests? Perhaps some of the people you know have found the solution to this problem of loneliness, and if so I'd like very much to know what it is.

"Returning briefly to Cindy, I wonder if it is wishful thinking when I surmise that she is repressing her incestuous desires toward me? As I have said, her interest in boys has never been evidenced by constructive steps to get dates, etc. It is difficult for me to believe that a girl as passionate as Cindy was at puberty, could have turned out to be a frigid woman—but it looks like that might be just what has happened.*

July 1

"I would like to comment on several of the points you made in your letter of a couple days ago.

"There is a thread of thought that seems to be woven into all of your letters to the effect that since most of the data on sexual offenses and offenders have been gleaned from low-level

---

provide it—in which case the risk of damage from violation of the incest prohibition would be avoided . . . You may decide to go ahead with this incest relationship; but, if you do, you must be ready to admit that it is your own self-interest, as opposed to your daughter's interests, that you are furthering. And you cannot, by means of more or less clever arguments, escape responsibility for any harm to your daughter that results."

* The most obvious interpretation would be that Cindy's desires remain fixed upon her father. For all practical purposes she might then be frigid—because she is unable to desire other men, and because she must reject the desire for her father, satisfaction of which would generate more guilt than she is able to endure.

people and those who have been apprehended, it is difficult to know the extent to which more intelligent, discreet, sophisticated people violate society's many prohibitions without ever coming to the attention of the authorities.

"I quite agree. But I venture the opinion, based on my own experiences alone, that, assuming my sexual *tastes* are fairly normal, and disregarding for the moment the degree of intensity or apparent recklessness with which *I* pursue the satisfaction of such tastes, the successful (undetected or unnoticed) violations are widespread. I believe it is fairly simple to, as you put it, 'persistently defy the prohibition' without any great risk of apprehension, provided that certain cautions are faithfully observed. Now I, *personally,* on occasion have disregarded some of these cautions and have taken the consequent risks. However, it seems to me that if the following 'rules' are observed and applied with intelligence, the risk then is minimal:

"1. First and foremost, never force a young girl, either physically or by mental coercion, into engaging in any kind of sexual activity. Lead her gently, step by step, and be sure that she is ready for the next step before proceeding from the previous one. Guard against frightening her and be sure that *she* enjoys the experience. The big problem here, I think, is *getting started.* Most of the school girls today have been mentally conditioned to fear greatly any approach by a strange man—and rightly so, considering the atrocities which have been committed on the bodies of innocent girls by brute force. So I believe it is almost out of the question to pick up a strange girl with the idea of having her cooperate in a mutually satisfying sexual experience, unless she just happens to be one of the very rare, thoroughly experienced juvenile prostitutes. Besides that, the risk of attempting to pick up a child is great. The best opportunities for developing sexual relations with young girls have occurred under circumstances where the girl has known me for some time, has liked and trusted me.* Almost without exception, when these conditions were present, the girl has

* It seems to be the case that female children more often are seduced by adults whom they already know than by strangers.

seemed quite willing to cooperate. (This last sentence sounds like I've had such experiences with dozens of girls. That is not at all true. The number is more like ten or twelve—in the group fifteen years of age and under. At nine years of age, Cindy was the youngest of these.) *Never* to the best of my knowledge has any girl reported her sexual experience with me to the authorities or to anyone else. So a summary of 'Rule No. 1' would seem to be: Be sure that the girl is relaxed and that she enjoys the relationship; if she isn't relaxed and if she doesn't demonstrate enjoyment, then *drop it*.

"2. *Always* take precautions against pregnancy in relations with a girl whose menstrual periods have started. I personally do not find that the use of a rubber prophylactic detracts appreciably from my own enjoyment of sexual intercourse and it seems to me that the protection afforded to both the girl and myself thereby makes it mandatory. I have never reached the stage of sophistication—or nerve—of a father I once read about who had his eleven-year-old sex partner fitted with a diaphragm which she wore whenever they had intercourse—which was for a period of some three years.

"3. To the maximum extent possible see to it that the atmosphere in which the intercourse takes place is pleasant and *absolutely secure*. How many times in case histories do we read of persons getting caught, literally, with their pants down? Countless times—and this seems to happen most frequently in incest cases. To my mind, this is nothing but unnecessary carelessness. Any man with a reasonable amount of intelligence should be able to plan his liaisons with his girl so that they are secure from all but the most unforeseeable intrusions.

"4. The man's conduct, in public, toward the young girl should be such that it will never serve to cast suspicion upon him. I think it matters very little what the *little girl's* public conduct is, since it's more or less expected that she will show some physical signs of affection for people she likes anyway. For example, a little ten-year-old daughter of a neighbor of ours used to climb up into my lap every time when Marilyn (my wife) and I would visit their home or they would come to our house. This went on for months—you know, the 'Uncle

Larry' bit—before I finally started fondling her genitals when we happened to be alone (there was no intercourse). My attitude toward her in the presence of anyone else was always tolerance and never was the slightest amount of suspicion directed toward us.

"It seems to me that the safest, most secure way for a man to practice nymphophilia would be for him to make an arrangement with a parent who was agreeable to such activities by his (or her, or their) daughter. I get the idea from some of your books, as well as those of other authorities in this field, that there do exist parents with such extremely liberal attitudes, but I have never found any. Personally, as a parent, I do not think I would ever introduce any daughter of mine to a man for the sole purpose of engaging in sexual intercourse and it is difficult for me to imagine a parent who would. But if there are, here in these United States, and in this present day and age, such parents of willing daughters, it seems to me that it would solve a lot of problems for the nymphophiles if they could get together.

July 6

"One of the questions asked in your recent letter is an easy one to dispose of, and I will take care of it without any further ado. This has to do with my sexual arousal with a nymphet as compared to that with an adult female. I can become aroused with an adult female partner (including my wife) *only* by entertaining a phantasy of a sexual experience involving a young girl. These phantasies take the form of one of my own past experiences or perhaps the experiences of others that I have read about in case histories. When I'm with an older girl for the purpose of sexual intercourse, I attempt to get her to describe her first experience—her age, the conditions under which it took place, her partner, etc., and then the image so created becomes *my* phantasy which I employ in the subsequent act of coitus with her.

"I would refuse intercourse with a woman over twenty years of age—the exception is my wife—and would prefer masturbation. I guess that, for me, intercourse with any girl over fifteen years of age is merely a form of masturbation any-way, although I do enjoy bringing *them* to the climax. I realize that all of this is inconsistent with my attraction to Cindy, who is now a fully matured woman. I cannot explain this inconsistency, except to venture the opinion that the arousal stems from my knowledge that, regardless of what may be her present age, she *is* my daughter and that, as a child, she was my sexual partner.

"On the other hand, I always become very quickly and intensely aroused by nymphets without any need for any kind of phantasy. I need but to look at a certain type of little girl, fully clothed, walking down the street, and I become sexually excited. For example, two or three months ago I saw a little colored girl, not over twelve years old I am sure, still in pig-tails, and at least *six months pregnant,* walking down the street. Immediately, I had an erection.

"Finally, I have to submit to your logic that militates against father–daughter incest. When it comes right down to it, it may be that the reason I am such a devotee of incest is the selfish one that my own daughters are quite readily available to me sexually, whereas, much more often than not, I have only been frustrated in my innumerable attempts to satisfy my crav-ing for youthful sex partners elsewhere.

July 7

"I will, as an addition to my brief note of yesterday, give you a considerably more detailed account than I gave previ-ously of my affair with Susan, the girl who was obtained by us from the orphanage. This more extended treatment may be helpful in giving you a better idea of my psychology and of my ways of behaving in these situations.

"By the time Susan came to us I had already developed a strong craving for young girls, although this appetite had not as yet been satisfied except in my phantasies. As you will recall, I suggested to Marilyn, my wife, that it might be a good idea to arrange to get one of the girls from the orphanage to come and live with us so that she could help with the housework, the child care, etc. Marilyn had no idea of my ulterior motives and agreed without hesitation to this proposal.

"The following day I called upon the superintendent of the orphanage and inquired as to whether such an arrangement could be made. Within the next week our conditions at home were investigated, our references were checked, and Susan was delivered to us by the superintendent.

"At age fourteen, Susan was a very quiet, shy, and rather unhappy-appearing girl. It was difficult to get her to eat very much and she didn't seem to be very strong or healthy. She was rather reluctant to talk about her background and about the conditions which had led to her placement in the orphanage. It seems peculiar, as I look back on it, that we did not inquire more closely concerning her background, but we didn't and I know—or remember—almost nothing about it.

"Almost immediately, I was filled with great compassion for this poor little underprivileged girl, and I determined to do everything I could in order to make her happy. We went out and bought her some clothing and toys, fixed up a pleasant room for her, etc., etc. Although our original purpose in getting her was, ostensibly, to have a girl living in our home who would be a helper and baby-sitter, what actually happened was that we continued to hire a baby-sitter most of the time and we took Susan out with us.

"One morning, about two weeks after she had come to live with us, she and I were alone in the kitchen and I took her in my arms and kissed her good morning, but rather casually. Later the same day, I entered one of the bedrooms where she was busy changing the baby and kissed her again, but this time passionately. She seemed quite agreeable to this advance.

"For the next week or so she and I embraced and kissed at every possible opportunity. Every chance I got I would manufacture an excuse to get Susan out in the car alone with me. I would take her to choir practice, take her out for drives in the countryside, etc. The necking sessions progressed rather slowly because, for one thing, *I* was frightened of the consequences and besides that I was wholly inexperienced in this kind of relationship. In fact, I was so naive as to really believe that no girl of that age had sexual desires or feelings. So what these embraces of ours amounted to were nothing more than 'soul kissing' and the touching of her little breasts outside her clothing.

"Then one warm spring evening Marilyn, Susan, and I were sitting out on our front porch enjoying the lovely clear night. It was still cool enough so that for comfort we needed a blanket over us, which afforded some protection for one of my arms and hands which were becoming progressively bolder in their explorations. After a while, I would think it was about ten o'clock, Marilyn said she was going to bed and asked if I was coming too. I said 'no' and told her I would like to stay outside for a while longer. Susan elected to stay with me, and soon we decided it would be more comfortable if we were to lie down on the porch sofa—which we did, facing one another.

"By this time I was highly aroused and we began to do some necking in earnest—although I still was not bold enough to put my hand on her genitals. I did, for the first time, slip my hand up under her blouse and fondle her breast *outside* of her bra. After a few minutes she asked to be excused for a little while, saying that she would be right back. Back she came and lay down next to me in the same position. Again, my hand slipped under her blouse, up to her breast, and to my surprise and delight the bra had somehow become unhooked in the back and was loose. She said only one word, very softly— 'Don't'—but she made no move at all to stop me. We lay there for a long time—probably an hour or more—during which I made no attempt to do more than hold her, kiss her, and fondle her now bare breast.

"After a while we decided that we had better break it up and go on upstairs to bed. Marilyn was still awake—it was then about midnight—and was quite put out with me for having stayed downstairs with Susan for so long. I am sure that by this time Marilyn was beginning to become seriously alarmed by the developing relationship between Susan and me, and we exchanged a few cross words over it. The upshot of this argument was that I left our bedroom, went into Susan's, and asked her if I might get into bed with her. Susan not only immediately said 'yes,' she also turned back the cover for me.

"We resumed our necking where we had left off downstairs and in a very few minutes I had managed to get her pajama top off. After a few minutes more of this necking, I rolled over on top of her and she spread her legs. We both still had pajama bottoms on and I still had not touched her genitals. Being at the peak of sexual arousal, I started the usual movements of intercourse, my penis slipping out and protruding from the fly of my pajamas and separated from her only by the fabric of her pajamas. At this point, my little Susan said, to my amazement, 'You might as well be inside me.' Immediately, I got off her, removed her pants, and then resumed my position. Intercourse was not easy. She was a virgin and also she was frightened. As I began to penetrate her vagina, it was obvious that she was experiencing a good deal of pain. Then she expressed concern about possibly getting pregnant. I was totally unprepared for intercourse with her as far as protection against pregnancy was concerned. I was as gentle with her as I could be. Several times I attempted a full penetration and each time when I reached the point where it was hurting her too badly I would withdraw and let her rest a while, fondling her with my hand. Neither of us slept at all that night and by morning we had accomplished complete intercourse, although I am quite certain that she experienced no orgasm that first time.

"Marilyn came into the bedroom while Susan and I were still in bed, at around eight o'clock in the morning. I don't recall the exact nature of the conversation in Susan's presence, except that it was reserved and there was no scene. Later that day, in private discussion with Marilyn, I somehow managed to secure her *permission* to sleep with Susan again that night, which I did.

"For the next two or three months Susan and I continued to have intercourse at every opportunity—and it kept getting better and better all the time. But while all this was going on, at the same time tension was mounting in our household and I began to see how much Marilyn objected to the relationship, and I came to realize that if we were to continue at all it would have to be done surreptitiously. So I told Marilyn that

I was sorry for the offense and promised that henceforth my relationship with Susan would be entirely nonsexual. Susan understood the problem completely and agreed to the solution I had decided on.

"From that time on we had intercourse in our house only when Marilyn was out. Those were the best times—we would take a bath together. I would dry her and then carry her nude into her bedroom where we would play together on her bed and finally wind up having intercourse. On one occasion, after we had finished intercourse and were just lying in bed naked side by side, both on our stomachs, she raised one of her legs, placed it across my legs, pressing her sexual organs against my hip, and said to me, 'Let's have another sexual intercourse.'

"We continued our outings in the car and on two or three occasions I checked in with her at a hotel. Very seldom during this two- or three-month period did a day go by that we didn't find some opportunity to have sexual intercourse. In our house, when Marilyn was at home, Susan would sit across the room from me with her knees drawn up in such a way that I could see right up her dress. That would always start the wheels turning in my mind—to find some way that I could be alone with her.

"But of course we weren't fooling Marilyn one bit, and, for her, the situation was becoming more intolerable with every passing minute. Finally, when I returned home from work one day, I found that Marilyn had taken Susan on back to the orphanage. By this time school was out for the summer and Susan had fallen into the habit of sleeping until late in the morning and leaving all the housework to Marilyn. She was really doing no work at all for Marilyn, which placed my wife in the position of having to wait on an adolescent who was supposed to be helping her and who was, in fact, my mistress—a fact that Marilyn knew perfectly well.

"After it was all over Marilyn gave me to understand in no uncertain terms that this kind of thing was intolerable and must never happen again.

"I was absolutely crushed—I imagine much the same as Humbert Humbert must have been crushed when he finally lost his Lolita. When autumn came and the children walked from the orphanage to school and back, I used to drive my car and park on a side street along their route in an attempt to catch a glimpse of Susan. On one occasion, by a ruse, I managed to reach Susan by phone at the orphanage. All she had to say to me was, 'Leave me alone, or else . . .' That was the end of it.

July 11

"This will be an attempt to answer your request for information about the language used by young girls (with whom I have had experience) to describe the sexual act, the genitals, etc.

"What I have to say about this particular phase of our mutual exploration must be viewed against a background knowledge of *my own* upbringing and attitudes about what constitutes acceptable and nonacceptable vocabulary. As you may remember, I was brought up to be, above all else, a gentleman. I was thoroughly taught that gentlemen simply do not employ such universally known and commonly used words as 'fuck,' 'screw,' 'cunt,' 'pussy,' 'cock,' 'prick,' 'ass,' etc., etc., in their conversation with anyone, least of all with females. Until fairly recently it was my belief that the use of such language in my conversation with a young girl, regardless of her niche in the social hierarchy, would be so offensive to her that it would frighten and alienate her.

"Hence, since these words were not a part of my normal vocabulary anyway, and since I could not have used them unself-consciously in any event, it is not surprising, I think, that the common 'four-letter words' were absent from most of my intimate conversations with my girl sex partners. As I have mentioned in an earlier letter, my experience has been, for the most part, that young girls are not very articulate in describing or referring to their sexual experiences, sensations, etc. For example, one conversation with a fourteen-year-old pickup went something like this (I had picked up the girl in my car just a few minutes before, and within ten or fifteen minutes we had reached a secluded parking place where we commenced necking with a minimum of preliminaries. She wore no brassiere and I unbuttoned her dress top for easy access to her breasts—which she seemed to enjoy. Then, as one hand started up her thigh, she spread her legs apart noticeably. Up to that point, there had been practically *no* conversation between us except for introductory remarks like—'My name is X, what's your name?' and her response, after getting in the car: 'Oh, I thought you were Y, who took me out once before.')

"So here starts the conversation (taking place with my one arm around her and the other hand probing and caressing her vagina all the while):

"*Me:* Do you like to do it?

"*Girl:* Uh huh.

"*Me:* Do you feel like doing it now?

"*Girl:* Yes, but I don't think there's time. I have to be at play practice in a few minutes.

"*Me:* (Opening trouser fly—girl reaches over and takes hold of my penis) Well, it won't take but a few minutes. Let's get in the back seat. (We did.)

"*Me:* How old are you?

"*Girl:* Fourteen.

"*Me:* (Removing girl's panties with her help) How long have you been doing it?

"*Girl:* Since I was eleven.

"*Me:* Who did it to you first?

"*Girl:* A boy in my class.

"*Me:* Are you still doing it with him?

"*Girl:* Uh huh.

(At this point the intercourse begins and the girl is obviously getting considerable pleasure from the action.)

"*Me:* Does it feel good?

"*Girl:* Uh huh.

(The intercourse is completed and we put our clothes back in place. We get into the front seat of the car and start toward her home.)

"*Me:* Did you like that?

"*Girl:* Uh huh.

"*Me:* You're lovely. May I see you again some time?

"*Girl:* Uh huh.

(Girl directs me to within a block of her house, where she gets out of the car.)

"*Me:* Good-bye sweetie.

"*Girl:* 'Bye.

"Not a very scintillating conversation, is it! But it *is* a fairly accurate representation of the full dialogue that took place between me and one of my nymphets, and it is fairly typical of the conversations which I've had with most of the girls in this age group. I refer now to the ones with whom I have had sexual intercourse.

"After having had my own sensibilities shaken a few times by girls whom I've been out with taking the *initiative* in using language which I would not have employed myself, I have now become fairly accustomed to using and hearing the girls use 'fuck,' 'screw,' 'cunt,' 'pussy,' and 'cock.' I distinctly remember picking up a sixteen-year-old and a thirteen-year-old here in my home city just a few years back. The sixteen-year-old was quite willing to get into my car with the explicit understanding that we would go off some place to have intercourse, but, at the same time, she insisted that the thirteen-year-old come along in the car too. In the car, I attempted to fondle both girls, but only the older one was a willing recipient of such advances. We drove to a secluded place in the park where we (the older girl and I) left the car with the thirteen-year-old sitting in it, and went into the woods where we had intercourse. When we finished and were walking back to the car, I asked, 'Doesn't your friend do it?' The girl answered me: 'Sure she *fucks.* She's just scared to *fuck* with you.'

"I have come to the realization that the use of such words is not shocking to at least a lot of girls and that many of the girls seem to be quite at ease when using them in their own vocabulary. In fact, it seems to facilitate communication with lower-class girls to speak frankly, in plain language which they are sure to understand, about the sex act rather than to use such 'high-sounding' words as 'intercourse,' 'penis,' 'vagina,' etc., which they may not have heard, or which they may think silly.

"Communication between a young girl and a mature man —especially when he is a stranger to her—is extremely difficult at best. Under these conditions the girls are simply not very talkative. It is the man who has to take the initiative in the conversation. I have found, however, that when the circumstances seem right and I *do* take the initiative in asking a twelve- or thirteen-year-old girl, for example, 'Have you started fucking yet?' or 'Will you fuck with me?' she is quite likely *not* to be shocked or startled and will answer, every bit as frankly, 'Yes, I have,' or 'No, not yet,' or 'Yes, I will,' or 'No, I won't.'

"One day last summer on my way home from work I stopped off at a shopping center to pick up some things at the drugstore there. Outside the store were four young girls (colored), standing by their bicycles laughing and apparently enjoying something very funny that was going on amongst themselves. As I got closer to them, I could hear that one of the girls was singing. They became conscious of the fact that I was watching them closely, and as I approached them one girl said to me, 'Mister, give us a cigarette.' I did so, and made some conversation with them for a few minutes, asking their names, ages, etc. Finally, I said, 'Look, I'll buy you a whole pack of cigarettes if you will sing that funny song for me.' They agreed, and I went into the store, got the cigarettes for them, and returned. The song was obscene, containing a number of verses, none of which I remember except for a line that went: 'Screw a woman, screw a woman, put it in her cunt.' These four girls ranged in ages from thirteen to fifteen. When the singing was finished, I asked whether one of them would like to go for a little ride with me, but I had no acceptances.

"Several months ago I picked up a seventeen-year-old girl on my lunch hour and went with her to her rented room where we got undressed in preparation for intercourse. When she got down to her panties she seemed to be a little embarrassed, and when I started to help her remove them she said, apologetically: 'I don't have very much hair on my pussy.' This seemed a source of shame for her (but, of course, of stimulation for me). Sure enough, she did have very scant pubic hair. As we lay down on her bed, she started to finger her own clitoris and I asked her if she did that a lot. Her reply was: 'I have to play with it every night before I can go to sleep.' This admission from her was a *rare* experience for me. I am quite interested in the practice of masturbation by young girls and I usually question the ones I am with about their habits in this regard. From the answers *I've* received, one would have to come to the conclusion that masturbation among girls is practically non-existent—which, as we know, is contrary to the facts. However, the vast majority of girls I have been with simply do not admit to any masturbatory practices at all. So, it was refreshing to find a girl who admitted quite frankly that she enjoyed masturbating before going to sleep at night.

July 14

"Since I value the relationship we have begun, and because I have hopes for its future development, I would not wish to jeopardize or to stifle it by some unintentionally inappropriate or improper request or question which might place you in a difficult position ethically. So, if any questions or requests which I may put to you do, in your opinion, constitute any breach of propriety, will you please attribute the fault to a wholly unintentional error stemming from my ignorance—and feel perfectly free to tell me, quite frankly, that the particular request or question which is offensive puts me 'off base.'

"With that introduction as background, I should like to amend my statement to you concerning my motivations in carrying on this dialogue with you—furnishing detailed material on my sexual experiences with the expectation that such information may, in the future, be published in one or more forms.

"It is quite true, as I told you, that I would like to help promote a better understanding and maybe to help the cause of other persons who share my sexual interests and cravings. But, as you may already have realized, I am motivated, too, by an additional factor. This is the hope that through my association with you, I, personally, will acquire information and knowledge not readily available to the general public which will help me to satisfy my own sexual appetites. For example, I should like very much to have access to a good collection of hard-core pornography—literature, photographs, motion picture films, etc., which are in keeping with my own predilections. I am sick to death of the cheap—as you call them, 'semipornographic'—paperback novels, which are really just 'teasers.' I have had very few opportunities to read 'hard-core' books and watch pornographic movies, and my only source here at home has recently dried up. That is probably all for the best, because he was a very low-grade character who is, besides everything else, a robber.

"Surely your work has made you knowledgeable in this area and I wonder if our relationship is not on a sufficiently high plane that you might feel yourself able legitimately to advise me in this regard.

"Incidentally, speaking about pornography brings to my mind an idea which I have had for some time and which, in all of my reading, I have never heard of. It has occurred to me many times that it would be very handy and pleasurable to have made up a life-size mannequin in the image of a very special nymphet. Some of the dolls made for children nowadays are very realistic in skin texture, consistency, hair, etc., and it seems to me that the incorporation of female sex organs in a life-sized doll would be easy enough to achieve. I believe that, for me, intercourse with such an object would be an improvement over ordinary masturbation and also an improvement over *actual* intercourse with a female who falls short of measuring up to the standards of my 'dream girl.' While I imagine that it would be quite expensive to have such a doll made to one's particular specifications, I doubt that the cost would be prohibitive to someone who really wanted it and had a fairly good income. Have you ever heard of such a thing?*

* Dolls more or less of the type proposed by Lawrence C. have existed throughout much of history. The late King Farouk is supposed to have had one. It is said to have contained a mechanism which, when triggered, would continue to operate for ten minutes or more, producing pelvic movements of the doll. The area from the upper thighs to about the navel was warmed as desired by hot

"This, in turn, leads me to my favorite masturbatory technique, which may interest you. I put a *lubricated* condom ('rubber') on my penis, then wrap a hand towel tightly around it. Next, I mount a bed, placing my penis which has been so wrapped between two pillows held tightly between my legs. Resting on my elbows, I look at one of the photographs of one of my favorite nymphets and commence the motions of intercourse. Frequently, I leave the rubber filled with semen on my penis and then repeat the procedure in about an hour. Of course, this kind of set-up requires the privacy of a hotel room, and so I employ the technique only when I am out of town on business trips. An alternative, and more convenient, technique, which can be followed just about anywhere, is to place the lubricated condom on my penis while it is flaccid; then, with my penis still flaccid, I place it through a roll of toilet paper (my penis won't go through when erect). After the penis becomes erect, I commence the back and forth motions of intercourse, while looking at a picture of one of my girls, until the ejaculation occurs. Of course, using the technique just described requires that the toilet paper roll be held steady with the penis moving in and out of the hole with the aid of the lubrication inside the rubber.

"Don't you think I may be onto something with my mannequin idea? If the girls can have their dildo and other phallus

---

water being poured into the doll. Even more sophisticated versions, some warmed and moved by electricity, are reported to have been developed in recent years. Japan is said to be the main source of these dolls, some of which are constructed to resemble international film stars.

It also might be noted that presently, in this country, "artificial vaginas" are being offered for sale through mail-order solicitation. I received an (unsolicited) advertisement for one of these about two years ago. According to the ad, it was very useful for obtaining semen specimens from bulls. However, since it came to me in New York City, where it is unlikely I would be raising cattle, one surmises that its effectiveness as a means of obtaining "semen specimens" is not limited to the bull. "Artificial vaginas" of various sorts also are sold in the Japanese "sex stores," and I have seen them from time to time in Europe.

forms, then why shouldn't we males have an artificial vagina built into a lovely doll which, among other things, would never grow up!

"To answer quickly some of the questions posed in your most recent communication:

"You are correct in guessing that I do derive *some* sexual stimulation as a result of writing these letters describing my sexual practices. I will have to leave it to you to decide whether this stimulation arises from my recalling in detail the actual pleasurable experiences, or perhaps from a kind of exhibitionism. I *think* it is the former, because, letter or no letter, I am stimulated to the point of masturbating to orgasm by recalling, for example, the details of one act of intercourse with Cindy.

"As regards my wife's knowledge of the affair with Cindy —she knew nothing of it until I became so burdened with guilt and determination to sever the relationship that I placed myself in isolation by taking the temporary position far away from home. At that time, just before I went away, I confessed the whole business to Marilyn in a spirit of deep contrition. Her reaction: shock, sadness, but, more than anything else, sympathetic understanding and forgiveness.

"I must admit to some puzzlement about Marilyn's whole attitude toward this and also toward some other of my extramarital sexual experiences that have come to her attention. Marilyn is an extremely intelligent, very well-read woman. She graduated from one of the best universities with an outstanding record of academic performance. She has always kept herself very well-informed about current events, cultural matters, developments in education, etc. As a wife, she leaves very little, if anything, to be desired. She is a good mother, a good cook, a good housekeeper, and so on. She is attentive to her personal appearance; she is sexually responsive, but not aggressive— which I would definitely object to. All in all, I am able to say, quite objectively, that she deserves to be rated tops as a wife. I would bet my life that she has never had sexual intercourse with any man besides me, and she has made it perfectly clear to me that she is deeply hurt and resentful of my extramarital activities.

"It seems to me that, by this time, Marilyn must know perfectly well that I am attracted to young girls, and she must know that it is likely that I may even disregard the incest taboo in order to satisfy my craving. But yet, even though she is not tolerant of my desires, she has taken no steps whatever to guard against another incestuous relationship being established in the family. Quite the opposite, for example, just last night Marilyn suggested that I take Sandra in the bathtub with me and bathe her at the same time I took a bath. Now, as you know, she is only five years old, and she's far from being an attractive sex partner to me at this point. On the other hand, I do get an erection when she snuggles up to me in bed or sits on me in the bathtub. What's more, *she* is quite aware of the pleasurable sensations which center around her genital organs. So—with the background knowledge of Marilyn's intelligence which I have given you, wouldn't you think that *she,* understanding the potential result of such intimate contact between Sandra and me, would guard against this kind of contact?* Just as sure as

* Concerning the reported behavior of Lawrence C.'s wife, much additional information, some of it coming from her, would be necessary before one could safely venture a comment. Is her behavior, in general, as he describes it? Or is he endeavoring to make her, in a sense, his accomplice—which might serve him as a means of diminishing his own sense of responsibility and guilt?

Concerning father–daughter incest cases generally, most of them, when reported to the authorities, are reported by the wife–mother. Sometimes this occurs as soon as the incident is learned of, sometimes only after the husband has been given many "chances." Of course, there must be a great many other cases where the incest is known to the wife but is never reported. As wife, she may be very reluctant to see her husband punished, to lose his services as bread-winner, to involve the family in scandal, etc. As mother, she may feel that her daughter can only be further damaged by what would ensue. Or, there may be a great many other motives involved. Occasionally, the wife may actively promote the incest—so as to keep her husband from having an affair outside the home, because of sadistic feelings toward the daughter, etc., etc. Or she may behave as this woman is described as behaving—consciously deploring her the world, Sandra and I would proceed into an incestuous relationship when she is ready, but for my deep concern about the possibility of such a relationship resulting in serious psychological damage to her. And, in this connection, you have just about convinced me of the absolute reality and unavoidability of such risks.

"As for the frequencies of my sexual outlets, until two years or so ago I was restrained to some degree by guilt feelings which accompanied acts of masturbation and extramarital sexual intercourse. Because of this restraint, my outlets would probably average about one orgasm daily from the age of fourteen. About three times weekly (since my marriage) these orgasms were attained through intercourse with my wife—and they continue to be so. However, today, without the old inhibitions, I average about two orgasms daily. If I happen to be particularly stimulated by a story, case history, or something of the sort, I may very well masturbate to orgasm three times within a period of three or four hours. When this happens, it is usual that I will have only one orgasm the following day. I have been waiting to experience a slowing down of my sexual activities—which was promised by the psychiatrist whom I used to visit regularly, and which, at that time, I actually hoped for. Now, I am very *glad* that I have the potency I do and I hope that it will stay with me.

"By the way, after discussing with you the matter of 'artificial vaginas,' I received in the mail, without my requesting it, an advertisement for an artificial penis made of a rubbery material and hollow inside, which it seemed might be even better suited to function as an instrument of self-gratification, fitting closely over the whole length of the erect penis. I then telephoned all over the city, seeking to buy one locally, and at last succeeded in ordering from one of the surgical supply stores a so-called 'CTD'—their abbreviation for Coital Training Device —and have been promised unfailing delivery by the end of this week. I'm quite anxious to give the thing a try.

husband's behavior and yet, as if unconsciously acting from motives of which she is unaware or but dimly aware, behave in such a manner that the incest is encouraged or facilitated in subtle ways.

"Also, before closing, I would like to supply you with a brief chart summarizing my relationships with nymphets as they occurred during the years 1940–1960. (On another occasion, perhaps I can make this chart complete; at the moment, I am uncertain of a few items outside this time period.) My chart follows:

Intercourse with Nymphets

DATE	NAME	PLACE	GIRL'S AGE
1940	. . .	————	14
1941	. . .	Dallas	14
1942	. . .	Chicago	14
1943	. . .	Albany	13
1946	. . .	Milwaukee	14
1949	. . .	New Orleans	14
1957	. . .	Chicago	13
1960	. . .	Chicago	13*

Sex Play with Nymphets—No Intercourse

DATE	NAME	PLACE	GIRL'S AGE
1941	. . .	Dallas	11
1947	. . .	St. Louis	13
1948	. . .	St. Louis	14
1951–2	. . .	Tucson	12–13
1952–3	. . .	El Paso	10–11
1958	. . .	Tucson	11

* This list does not include Lawrence C.'s daughter. Names have been deleted by R.M. Note the age difference between the girls listed above, with whom coitus was had, and the girls listed below, with whom there was no coitus.

"This listing refers, on the one hand, to girls with whom I had intercourse (coitus) one or more times, and, on the other hand, to girls with whom I had sex play—including mouth-genital stimulation in one instance—but no actual intercourse. These are the relationships, in that time period, which I am able to recall at the moment.

"As I have told you, I contest the contention that child prostitutes exist in most large cities. It may be so, but I have yet to make a good connection—and, as you know, I have made a diligent search.

"Anyone who is interested and takes the trouble to investigate the matter can find plenty of evidence to support the view that there really are lots of nymphet-age girls who would be willing to engage in sexual relations with mature men—and who would genuinely enjoy taking part in such relations. But the problem of getting the willing girls and the desirous men together—especially under reasonably safe circumstances—seems immense and almost insurmountable.

"For many reasons of which I'm sure you are aware, it is nothing less than foolhardy to approach an underage girl on the street—even though she may be perfectly willing and even eager. One needs the security afforded by an adult third party —whether that person be a permissive parent or some other adult who is in a position to supervise (if that is the proper word for it) the sexual activities of the child—to arrange for a suitable meeting place, to see to it that she is adequately protected against pregnancy, to take precautions against physical harm to the girl by thoroughly checking her partners, and so on. There *must* be such permissive-minded parents who are, at the same time, discreet and understanding of the vagaries of sexuality which make such relationships extremely attractive to some people.

"As you know, I have been struggling for some time with the question of whether or not to deliberately establish, for the second time, an incestuous relationship with one of my daughters. I have just about decided, after thinking the problem through as thoroughly as I can, and after considering the large amounts of scientific and other information you've provided, that for the sake of the girl I should avoid this. As you have pointed out to me, the desire to raise to adulthood a happy, well-adjusted person and, at the same time, to have her as a regular sex partner from age ten or so, is akin to wanting to have one's cake and eat it too—at least in our society. On the other hand, my desire is great and it would appear that this craving can be most easily and readily satisfied by my daughter —who, at this point, promises to be just as willing to cooperate in a few years hence as was her sister before her. Whether my judgment prevails over my passion in this situation remains to be decided. I do think that the answer will depend to a very large extent upon whether I am able to establish a contact with someone who will help me—or, I should say, who will make it possible for me—to satisfy my desires through relationships with young girls other than my daughter, on something approaching a regular basis.

"By the way, the CTD—Coital Training Device—has arrived, and is OK, but that's about as far as I can go. It's a damned poor substitute for a genuine vagina!

August 7

"I can only be thankful that I had no liaison with some delightful nymphet all set up for this coming weekend. My pleasure would fall far short, I'm afraid, of what is usually possible for me in such situations.

"The sad fact of the matter is that I am temporarily 'out of action.' Last Monday was the day I decided on to give my 'CTD' a real test, and before I caught on to what was happening I had really inflicted some pretty painful damage on myself through irritation. I am still raw in spots—too much so for intercourse to be comfortable—but, fortunately, it is healing up rapidly now. This misadventure happened notwithstanding my considered use of the prescribed lubricant.

"In a way it is sort of funny. I suppose that I got what I deserved.

"You might be interested to hear just how this irksome wound was sustained.

"Monday morning, I masturbated with the thing (CTD), and then left it on. Later, around noon, I walked to a section of town where the prospects of making contact with amateur prostitutes are fairly good.

"There, after two or three unfruitful attempts, I encountered what appeared to be a competent pimp who assured me that he could provide exactly the kind of girl I was looking for. So I met with him and the girl at the place appointed and, although she was rather attractive and, as specified, quite small, she just wasn't young enough—probably she was twenty-five or so—to suit me. I declined with regrets and apologies to all—at which point the man said: 'Well, then I'll fuck her'—which he proceeded to do in my presence.

"I've witnessed this kind of thing only a few times before and I found it extremely exciting—so I masturbated again while watching the two of them have intercourse. He was into her and finished long before she had a chance to climax—and when he withdrew he left her all worked up but unsatisfied. So, even though she left me quite cold, I felt sorry for her and decided to see what I could do, with the help of my 'CTD,' to bring her to orgasm. I was successful—but got nothing out of it myself.

"In the meantime, the man had left and the girl introduced me to another girl who lives in the same apartment building—a seventeen-year-old—who said she would be unable to have intercourse until the following day because she was having her period.

"Monday evening, I masturbated a third time, once again using the 'CTD,' and only then did I begin to notice the soreness. It developed that I had rubbed the head of my penis until the thing was raw.

"I suppose it will be a good idea to give it a rest for a while, huh?

September 1

"Apologies for my long silence, but the burden of work around here has been almost unbelievable!

"Last week I had to make a quick trip to Chicago on business and I took my daughter Sandra along with me. I had a sitter for her during the day and then we spent the night together at the ——— Hotel. At the present time, Sandra is just about the same size and shape as the little girl whose picture I recently sent to you. In due course, I will tell you all about our evening. For now, suffice it to say that it was nice. I just hope I won't find cause to regret it later on.

September 15

"Well, business has now slacked off a bit—thank God!—and I am exhausted. What a grind!

"Unfortunately, at this point I simply cannot remember what material I have given you and what I haven't. Further, your letters to me, which provided me with some guidance in the matter, no longer exist.

"Perhaps I am excessively cautious, but I thought it unwise to take a business trip I made recently and leave all the correspondence we have had during the past months here in my office while I was absent. Therefore, I took the whole lot of it along with me to St. Louis. Then, when I sought unsuccessfully to find some safe place in the hotel room to put all the correspondence, plus a bunch of books and pictures I also had brought, I began to get nervous. Finally, as a last resort, I went ahead and destroyed the whole business.

"Was I overcautious? Perhaps, but possibly this very overcautiousness is what has saved me from a lot of trouble in spite of my proclivity for sexual expression of types which are unacceptable in our society.

"I haven't forgotten, of course, that I promised to supply you with details concerning my overnight experience with Sandra in Chicago some weeks ago.

"First, I should remind you that Sandra soon will be six years of age. She is really too young and too small to be very stimulating sexually, except for the fact that I can conjure up a picture of Sandra some five years hence when she very definitely will be desirable to me.

"Secondly, while we had complete freedom in Chicago, with plenty of time for uninterrupted play, this was very definitely not the occasion of her introduction to sexual experience with me. In fact, for a long time I have been fondling Sandra whenever she sits in my lap, crawls into bed with me, etc., always provided, of course, that there is privacy. She reciprocates this manual fondling quite, quite willingly.

"During the last year or so, sex play with Sandra has progressed to the point of interfemoral (between the thighs) intercourse, and also *mutual* mouth–genital stimulation. Opportunities for interfemoral intercourse naturally are somewhat limited because of lack of privacy and the danger of interruption, but we do manage it about once a week. It is customary that I help Sandra to get ready for bed while Marilyn is downstairs preparing dinner, and almost always during this process of getting her into her pajamas, she will lie back on the bed, spread her legs apart, and I will suck her little cunt for a few minutes.

"I believe that Sandra thoroughly enjoys this kind of sex play. I base this opinion on my careful observation of her hip movements, the increased tempo of her breathing, and the spontaneous way she spreads her legs to receive my hand or my mouth or my penis. (I would surely like to have your opinion as to the extent that a six-year-old girl is really capable of being sexually aroused, whether it is possible or probable that she reaches orgasm, etc.)

"As I have probably indicated to you already in some of my previous letters, one of my principal concerns has been whether a little girl can possibly appreciate the necessity for absolute secrecy about such a relationship—and, even if she does understand, whether she can be depended upon to keep the secret inviolate. Even while my intellect produces negative responses to both questions—something that has caused me a considerable amount of worry—actual experience over a period of years with Cindy when she was a little girl, and now Sandra, indicates that they *do know* enough not to tell and that probably the relationship means enough to them that they would not risk bringing it to a swift end by revealing its existence to anyone else.

"In any event, Sandra and I went to Chicago, where we stayed together, as mentioned, at the ——— Hotel. I had asked Sandra how she would like this, and she was all for it. In my discussion of the planning with Sandra, I explained to her that our spending the night together in the hotel would give us a wonderful opportunity to 'do it together'—which is our standard terminology for sex play—and so she understood quite fully just what it was that I had in mind.

"During the day she had a fine time with her 'sitter,' visiting the shops of interest, having ice cream sodas, picking out a lovely doll for herself, and so forth. I took her to dinner around seven o'clock, and as soon as dinner was over she was ready to go up to our room and get undressed so that we could 'do it together.' So up we went, got undressed, took a leisurely bath together, and then got into bed. She snuggled up to me and we began our sex play, which included mutual fondling, mouth–genital stimulation, and, finally, after about an hour, ended with interfemoral intercourse.

"The really nice part of all of this was that there was no hurry, no fear of interruption, and no worry about covering up the evidence, which is always one of the big problems at home. For example, at home I always have to worry about traces of semen being left on the sheets, the towels, the handkerchiefs, etc.—even on Sandra. In the hotel room there was no need for such concerns and one could be totally relaxed.

"I have started working on Sandra's hymen with a lubricated little finger in the expectation that, over a period of time, I can assist in preparation of her genitals for actual intercourse with a minimum of pain. As I think I have told you, I did the same thing with Cindy, starting when she was eight, and by the time she was ten there was no difficulty at all in effecting full penetration of her vagina with my penis. Until learning recently of an incest case involving an eight-year-old who had intercourse with her father, I had always thought that ten was extremely young. However, assuming that my relationship with Sandra is going to continue and develop into full-fledged incest, I am all for intercourse at the earliest age at which it can be accomplished without pain or injury to her.

"Whether it will continue or not is another thing. You just about had me convinced that the risks to her emotional well-being and the possible disruptive effects upon the whole family, militated too strongly in favor of stopping all sexual play with Sandra. I think you are probably one hundred per cent correct, and I think it is still not too late to nip the relationship in the bud without Sandra's even remembering it—except possibly very vaguely. But whether I will do it or not remains to be seen. The attraction is very, very powerful and difficult to resist.

"Oh—one more thing, which I think can be disposed of quickly. I'm afraid we are going to draw a near blank when it comes to a description of my erotic dream life. I have *never* had an orgasm in my sleep. I have erotic dreams *very* infrequently, and even then it is most difficult for me to recollect any of the details. Once in a great while—probably no more often than once a month or even every two months, as far as I can remember, I would dream about some attractive young girl. For example, on one recent occasion, I dreamed about a pretty, blonde, ten-year-old girl who used to come to our house back a number of years ago. As best I can remember, in the dream I played around with her with my hands a bit, and perhaps removed a portion of her clothing, but I am not at all sure of this. I do think I was highly excited sexually, but actual intercourse never took place. This is how it is with just about all of the erotic dreams I am able to remember—they nearly always stop short of intercourse, and they certainly stop short of orgasm.

"It occurs to me to be extremely regretful that my present attitudes and beliefs about sex could not have been formed much earlier in my life. I had no idea—and would never have believed—how much of a prude I really was for so many years. What suffering and guilt this caused when I repeatedly violated the ridiculous code of sex ethics that I had been brought up to believe in! How that pain detracted from the pleasure that was inherent in the sexual acts themselves!

January 11

"I will write to you within a few days and attempt to offer some explanations for my failure to be more productive during the last several months. The plain fact of the matter is I just haven't been in the proper frame of mind.

"You describe in one of your books an incest relationship

between an eight-year-old girl and her father. If it is not too much for me to ask, and if granting my request would not violate ethics on your part, would it be possible for you to let me see the detailed history of that case—of course with names and any other identifying data deleted or altered?

"You know, I am sure, that I derive a great deal of pleasure from reading such material. It is, for me, about the next best thing to that which is so rare that it is practically unattainable.

March 23

"You surmise that there *must* be some conflict between my religious beliefs and my sexual behavior. Here, I find myself to be in disagreement with you. There was undoubtedly a period—a terrifically agonizing period for me—when there *was* a conflict between my personal behavioral patterns and my religious beliefs. But I do believe that no such conflict exists today. As I think I have said, I have no qualms of conscience insofar as my sexual practices are concerned. My only concern, sometimes, is that by supporting a religion and a church that perpetuate a sexual ideology which I have rejected, I may be in violation of my own intellectual integrity. However, even with the various churches there presently exists a very broad spectrum of opinion as to what is sexually right or wrong. Also, I do not think that it is necessary for me to agree with my church on every particular point of its moral code in order to approve of its overall goals and so be able to give it, in general, my support.

"To round out the background concerning my sexual behavior, I have had a few homosexual experiences—but most of them were while I was in high school and during my first years at college. Most of these have been in the nature of experimentation and, honestly, it just does not appeal. I *do* enjoy masturbating along with other males who are doing the same. I don't mean mutual masturbation—because I can handle myself, control the level of excitement, much better than when someone else is doing it for me.

April 15

"What's been happening in recent months?

"Not much, really. As far as incest is concerned, you have convinced me—and I give you the full credit for this—that the potential damage is too great. I have just about dropped the idea of ever again allowing myself to get involved in an incestuous relationship. We'll see.

"As for relations with other nymphets (genuine nymphets, that is), I have had to face the unhappy reality that I am just not young enough any more to be physically attractive to them. And satisfaction of this appetite by purchase is not only extremely difficult and expensive, but it's a damned poor substitute for a girl whose heart is really in what she's doing. Honestly, if the girl doesn't enjoy, or at least make a very good pretense of enjoying, sexual play with me, I get nothing much out of it.

"Just to give you an example, two or three months ago a colored woman did, for a wonder, actually produce for me a genuine twelve-year-old (instead of trying to fool me by putting a short skirt, pigtails and a hair-ribbon on some young woman in her late teens or older, as so often has happened). But this poor little girl had obviously been pushed into the situation against her will, and she acted like a scared rabbit and began to cry. To have gone ahead would have been out-and-out rape, so I just left the place—a very frustrated man, believe me.

"I continue to pick up an occasional eighteen- to twenty-year-old (and try to pretend that she is younger). I continue to enjoy frequent masturbation and to have intercourse with my wife two or three times a week.

"So much for my current sex life.

May 12

"From the very beginning of our long dialogue, I have kept in mind at all times the condition under which it was initially undertaken: that it was to be clearly understood as an exploration and discussion of a subject of mutual interest, and that under no circumstances should it be considered in any way akin to a doctor–patient relationship.

"So be it.

"But *something* is—and probably has been for quite some time—happening inside me to change my whole attitude about sex and to markedly alter the pattern of my sexual behavior. I don't understand it and I don't even know whether the change is temporary, permanent, or whether it is just a phase I'm going through. In any event, I am going to attempt to explain the symptoms to you and ask whether, even in spite of our agreement, you might be able to shed some light which could assist me in arriving at a better understanding of myself.

"You have the full background, just as thoroughly and as honestly as I have been able to give and explain it to you over a period of nearly a year. You know that at some point within the last several years—perhaps two or three years ago, I'm not sure exactly when—I started out upon the long road of transition from very strict, puritanical attitudes about sex (which ran headlong into conflict with my personal behavior, causing me no end of agony), and started moving toward a much more liberal—and more realistic—concept of sexual behavior. I don't know, really, whether this gradual change of attitude came about as the result of an objective, intellectual conviction, or whether it may have been just a machination devised to soothe a troubled conscience—to suppress deep-rooted guilt.

"In any event, when I finally arrived at the liberal end of the road and at the point where I could accept and fully enjoy various kinds of sexual expression without any shame or guilt, I rebelled quite strongly against the puritanical ideals. I powerfully resented the fact that so large a portion of my life has been wasted insofar as a full enjoyment of sex was concerned. By this what I mean is that I very strongly resented and regretted the fact that *never* had I been able to enjoy the pleasure of even masturbation, to say nothing of extramarital intercourse, without suffering enormous guilt, depression, self-condemnation, and all the rest.

"My feelings of rebelliousness and resentment then were expressed through an increase in my sexual activity. Now I could fully enjoy and savor any kind of sexual expression, just so long as I didn't believe that in so doing I was trampling on any other person's rights or feelings. So, I resolved that I was going to make up for lost time. I don't believe a single day ever went by, for about a year and a half or two years, up until about just one month ago, when I didn't experience orgasm at least once—sometimes two or three times—through masturbation, extramarital coitus, marital coitus, or a combination of two of these or even all three.

"As you are aware, I bought really prodigious amounts of nudist publications, in order to obtain the pictures of nymphets that they included. I read all of the sexual case histories I could possibly lay my hands on. And I read just as much pornography as I was able to find. Many, many is the lunch hour (often of two to three hours!) that I have spent wandering through the poorer sections of the city—always looking for, and once in a while managing to find, a young girl.

"At this point, I think that I should say something more than I have said up until now about the sexual relationship that had existed between my wife, Marilyn, and me. I have told you that all throughout our married life we have had intercourse about two or three times a week and that the relationship always seemed to be mutually enjoyable and completely satisfactory. Well, perhaps I was wrong.

"Even with my wife, the old puritanical ideas prevailed—much modesty in the bedroom, a minimum of foreplay (probably not really foreplay in the true sense of the word since it included *no* manual manipulation by either of us, no oral–genital stimulation, etc.). I didn't really feel fully relaxed in the matter of sexual relations with Marilyn—possibly because I had her on a pedestal, which rôle was in conflict with a deep-rooted idea I had that sex was shameful and dirty. So much for the past.

"About a month ago my newly-found liberation from puritanical sex began to take expression in my own bedroom at home. Without the exchange of many, if any, words on the subject, I was able to get the idea across that 'this is good, it is fun, it is nothing to be ashamed of, let's just relax and enjoy it.' Marilyn went along with that idea completely.

"Now, almost every night before going to sleep and in the

morning upon awakening, we participate in mutual, unin-
hibited sex play which I find absolutely delightful. Sometimes
this ends in intercourse and sometimes it doesn't, depending
on how we both feel. I've only just discovered that there is
more to sexual enjoyment than the orgasm—that it isn't necessary to reach orgasm every time sex play is started. In fact, I
believe that I—and perhaps a very great many other men—
are (or have been) 'orgasm happy.' Thus, we have had no idea
how much pleasure is to be derived merely from relaxed,
gentle sex play, saving the orgasm for the next time or possibly
even the next time after that.

"Anyway, I find myself becoming less and less interested
in extramarital sex. During the last couple of weeks I have
looked at my pictures of nymphets, as usual, and, on a number
of occasions, started to masturbate, but I found that I just
didn't care enough about it to finish. Likewise, I'm not sufficiently interested in having a young girl to make the effort to
look for one or to spend the money to pay for her if I should
find one. Remember how anxious I was at one time to spend
as much as one hundred dollars for a weekend with a nymphet?
I wouldn't do it today (although I can't be sure whether by
tomorrow, or next week or next month, I may not be after the
same thing again?).

*"Could it possibly be that, at this late date, I am finally
growing up?*

January 10
(about eight months later)

"I had a lovely seventeen-year-old colored girl yesterday
afternoon—but as usual it was one of these 'quickies' where
the proprietress comes and knocks on the door after thirty
minutes and tells you to hurry up and leave. This one—the
girl—is really nice enough to spend a weekend with. . . .

"By the way, perhaps you will enjoy one of my most recent
'phantasy girls,' and the picture (clipped from a nudist magazine) is enclosed. Her two companions in the photo are quite
nice too, but the little thing in the middle, facing the camera,
is just delightful, I think."

COMMENTS

The true nymphophile is an adult male who is sexually attracted principally or exclusively to young girls. Usually, the girl is prepubescent, and typically the preference would be for a girl of eight or nine to twelve or, possibly, thirteen years of age. It may be the ideal, as was the case with Lawrence C., that the signs of approaching womanhood are just becoming manifest. Also, for practical reasons, the nymphophile probably would prefer that the girl be sufficiently developed physically so that vaginal penetration may take place without unusual pain or injury to her. While fondling and oral–genital contacts with the young female undoubtedly occur with a greater frequency than does coitus—and more will be said about this later on—I think it erroneous to say that those activities are preferred to coitus by the offender, at least when it is of the nymphophile we are speaking.

Nymphophilia, like almost all other sexual aberrations, has had a certain number of famous representatives—among them, the writers Dostoyevsky, Ruskin, and Lewis Carroll. Dostoyevsky may have been overtly nymphophilic only for a time.* However, the theme of the child as a sexual object appears repeatedly in his work and is associated with sadism. During Dostoyevsky's life there were many rumors to the effect that he had had relations with female children and even that he had raped a little girl. Stavrogin's description, in *The Possessed,* of how he raped a twelve-year-old and then forced her to kill herself, did nothing to quiet the rumors.

Marc Slonim writes that "In a letter to Leo Tolstoy, Strakhov repeated the story that Dostoyevsky himself had supposedly boasted of having had sexual relations with a little girl who was brought to him by her governess while he was taking a bath." And Dmitri Grigorovich, a writer and friend of Dos-

* Cf. Albert Moll, *The Sexual Life of the Child,* Macmillan Co., New York, 1924, pp. 233–34. Moll remarks, with reference to his statement about Dostoyevsky, that "from the circle of my own acquaintanceship, I have learned that such a tendency may exist in those who are in other respects morally and intellectually sound."

toyevsky's since his youth, related that "during a trial over the rape of a ten-year-old girl, Dostoyevsky had become inflamed with passion for her and, even though he had never set eyes on the child before, had followed her out of court and *used* her. All of this had supposedly taken place in the early 1860's."*

Slonim, after considering the evidence, concludes that "One thing is indisputable: the theme of corrupting minor girls sounds so often in his works, and he reverted to it so frequently in his conversations, that it assumes a persistent, if not a truly manic character. . . . Whether any ten- or twelve-year-old girl actually had come into his life, to the impairment of her morals . . . we do not know and probably never shall. But that a sexual fantasy of this sort dwelt within him and that he was hag-ridden by it appears undeniable. . . ."**

In the case of John Ruskin, he was attracted progressively throughout his lifetime to younger and younger females, this consistent "regression" culminating in his love for a nine-year-old girl, Rose la Touche, when he was forty. Ruskin is known to have been impotent with mature females (and to have suffered greatly from guilt resulting from masturbation). Apparently he refrained (or had no opportunity) from establishing a consummated sexual relationship with a child.† Lewis Carroll (the Reverend Charles Dodgson) also is not known to have sexually consummated any of his numerous attachments to children. However, he from time to time had difficulties with parents of little girls whom he openly kissed and fondled (and also sketched and photographed in the nude). He considered the young male friends of these girls to be his rivals and showed his hostility to them openly. Usually, but not always, Carroll terminated his friendships with girls when they reached an age and stage of physical development at which they no longer attracted him. Out of his feelings for the child Alice Liddell

---

* Marc Slonim, *Three Loves of Dostoyevsky*, Alvin Redman, London, 1957, pp. 276–77.

** *Ibid.*, pp. 278–80.

† See, for example, Allen, C., "The Problem of John Ruskin: A Psycho-Sexological Analysis," in Pillay, A., and Ellis, A. (Eds.), *Sex, Society and The Individual*, International Journal of Sexology, Bombay, 1953.

came *Through the Looking-Glass* and the other much beloved *Alice* stories.*

Such "decadent" writers as Charles Baudelaire and Aubrey Beardsley also found little girls sexually attractive, or professed to, but this should be regarded as much more a matter of libertinism than of anything resembling nymphophilia. To mention one more name, Edgar Allan Poe has been charged with having, amongst his various alleged aberrations, nymphophilic tendencies. However, the girls to whom Poe was attracted were, while young, still somewhat older than those who would be most attractive to the nymphophile.

Doubtless a number of other well-known persons, from different fields of human endeavor, could be with assurance added to the list if the facts of their lives were better known to us; but a deviation of this type is usually kept a very closely guarded secret. Among present-day figures, there at once comes to mind one of the men who has been most instrumental in fashioning our "liberalized" sex behavior code. His desire for little girls was not much of a secret, and neither was the fact that he had no moral scruples about satisfying the desire whenever possible. As with so many other of our sex behavior theorists, we can only speculate as to the effect of his personal problem upon his research and the conclusions ostensibly derived from it.**

Historically, the sexual relations of adults with children have been so commonplace, and so often sanctioned by various societies, that doubtless many nymphophiles simply passed unnoticed.† Thus, although records of many aberrations as

* Allen, C., *ibid.,* p. 250; also, "Weaver of Wonder," in *MD,* September, 1965, pp. 216–23.

** If there is a book that cries to be written, it is one about the sexual problems of sexologists. So many have been deviates of one sort or another, or afflicted with impotence or other serious problems, that society, which is being strongly influenced by them, is entitled to a careful study examining their work for possible bias. The job would not be a popular one, but it ought to be done.

† Of course we do know about some. For instance, a Chinese figure who has come down to us is the Emperor Yang Wang, of the Sui Dynasty, whose preference for girls between the ages of six and ten was notorious.

they have existed throughout history are abundant, we rarely
encounter any mention or hint of nymphophilia—though, of
course, we do find a great many references to adult–child sexual
intercourse. As a possible exception, the Arabs long have recognized a special adult male craving for immature females, which
they term "nymph madness" (khebl-hhūrī). Even here however, the appellation seems to be applied to many males other
than nymphophiles—although doubtless not to the Prophet
Mohammed, who deflowered his child bride, 'Ayisheh, when
she was six years of age. Thus, the history of nymphophilia is
obscure, and there is little in the way of relevant psychological
speculation or even awareness of the problem as a special one
apart from the general problem of adult–child intercourse.

In fact, even at the present time there are no sufficiently
extensive and convincing studies of the true nymphophile, such
as Lawrence C., as he exists in our society. We have had, recently, some extensive reports on the adult sexual offender
against children; but only a minority of these are nymphophiles,
and the nymphophile is not adequately separated out from the
other offenders.* Neither do various older, but still modern,
studies from our own and other societies tell us very much that
is useful concerning this problem.

As regards observable characteristics and overt behavior
of the general run of *apprehended* sex offenders against female
children, among whom some nymphophiles would be included,
one notes that the offender portrait emerging from the most
recent studies differs in significant ways from some of the long-
standing stereotypes.

For example, in perhaps around two-thirds of all cases, and
certainly in a high percentage of cases, the offending adult has

---

* Cf. Mohr, J. W., *et al., Pedophilia and Exhibitionism*, University of Toronto Press, Canada, 1964; and the latest of the several
"Kinsey reports" (Gebhard, P. H., *et al., Sex Offenders*, Harper &
Row, New York, 1965), which terms "somewhat unfortunate" the
authors' own heading "Pedophiles," remarking that "these men
evidently did not consciously prefer children as sexual partners, but
simply found them acceptable." (p. 74.) Obviously, the nymphophile (or pedophile), as represented by Lawrence C., is a bird of
quite another feather.

known the child previous to the commission of the offense—
neighbors, friends of the family, and relatives appear to be involved much more often than usually has been supposed. Thus,
the stereotype of the typical child-molester as a furtive and degenerate stranger no longer is acceptable. This new evidence,
along with the fact that the greater number of sexual offenses
against children take place in their own homes or under similarly sheltered conditions, makes it evident that the usual police
precautions, such as surveillance of playgrounds and school-
yards, at best are effective against only a minority of potential
offenders.

Another casualty of recent research is the belief that
elderly males constitute a majority of the offenders against
children. For example, Mohr and his coauthors report* that
"The ages of pedophilic offenders indicate the existence of
three groups: the adolescent group, with a peak in puberty; the
middle-aged group culminating in the mid-to-late thirties; and
a senescent one in the late fifties and early sixties. All data
agree that the senescent group, which often has been described
as the predominant one, is actually small in comparison with
the middle-aged group. The adolescent group is at its height
on the borderline of the definition of pedophilia, because the
offender himself is likely to be in puberty. . . . In addition to
those in the three age groups, there is a small group of chronic
offenders who remain prone to pedophilic acts, whereas for
the majority of offenders pedophilic acts are more or less in-
cidental occurrences."

Among these chronic offenders, of course, would be found
the nymphophiles. However, even a "chronic offender group"
is not made up of nymphophiles exclusively. One might also
find in it, for example, some conscious sadists who prey mainly
or exclusively on children. The popular notion of "childish
innocence," linked to that of sex as dirty and degrading, can
make of sexual relations with a child—regarded as a defiling of
the purity of the child—a source of gratification even when no
violence is employed. Some exhibitionists, who also must be

* *Ibid.*, pp. 41–2.

suspected of sadism, prefer or need children as the objects of their acts. Also, there are impotent or partly impotent males who do not really prefer young girls, but who experience shame when they fail with older females and so may limit their activities largely to children. Nor do these various types of individuals exhaust the list of those who might be found in a chronic offender group along with the nymphophiles.

To return to the subject of exploded stereotypes, it long has been thought by many law enforcement officials and also writers on sex problems that most offenders against children are, when not senile, of low intelligence or mentally retarded. However, we now have good reason to believe that the intelligence of the average offender falls within the range of the normal. On the other hand, it is true that mentally retarded individuals do commit a disproportionate number of offenses of this type.

Another almost certainly erroneous belief, that has fairly widespread if not general acceptance, is that use of various prohibited drugs, such as marijuana, cocaine, and heroin, is likely to precipitate acts of sexual aggression against children (and others). Recent studies of offenders lend no support to such a notion. On the other hand, consumption of alcoholic beverages —the drug our society does allow to be consumed—is a significant factor in the commission of a large percentage of all sex offenses, including those against children and young girls.*

Yet another misconception, often encountered, and recently subjected to statistical challenge, is that the sexual contact of adult males with prepubescent females usually takes the form of (or includes) coitus. But the fact, which by now seems established well enough, is that fondling of the genitals and

* Of course, in assessing these last statements, one does well to keep in mind the extent to which use of alcohol exceeds the use of the other drugs mentioned. Even so, there can be little doubt that alcohol intoxication is more likely to result in violation of sexual taboos and laws than is the intoxication produced by many prohibited drugs, certainly including heroin and the other opium derivatives. Use of marijuana and cocaine not infrequently is associated with sexual activity; but this seems to be very largely limited to the group that is involved in the drug use.

some other body parts is an act of much more frequent occurrence than that of vaginal intercourse. Also more frequent than
vaginal intercourse are mouth–genital contacts—the adult more
often orally stimulating the genitals of the child than the re-
verse. However, oral performance by the child, and also re-
ciprocal oral contacts, are not uncommon.*

As concerns these greater frequencies of fondling and
mouth–genital contacts, as compared to coitus, it is proposed
that these "immature" acts are evidential of the immaturity of
the adult partner. Possibly this is true in some cases, but there
are also other reasons for it. For one, the adult male may believe, whether rightly or wrongly is beside the point, that the
girl is too small for vaginal intercourse and would be injured
by it or would suffer too much pain. Especially in the case of
the nymphophile, who would like to give his partner pleasure,
and who typically insists on his concern for the child's welfare,
the thought that coitus would hurt or injure her is a strong
deterrent and often leads him to settle for other types of contact.

Particularly with regard to fondling, it should be noted
that many such acts are accomplished under conditions where
privacy is uncertain and which thus do not allow for coitus. A
hand on the girl's genitals may be quickly withdrawn; when
coitus is interrupted, restoration of the appearance of propriety
is likely to take somewhat longer. Oral–genital relations, too,
are less hazardous when there is a possibility of interruption. A
man who repeatedly has performed cunnilingus on young girls
in a public park relates that his practice is to kneel in front of
the girl while she is seated on a park bench, or, occasionally, in

* It might be well to remind the reader that the whole discussion is about male offenders against female children. When
homosexual offenders against male children are considered, many of
the data change substantially. (For example, there are comparatively
few homosexual offenses against boys younger than fourteen years.
This seems to puzzle some writers who are so psychologically
oriented they seem unable to consider any obvious, practical explanation. But the fact is most homosexual offenders against boys
want one who is old enough to ejaculate. It is certainly debatable
whether there exists a homosexual counterpart of nymphophilia.)

a swing. If approaching footsteps are heard, he is able to hastily pull the girl's skirt down and then, if need be, he pretends to be tying her shoe lace. Like Lawrence C., this man is very adept at making friends with children and, so far as he knows, has never been reported by any girl with whom he has had relations.

When the situation allows for it, masturbation by the male is a usual accompaniment of his fondling of the child or of his mouth–genital contact. This is when the child cannot be induced to provide the manual or oral stimulation. However, some men are able to reach the climax without any handling of their own genitals, the stimulus derived from the fondling or cunnilingus being sufficient to trigger the orgasm response.

That the offender against children generally, and the nymphophile in particular, tends to be an "immature" personality often has been stated. The immaturity may be described as general or as "psychosexual." When this psychosexual immaturity or "infantilism" is defined in terms of desire for an immature sex object, we are merely playing with words. Nymphophilia or pedophilia, as terms, already cover this same ground; and these are certainly not further illumined by speaking of psychosexual immaturity. More often, however, further signs of immaturity are said to have been detected in the nymphophile. For example, an inability to delay the gratification of appetites and wishes, along with a low frustration threshhold, often has been described. Sexually, such an individual might be likely to select a child rather than go to the trouble of gaining the affection of an older girl or woman. However, while this might help to explain some offenses by males who find children "acceptable," it does not appear to shed much light on the problem of the nymphophile who has little or no desire at all for older females.

Immaturity can manifest itself in many ways, including performance of the sexual act. For example, insistence on swift gratification may lead to omission of foreplay and to the male's striving toward his climax with all possible haste and with no concern for the feeling and satisfaction of his partner. We find little of this in the case of Lawrence C. (or in the few other

cases of nymphophilia of which I have first-hand knowledge).
Lawrence C. omits foreplay only with his wife, or did so up
until recently, as he describes; his control is superior and he
takes considerably longer to reach his climax than does the
average male; and he usually expends whatever effort is needed
to bring his partner to orgasm—in fact, in relations with older
females, he derives more pleasure from the partner's orgasm
than from his own. Apart from sex too, it should be pointed
out, he displays the ability to defer gratification of his desires.
His successes in several business careers have required that he
possess such capacity. And he displays it in various other areas
of his life as well.

On the other hand, he does consider himself to be immature—and speaks of his hope that he is "finally growing up."
Also, as has been noted of other nymphophiles, he has a peculiar ability to associate with children on their own level. There
indeed may be something curiously childish about such men.
But whether they have cultivated this trait, the better to pursue
their erotic fulfillments, or whether the childishness preceded
consciousness of the nymphophilia and is directly related to it
—these are matters requiring further study.

To examine the fairly copious literature of nymphophilia
or pedophilia) is to encounter an abundance of speculation, very
little of it having much value except as a record of confusion
and error. As noted, nymphophiles are rarely ever adequately
separated out from the other varieties of sex offenders against
children; and some studies take as their definition of "child"
whatever legal criterion may have been operative at the moment
in that particular place. Thus, we actually have "scientific" discussions of "pedophilia" which fail to differentiate between
offenses against girls of eight on the one hand, and girls of
eighteen on the other.*

* On this basis of legal definition, we also have offenders
against "children" twenty years of age! As the authors of the aforementioned Kinsey report on *Sex Offenders* observe, this places us
in the idiotic position that a Miss America or Miss Universe, presumably the most desirable of females, would be considered too
young to have sexual relations in some states. One might add that

Especially when all offenses against female children are considered to be nymphophilia, we are likely to encounter such an explanation of the conduct as "feeling of inferiority." The inferiority feeling, it is said, prevents the male from establishing a sexual relationship with an adult female. Then he turns to children, with whom he is able to be more at ease. But this, of course, does nothing to explain nymphophilia, since for the nymphophile the child is in no sense a conscious substitute for a preferred older partner. Neither do "timidity," "impotence," or even "pubic hair phobia" explain nymphophilia, although the first two may account for some child-molestings. In the case of the last-mentioned, one wonders if some lady could not have been induced to shave?

Probably the most commonly accepted theory as regards causation is the Freudian one which advances the notion of an unresolved Oedipus complex. Here, any mature female is equated with the mother. And, since coitus with such a woman thus would activate the unresolved conflict, the desires are fixed rather upon children. Yet, once again, it would seem that at most we have an explanation only for rejection of the mature female as object of desire. The nymphophile's specific desire for the child still goes unexplained despite some attempted amplifications. Also, one wonders, were this theory valid, would the nymphophile, in so many instances, prefer a child whose breasts, though small, have started to develop; who has scant, but not entirely absent, pubic hair; and who, in other ways, gives evidence of approaching womanhood? Why would he not prefer a still younger child who exhibits even less evidence of her femaleness? Or does the nymphophile, possibly, seize upon these signs of the female because he does crave femaleness in the sex-object, but can tolerate only limited amounts of it? If that is the case, then might he acquire this deviation rather

the individual who succumbed to the temptation to have intercourse with one of these beauty queens, might eventually wind up in the literature as another statistic in some study of nymphophilia or offenses against children. As I have remarked in another volume, Judge Morris Ploscowe is both realistic and wise in arguing for an age of consent of fourteen years.

than, say, homosexuality for the reason that he is able to tolerate somewhat more of the feminine than can those homosexuals who also are in flight from woman and possibly from incest?

That the nymphophile may in childhood have had some erotic experience with a young girl that has caused him to fix his desires upon such an object would seem to be another possibility. However, here one is obliged to admit that the crucial experience, if it occurred, often has remained inaccessible whatever the psychotherapeutic method employed to bring it up into consciousness. Therefore the theory, while appealing to "common sense," cannot presently be verified if advanced as a general one intended to explain all cases. Also, with regard to this and some other theories, we are left to wonder how it is that a good many persons become aware of their deviation only after a period of fairly successful heterosexual functioning on an adult level, as occurred with Lawrence C. Nymphophilia is not the only aberration that often makes itself manifest only after such a period of apparent normalcy; and the question of why the deviation does not operate at full force from the beginning of the overt sexual life is one that remains to be adequately answered.

The case of Lawrence C. raises many other questions too, and some of these will be dealt with in the discussions of incest and sexual behavior of children which will follow. But first at least a few words should be said concerning the possibility of a sadistic component of nymphophilia.

While some writers on this problem of nymphophilia are inclined to believe that most or all nymphophiles are sadists and even possibly potential lust murderers, there seems to be no sound basis for this view. As noted, there are sadists who prey primarily or exclusively upon children; but these seem to be a quite distinct group apart from the nymphophiles. Nymphophilia does sometimes lead to murder, but not to lust murder; rather, in these cases, the nymphophile panics and kills the child to prevent his own exposure. The murder does not, however, give sexual pleasure and therefore should not be seen as lust murder.

On the other hand, there often does seem to be the sugges-

tion of a sadism or at least a cruelty—perhaps "immature" and
akin to children's cruelty?—that manifests itself not in physical
violence or brutality but rather in more subtle, psychological
ways. Typically, the nymphophile insists upon his affection for
children and stoutly denies that he wants to harm them in any
way—he is, he will maintain, at worst a seducer, never a rapist
or inflictor of pain.* He points at once to his various precautions against inflicting physical injury, adding that he even
denies himself coitus when need be. Such an individual takes
pains not to frighten the child he seduces—and he comes to the
relationship bolstered by all kinds of rationalizations he has
made to convince himself that the child will not suffer as a
result of the sexual episode. Often he will persuade himself—
and sometimes, of course, this has basis in fact—that the advances actually were made by the child, who hinted in various
ways her willingness to engage in erotic activities with him.

Yet, it is usual that guilt results from the nymphophile's
acts—meaning that the rationalizations and self-deceit have
been less than completely effective. This is likely to mean, too,
that the nymphophile does believe that the child is likely to
sustain at least psychological damage from the activity with
him. And we must at least leave open the question of whether
this possibility of harm does not intensify erotic excitement or
even serve to make possible the gratification.

* While these insistences may seem calculated to gain some
sympathy from other adults, it seems probable the nymphophile
himself believes in his "good intentions," at least partially.

Incest in Its Relation
to Nymphophilia

Not every nymphophile has the potency for sexual intercourse with a mature female. However, some do, and these individuals, like other men, usually marry and produce children.* Often, because they are extremely fond of children—a more general as well as a sexual fondness—they have larger families than most. Thus, without any conscious calculation in most cases, they open the way for a succession of incestuous relationships.

When the nymphophile marries and his wife has a daughter, the potential for incest always is present as the daughter

* The nymphophile's potency often is made possible, as was the case with Lawrence C., by his ability to phantasy sex contact with a "nymphet" at the time when he is having an actual sex experience with his wife. In fact, the use of phantasies gives some potency to various types of deviates, who thus are enabled to marry. Some homosexuals, for instance, employ phantasies of male contacts and so are able to perform erotically with their wives. In cases of extreme inversion, the man may phantasy that he is the female partner in the act, while his wife is the male. Nor is it unknown for wives who are unresponsive to the image of their husband to phantasy intercourse with some other male while the unwitting spouse performs the very act that accomplishes his own psychical cuckolding.

reaches an age when she begins to exhibit those physical characteristics to which her father is powerfully attracted. What
greatly increases the chances that incest will occur is the difficulty the father is likely to be experiencing in his efforts to
secure sex partners outside the home. Moreover, should the
father make a sexual approach, the little girl is much less likely
to offer resistance than she would be if the same thing happened when she was adolescent or older. One study indicates
that of girls under ten years of age, only ten per cent will resist
seduction by the father;* other studies suggest that only about
half will offer some resistance to an incest relationship at this
age or thereabouts. In any case, the girl is much less likely to
try to reject the father's authority and demands at the age
when the nymphophile would find her most attractive than
she is at the later age when an incestuously inclined but non-
nymphophilic father would be more likely to make the same
attempt.

Some nymphophiles, for reasons of morality or inhibition
or whatever, refrain from acting out their aberration with anyone; others exempt their daughters from their practices, out of
love for them, because the incest ban is too powerful, or for
some other reason; but it would appear that for the nymphophile who has a daughter of appropriate age, the temptation
to incest is always present and usually is very difficult to resist.
As noted, one reason why the nymphophile is more tempted to
incest than are most other men is that he typically remains in
a state of sexual frustration, at least in this society. His desires
are difficult and dangerous to satisfy, so that the frequency of
his contacts is low. The sexual intercourse with the wife is performed with effort and mainly out of a sense of obligation or as
a means of keeping the marriage viable. Such sexual acts "do
not really count," give minimal pleasure, and do not contribute adequately toward release of sexual tensions. This
chronic frustration then is repeatedly brought to mind and intensified by the proximity of the daughter. Under such conditions various stimuli, such as, the visual ones of seeing the girl
nude or in underclothes, night wear, etc., excite desire and

* Gebhard, P., *et al, ibid.,* p. 224. (Footnote).

may come to be interpreted as sexually provocative acts directed by the daughter toward her father. Still more importantly, in the case of these young girls, there often is the additional stimulation of types of close and affectionate physical contact that are reacted to sexually by the father—hugging, kissing, sitting on the lap, and so on. All of this not only intensifies frustration, it also provides the mental stuff used by the man to persuade himself that his daughter is just as eager to establish an incest relationship as he is—so helping to justify, as he sees it, his actions in bringing that relationship into actual being.

Another factor that can be of considerable importance is the nymphophile's dream of a permanent or, if not that, fairly long-lasting sex–love relationship. This he necessarily must try to find with a child, since only a child can elicit from him a full measure of passion. However, if but for the most obvious reasons—surveillance of the girl by parents or guardians and her limited free time and freedom of movement—a sex–love relationship with someone else's child is almost impossible to establish. It is also almost impossible to establish because of the immaturity of the child's emotions and thought, but this aspect of the problem is much more easily overlooked or rationalized away.

Once the incest relationship has been established, the nymphophile is very likely to persuade himself that it is at least an approximation to the authentic love he has been so desperately seeking. Of course it is not, since the daughter has neither the emotional wherewithal nor the highly developed capacity for rationalization and self-deceit that her father possesses. However, for him, while imperfections may be recognized, the craving for love still may find its greatest possible measure of fulfillment in the incest, as we have seen occur with Lawrence C. Thus, when the relationship comes to an end, and if there is another daughter available, the nymphophile is strongly motivated to begin another incest relationship, expecting to find in it the same important rewards that he derived from the preceding one. And the second time the step is easier to take, resistance to the idea of incest already having been overcome.

When the progress of an incest relationship is not interrupted by the action of some third party, it may last for a
number of years, the duration frequently depending on how
old the girl was at the start. The father is likely to terminate
the relationship because his guilt feelings are too strong, because (in the case of the nymphophile) the girl reaches a stage
of development when she no longer is attractive to him, or because the possibility of pregnancy introduces a risk he is not
prepared to take. Of course there may be still other reasons,
but the ones just cited are among the most common. When the
incest is not terminated by the father, the girl is likely to insist
upon an end to it eventually. Her guilt may be the main factor
or, as she becomes older, she may acquire the strength to break
off an intimacy she did not want but felt unable to resist. Or
she may develop an interest in some male closer to her own
age and so lose sexual interest in her father as she might in any
other lover. Again, there may be a variety of possible motives
in addition to those mentioned, but those cited are the ones
most frequently described.

Unless his feelings of guilt are too disturbing, the nymphophile is likely to exhibit more sensitivity, intelligence, and general *savoir faire* in an incest relationship than are nonnympho-
phile males in the same situation. He has his past experience
with other children to draw upon; and he may possess a much
better ability to communicate with the daughter than most
fathers have. Also, in the majority of cases, he is dealing with
a younger and therefore more passive and malleable girl. Because of these factors the relationship may seem to move along
comparatively smoothly with little or no evidence of psychological damage to the child. The child, in fact, may take considerable pleasure in most aspects of the relationship, although
she is rarely so enthusiastic and unworried a participant as the
father may claim to believe or would have any confidante
believe.*

* Apart from the possibility of exposure, which always hovers
darkly over incest relationships and generates tension in the participants, there are a great many related problems that tend to come
up—for instance, the father's ability to administer discipline may

In such cases as that of Lawrence C., where the incest is ended without third-party intervention, psychological damage to the girl may become apparent only after termination and as she grows older. Doubtless there are cases where such damage was very slight, but the evidence for this is less clear than is the evidence of damage we do find in the numerous cases of subsequent fixation upon the father, homosexuality, promiscuity, prostitution, frigidity, etc., which seem to be directly referrable back to the incest. In any case, whatever the percentages and degrees, there can be no doubt at all that the transgression against the incest prohibition carries with it a significant risk of some severe damage to both parties. Self-punishment occurs somewhat as it does in the case of violation of taboo.

---

be impaired; and the girl's position with respect to her mother may be altered in multivarious ways, both when the mother is and is not aware of the incest. These and a multitude of other problems are described in my book, *Patterns of Incest,* and it would not be practical to try to deal with the same extensive materials in the present volume.

Nonincestuous Adult–Child
Sex Relationships

When the potent incest prohibition is not involved, the risk of psychological injury to the girl in the adult–child sex relationship naturally is diminished. Probably such relationships are not *necessarily* damaging at all in the sense that they must be severely traumatic and productive of a neurosis or some other mental or emotional disturbance later on. On the other hand, even under the best of conditions, it is doubtful that the child has very much to gain by beginning her sexual activities before puberty; and the temptation for the adult to exploit the youthful partner is inherent in the relationship with its heavy imbalance of power. Also, in the United States today, there are a great many cultural factors, especially illegality and censure by society, which work to make such relationships damaging even though there may be nothing essentially damaging in them. That we are presently paying a higher price than need be for protecting children from sexual exploitation is probable; if we ever care enough to give the matter thorough study, we probably can give as much or more protection while reducing emotional penalties which may fall as heavily on child as on adult participant in these cases.

Some limited evidence indicates that the damage to

"molested" children, when there is damage, is much more often and to a greater degree the product of highly emotional parental and other *reactions to the behavior after its disclosure* than it is a product of the actual sex experience. Thus, when it is revealed that a child has been involved in a sexual episode great care should be taken that no damaging response to the event is made by parents, law enforcement officials, or anyone else with whom the girl comes into contact. The consensus now seems to be that it is especially undesirable for children to have to appear in court in such cases. No doubt. At the same time one wonders about the extent to which the child's absence from the court proceedings must work to the detriment of justice, whether the handicap be on prosecution, defendant, or both.*

Before concluding, I will comment briefly on one other question Lawrence C. raises—that of the normality or abnormality of desire for prepubescent girls. Of course, in Lawrence C.'s case, the evidence for sexual abnormality is overwhelming. Speaking generally, however, the proof of the aberration lies not in an individual's being attracted to a young female, but in his being principally or exclusively attracted to such females while, at the same time, his ability to experience desire for a mature partner is impaired or altogether lacking. Such a condition as the latter we describe as nymphophilia, and the fact that another, normal male might be attracted to the same girl is in no way a proof for the nymphophile's normality.

It cannot be denied that much of human history testifies to the fact that a normal male may experience desire for a girl of, say, nine or ten years of age, not to mention older females who still exhibit some signs of immaturity. After all, the common law age of consent was ten years. The Babylonian Talmud speaks of three years and one day as the age when "marriage by coition" may be considered legitimate. The famous French

* It always has to be kept in mind that there are countless instances on record of children making false accusations of sexual molestation against adults. The accusation cannot be simply accepted without question. Protecting a child from psychological injury, while also protecting the rights of the accused, is a matter of the most extreme difficulty.

jurist, Jean Bodin, in the Sixteenth Century, placed age of consent at six years—and, in the last century, the French penal code fixed it at just eleven years. Among the ancients, religious prostitution, compulsory for all girls in some places, began when the girl was at least as young as seven and often continued up to the girl's puberty, when her obligation ended and she married. These, along with a great many other similar laws and customs, do not establish the existence throughout much of history of an epidemic or pandemic nymphophilia. Neither do they at all prove the wisdom of sanctioning the sexual relations of adults with children, as occasionally might be argued. What they do testify to is the fact that a male need not be sexually or otherwise aberrant to find a young girl desirable.*

As concerns this whole problem, in our society mental soundness may consist much less in never being erotically aroused by a child, than in having the capacity to resist the desire and to limit sexual activity to females who are mature enough to participate as approximate equals in the relationship.

* At least not when the girl is physically capable of coitus or appears to be so. Hopefully most civilized men of today *have* evolved beyond the possibility of seriously considering sexual intercourse with even less mature girls.

PART TWO

Bestiality: Human—
Animal Sex Contacts

PART TWO

Bestiality: Human–Animal Sex Contacts

"Heterosexual" Bestiality

Since publication in 1962,* of a lengthy report on human–animal sex contacts, I have accumulated some unusually detailed autobiographical statements concerning such practices. Those now to be presented to the reader are probably the most extensive accounts of bestiality ever to be made available to students of sexual behavior. First, however, and as a kind of introduction, it is worthwhile quoting from an informative letter sent to me by a Mississippi cattleman and university graduate. This gentleman has taken a keen interest in animal contacts as practiced in his area for almost half a century. He writes:

"I absolutely agree with you that legal reforms are needed. Bestiality is an offense that hardly warrants the very severe penalties now imposed in some states.** The State of Illinois,

* Masters, R. E. L., *Forbidden Sexual Behavior and Morality,* Julian Press, New York.
** U.S. penalties range from a year's imprisonment up through life at hard labor, though a few states have a fine and/or imprisonment penalty. The average sentence, a few years ago, was two to five years' imprisonment. However, many sentences are suspended under various conditions, such as agreement to enter psychotherapy —not warranted unless on some other grounds, but certainly preferable to imprisonment.

in its new penal code, no longer punishes this practice as such, which seems a sane position. In my own locality, although there are many cases, I have never known the law to interfere, although they would have had to do so, of course, had anybody wanted to make a complaint.

"What I now am writing you is personal knowledge, not hearsay; also, in some cases, personal observation—concerning a kind of behavior that has occurred in this locality just as far back as I am able to remember. It has been practiced by all ages. Of course the juveniles have the edge, but you can find bestiality, too, among the well-to-do people, the Negro or white tenant, and others who are, or have been, in cattle or farming, or who have otherwise had the opportunity for such sport.

"I have always observed that these people, when they know right where one stands on the subject, will confide their experiences with a great deal of pleasure. They seem to think it not morally wrong and they only fear the law or the chance of becoming a social outcast. They get enough pleasure from their practices to compensate them for all the risks they take, and those I have known seemed just as well-adjusted as anybody else. Incidentally, I am referring to human male–female animal contacts. I am not personally aware of any contacts between human females and animal males, although I am informed that such acts take place as exhibitionistic performances at private gatherings in New Orleans.

"I have seen males who are having relations with animals go to quite a bit of trouble to prevent other people from learning about their secret—such as, specially constructed barns, some air-conditioned, with all equipment needed. This includes sanitary facilities and cattle breaks, to train the animals in. You can be assured that these are well hidden, with easy access, etc. Most of the bestiality is with heifers from six to twelve months old; of course, the cows are used too, but the heifers (about waist high) are used as a rule. There will be eight to ten in a 'harem' when the man can afford it. They are not started training too early because of their discomfort. The teaching seems to be mainly kindness and handling, halter breaking, giving a few tidbits, such as, sugar. The animal is put in break—that is padded to protect both calf and operator —then the 'woo' begins by insertion of an artificial phallus that is lubricated and worked gently until the animal is quite ready and bows its back, bringing the vagina down to the proper level of the zooerast. After several sessions the break may not be needed—the animal is happy to participate.

"The jackpot that every operator looks for is when the animals rut or come in heat for the first time. The size may by now be a problem, but the zooerast still will tell you that you haven't lived until you've had what they call a 'heat ride.'*

"During my many years as a rancher, sometimes with quite a few tenants on my place, and from observations around the stockyards as well, I have personally become very tolerant as concerns these practices. I have yet to see it harm *man* or *beast*, and no matter what the public opinion may be, in several cases I have seen a lot of good come out of it—even some mental problems solved, unless I am very much mistaken. It is my thought that these animal contacts make men out of boys in a good many instances, and in some others the bestiality spares the community some much worse ills that would have occurred had this barnyard therapy not been available when and where it was needed."

I think that the point of view expressed by this correspondent in his concluding remarks is a mature and reasonable one, especially as concerns the practices of farm youths and some other persons for whom the animal contacts are in no sense the products of a perversion. Such acts should be thought of, rather, as akin to masturbation—performed, as masturbation may be, not out of preference or because of incapacity, but because of a lack of opportunity for heterosexual inter-

---

* This writer applies the term "zooerast" to anyone having sexual relations with an animal. Others limit the term to anal intercourse with an animal. It might be pointed out that another, similar term—*zoophilia*—is often used either as a synonym for bestiality or as a term for predominant or exclusive desire for animals—i.e., for bestiality-as-perversion. Zoophilia also sometimes refers to any sort of excessive emotional involvement with an animal.

course. On the other hand, bestiality certainly may be a part of a larger pattern of neurosis and self-damaging behavior; then, while tolerance still is warranted, the behavior is much more significant for the person and its continuance may be harmful even when there is no risk, or almost no risk, of detection and subsequent punishment. We will see that in the following case, the bestiality is productive of very strong feelings of guilt (although guilt at first is denied). The case is presented in a series of several brief and one long autobiographical statements by the author, a Wisconsin farmer in his mid-30s, who places the animal contacts in an overall context that includes also both heterosexual and homosexual experiences. Among the data provided by this farmer, whose account contains much unusual information, were photographs illustrating some of the contents of his "confession"—photographs which certainly go far to establish its authenticity.

The initial document was offered just following the informant's reading of my aforementioned discussion of bestiality and included the following excerpts:

"What I have to say is on the basis of my active participation in, and first-hand evaluation of, bestial relations with various common female farm animals over a period of some twenty years. Having been reared on a Wisconsin farm, and having chosen farming as my life's work, I have had ample opportunity to avail myself of this diversion as a satisfying sexual outlet with considerable regularity since shortly before my thirteenth birthday. Perhaps it is largely due to the fact that I began this practice at so youthful an age that I now have little or no moral inhibitions, but rather look upon this form of sex with considerable pleasure and renewed anticipation. Yet, I hasten to add that I am not so enamored with bestial relations that I consider them to be quite on the same level as heterosexual sex. Having married a girl who enjoys sex as much as I do, I could not excuse my bestial intimacies on the grounds that no other form of sex was available. Not that I feel an excuse to be needed. I enjoy home cooking and greatly prefer a meal around my own table, but for variety (the spice of life) I also enjoy an occasional meal out. I suppose it depends on the circumstances and the opportunities at hand to a certain extent. And one is apt to become encouraged to variety if there are certain inducements.

"At this point I have in mind a particular inducement, and it is one that conflicts with your expressed observation that among female animals ordinarily only monkeys and apes solicit human partners. I refer to the fact that I find myself being sexually solicited from time to time by various females of the swine species. This is a phenomenon which I have never recognized in relations with cows or heifers, ewes, bitches, or mares. In recent years, since horses have vanished from the farm scene, this species is no longer available, but I have had enough intimacy with all of these other species that I am quite sure I would detect a sexual advance if any one of these kinds of females would make it. Perhaps this solicitation on the part of sows and gilts accounts at least partly for the fact that it is with these animals that I enjoy the most frequent and satisfying sexual experiences. Of a surety, there is a wide range of responsiveness and/or passion for sex evidenced between various individuals. This range extends from the sexually frigid individual which will scarcely stand, even though she is fully in estrus, while being mounted by a boar, to the rare red-hot individual which will make sexual advances to a male of almost any species and without any previous experience. The animal shown in the first two photos I am sending you was just such a hot one. I know it for a fact that at the time these pictures were taken no previous sexual advances of any kind had been made to me by this sow. However, it is possible that her interest was awakened by seeing me performing coitus with another sow or gilt. It is not at all uncommon for other animals in the herd to observe with what seems to be great interest the act of sexual mating as it is in progress in their presence. I have found that this is just as likely to happen when I am the male involved as when a boar is so engaged. Especially is this inquisitiveness demonstrated by other females which also happen to be in heat at the time. Their investigation is usually focused upon the site of our genital coupling and the sexual stimulation derived by these animals, as a result of their observations, is quite often evident by the aroused intensity of their rutting activity. Immediately following intercourse, a sow or gilt, which has thus been served, attracts the almost exclusive attention of the other females in estrus. The resultant engorged and wet condition of the recently inseminated sow or gilt's vulva, which is sometimes also smeared with exuding ejaculate, seems to be not only extremely fascinating but, without question, erotically stimulating to the other individuals in rut, and also occasionally to other females in the herd as well. Perhaps the odors connected with the semen of the boar are more sex inciting to a sow or gilt, but it is quite plain that they are also aware of what the semen of a man is, when they see or smell it, to distinguish it sensuously, even without their having experienced sexual intercourse with a human male themselves. At any rate, on this occasion recorded by the photographs, being acutely aware of this sow's lasciviousness and *obvious display of her desire for my cock,* I determined to find out just how far she would go. Assuming the completely passive position, and yet making myself available to her investigation and advances, I found that instead of giving up her pursuit upon finding me to be non-aggressive, instead she seemed to become more insistent. She was of course intensely interested in examining my nude body, which I freely allowed since she was gentle, but there was no mistaking what area of my anatomy she found to be the most intriguing. Also, without any hesitation, she repeatedly mounted me when I assumed the proper (all-fours) position and even attempted simulated copulatory thrusts which, understandably, I found difficult to bear on account of her disproportionate weight. Without a doubt, she knew what she wanted and where it was. And I will have to confess that she knew just how to go about getting what she wanted. When I finally proceeded to the active role, I found her receptivity to be equally outstanding.*

* A female animal in heat will often mount another animal, or at least certain species do this. Just how this behavior is to be interpreted, apart from its being a sign of frustration, I am uncertain. Ordinarily, the other animal mounted is a female of the same species, but this action also is fairly often performed upon animals

"I know that I have not the means to support my asser-
tions concerning the sexual aggressiveness of the female animal
in bestial relations. But some of the photographs bolster my
case. The one photo of myself alone in the nude is included to
let you evaluate for yourself the degree of sexual excitement
which is always the case with me as I contemplate and experience bestial relations. Perhaps the fact that I consistently am in
a state of extreme erection throughout the whole experience
from and including all the preliminaries on up until detumescence takes place following ejaculation, makes a great difference in the satisfactory progress achieved in the relationship
itself."

In the following, lengthy second statement, the man just
quoted places his animal contacts in the context of his overall
sexual life and also provides materials concerning his background and beliefs. He writes:

"*Biographical Background:* I was born in 1932, the second
of three children, and the only son. One sister was a year my
senior, the other five years my junior. My parents had both
come to this country from Germany when they were not yet in
their teens and both of them lived their whole lives on farms.
My father was very largely self-educated; my mother completed
high school. They still are living, but some years back they
moved into town and left the farm to me.

"Father was a man devoted almost exclusively to his work,
except that he related his husbandry of the soil to his duty as a
steward of the Supreme Being. My parents' marriage seems to
have been a happy one at all times and always was marked by
extreme consideration for each other and also for us children.
Discipline was administered fairly when, to their knowledge,

---

of other species if they are at hand and the size is such as to make
the act possible. A sow or gilt in heat, for example, will attempt to
mount a dog, a sheep, or a goat, so that it is not unusual that a
sow might attempt to mount a human male if he presented himself
in the proper posture. As concerns cross-mating, swine have been
observed to mate with sheep, although apparently, despite a few
claims, the cross is not fertile.

the clearly laid down rules were broken by us kids. They did what they could to instill in us a deep religious consciousness and to teach us the true values of life as they saw them. Aside from the matter of sex, I think it is fair to say that all three of us responded to their training in the way they intended we should. Concerning sex, I don't remember that any training ever was given us, except that my sisters both were taught to take care of themselves during their periods. To the best of my knowledge, the sex life of my younger sister has always been completely conventional. My older sister, however, was very sexy when she was young. She was also very popular and active socially. My relationship with her was close and I will discuss that further in a moment.

"As to education, I attended a West Coast college where I received my degree in animal husbandry. My wife, who I met during my years as a student, also has a degree, but in arts and sciences. We were married upon graduation and now have three children. Since then, we have lived here on the farm where, most likely, we will remain for so long as it is possible to make a decent living farming.

"*My Religious and Philosophical Beliefs:* This may be the most difficult of the whole series of topics I have set myself to cover. To rationalize what I profess to be my religious and philosophical convictions in such a way as to fully convince that I actually have, up to this point anyhow, not any, or very few, inhibitions regarding my sexual conduct in the light of these convictions, may well be impossible as my beliefs may seem to be inconsistent with my acts, to say the very least. Since consistency is otherwise the very element which impresses me most about the religious tenets to which I hold, it is puzzling to me, to a certain extent, why I should not also desire consistency and compliance with the rules in the matter of sex. Perhaps compliance with the rules, simply because they are rules, does not seem to me to be sufficient cause upon which to base my conduct. And for me whose religious convictions are otherwise well established, such defiance of God's law amounts to what I recognize as heresy of the first degree.

"Let me hasten to say I find it inconceivable that anyone

who lives as close to nature, and who lives as simple a life as I enjoy, could fail but to recognize the real existence of a Supreme Creator. Except in the matter of sex, and I say this truthfully, I am aware of His power and His influence in all that I do. I find happiness in doing what I know He wants me to do, and I am sorry whenever I do something I know He would not approve. EXCEPT IN THE MATTER OF SEX. Consequently, I am active in my church and find much spiritual satisfaction in this work. Yet, I am not sorry or ashamed because of my sexual conduct.

"Now as to the Christian teaching about sexual morality, true, I am constantly being confronted with my own inconsistent position—in much the same way that the rich young ruler was confronted by Christ concerning his shortcoming—which was the love of money. But like that rich young ruler, I find that I have no desire to mend my ways, because of my attachment to these practices I find to be so enjoyable.

"I truly do enjoy sex in most forms, specifically the forms in which I take the masculine role. When I consider the many sexual opportunities that come to me, I find it impossible to understand why God would object so strenuously when I avail myself of my potential for enjoyment. It would be like giving food to a starving child and then forbidding him to eat it. If, in any way, my sexual conduct would infringe upon the rights or injure the person of any other human being, then I could understand His objection and I am sure I could not then consider that activity desirable. Since my family, and all of my acquaintances, who do not share my interest in sexual deviations, are not aware of my conduct—my conduct, as such, cannot possibly harm them. I have taken every possible precaution in this regard . . . In my case in this matter the question isn't what others think of the total religious or philosophical position in which I stand. The question is, 'Why do I stand where I do?' and, as it is, I don't care enough to bother to try to find the answer. Maybe some day I will and maybe I never will. It may be possible that my sexual conduct has been determined by personal experience, begun at an early age and now established firmly as habit, instead of being influenced by religious convictions. By the time I had become aware of a true belief in God, I was already devoted to sex as exotic, both the practice of it and the gathering of information concerning it.

"*My Early Sex Experiences:* My earliest recollection of anything of a sexual nature has to do with my sister, Karen, who was about a year older than myself.* It was from her that I learned all about the birds and the bees. When we were growing up, the house was not too large and Karen and I had to share the same bedroom long beyond the time when we should have been separated. There was no modesty whatever between us, and as a result of this intimate familiarity I was able to note, with no little amount of curiosity, the various stages of her sexual development, and later on she was able to do the same with me. As her body developed, so also did her sexual urges become awakened. Thus, when I was about ten years old and she was eleven, there began between us a progressive relationship of sexual familiarity occurring at night after we had snuggled in beside each other in the bed. (We used the same bed in winter since there was no central heating and the room would get pretty cold in the dead of a Wisconsin winter.) She, through conversation with her girl friends, had all the information that was necessary about sex, and as I recall it was pretty accurate in most ways.

In almost all of the intimate activity during the first couple of years after I was ten, the initiative was hers although I, mainly out of curiosity and a liking for intrigue, was indeed a willing partner. At first the relationship included merely the tickling and fondling of each other's bodies, but as time went on we progressed to mutual masturbation. She taught me how to do it for her so that she could gain the maximum pleasure and also performed it on me, even though the maximum result would be only a good, stiff erection. Finally one night, when I was twelve, we agreed to try and have intercourse. It was good, so very good in fact that she had a number of orgasms before we retired in exhaustion. As yet, of course, I had not been able

* The reader is reminded that in this book all names, dates, places, etc., that might serve to identify the research subject have been altered according to the usual procedures.

to ejaculate but my physical development was such that I felt this phenomenon would be achieved in a matter of weeks or a few months at the most. Once having experienced this mutually delightful act, we repeatedly engaged in it regularly (two or three times during each week). Throughout each act she was very passionate and we kissed each other deeply and almost continuously as we took our pleasure. It was about two months after this had started that I gave her my first load and, as I recall, it took us both by surprise. I can see her face yet and the anxiety nigh on to terror which was plainly evident. Although, by this time, I had begun to grow a few hairs on my pubic region, she had no doubt underestimated my capabilities. Of course neither of us knew or contemplated the likelihood of adolescent sterility,* so the following few days were trying ones for both of us. Anyway, this experience proved to be the end of our sexual relationship. Now, at the very time when my need and desire for sexual outlet had become full blown, Karen would no longer, out of fear I am sure, continue to share it with me. When, not too long afterwards, another room became available, she moved into it and I was no longer permitted even to see her scantily attired or in the nude. And to top it all off, sex was from then on a taboo subject between the two of us, a ruling she laid down in no uncertain terms. We did, however, remain very close in other ways and still are quite close at the present.

"My first resentment at having been rejected as her lover was short lived. Young though I was, I think I recognized that our incestuous relationship was probably not in her best interest. I truly loved my sister and it was a love which transcended the physical desire I had for her body even though that desire was as intense as any I have ever felt for any girl, including my wife. It remained that way for a long time and as a consequence I felt and exhibited very little interest in any other girl up until my last year in high school. Karen, on the other hand, began to go out on dates soon after the end of our

* "Adolescent sterility" is mentioned in a book of mine, which this man had read. The term refers to irregular early ovulatory processes tending to diminish the chances of adolescent conceptions.

sexual relationship. But I think that, up until her marriage, I was the only boy who ever had her.

"Karen had never told me about the possibility of my masturbating to the point of ejaculation and I had not, strangely enough, acquired this information elsewhere. So I was to experience a couple of months of continence until the last weekend of August when my next erotic relationship took place. As I reflect, I had no doubt been so completely engrossed in my relationship with my sister that I had not even wanted to talk about sex with anyone else. Otherwise, it seems to me, I surely would have come upon such information from some of my contemporaries. As I was to learn later, sex was of major interest to most of the boys my age or slightly older; and while I was ahead of most of them in practice, I lagged far behind in the theory.

"I have established that my next sex contact took place on a Tuesday night and Wednesday forenoon, a little less than two months from the time of my last copulation with my sister. The family had gone away for overnight, leaving me at home to take care of the chores, and it was arranged that my uncle Fritz would come over and keep me company in their absence. He was, at the time, fifteen years of age and was thought to be more dependable than he really was.

"To state it very plainly, that evening, night, and morning sufficed for me to be introduced to masturbation and also to a large number of facts and some superstitions about sex. This started almost as soon as the family car had turned the corner out of sight, and it began with Fritz telling me a lot of sexy stories that I think were intended to excite me and make me a willing partner in what was yet to come.

"When it was visually evident (I was wearing tight jeans) that I had an erection, Fritz began talking to me about sexual development and invited me to compare my physical attributes with his. This I was reluctant to do, never having shared sex with anyone but Karen, even to the extent of exposing my nude body. But he kept on talking until my curiosity was aroused and I agreed to take off all my clothes if he would also take off his. That, evidently, was just what he had in mind, and after the two of us were stripped he then proposed that we should take turns 'jacking off.' Believe it or not, I had never heard this term, and he had to define it for me and also even had to give me a practical demonstration of how I should operate on myself to achieve ejaculation. Once he had demonstrated, I complied, though still embarrassed, after first putting on a condom he gave me since he said that he wanted to save our semen and feed it to the chickens. (This we did, emptying the condoms on their food and watching them consume the semen-soaked mash.)

Fritz then proceeded to take his own turn, requesting that I watch him while he masturbated. Never having seen a sexually well-developed male with an erection before, I was much impressed by the extent of his development. Furthermore, unlike myself, he was circumcized, and this difference in the appearance of his penis, which was also much larger than mine was at the time, drew my interest.

"I don't remember exactly, but I think that by the time the family returned, we had each repeated the act at least three and possibly four times each. Part of the time we masturbated one another, with Fritz giving me detailed instructions as to the speed of my wrist movements, how to hold his penis, and so forth.

"It was not long after we had started these activities that I lost my reserve completely and discovered that this new act was most enjoyable. In between times, Fritz told me a lot of dirty stories, some jokes, and also some accounts of sexual intercourse he said had taken place between boys and girls in our community. He urged me to have my first intercourse as soon as I could, since this would 'make a man' out of me. (I remember feeling quite superior at the time, since in fact I already had had such intercourse, while I doubted that Fritz had been equally fortunate.)

"Then finally my cousin very strongly recommended that I should have sexual relations whenever possible with various female farm animals, a possibility which, up to that time, I had never thought about. I was so naive and in awe of his superiority, both of sex knowledge and capability, that I believed every last word he said and resolved to do all he recommended. It never occurred to me to inquire if he practiced what he preached, perhaps because his presentation already implied first-hand knowledge. Now, however, I am inclined to think that he poured it on just to amuse himself by observing my gullible response.

"Anyway, I did proceed, from that weekend on, to follow his advice on all points. I began masturbating regularly, sometimes even more than once a day and, at the very longest, going not more than three days without enjoying a repeat performance. Often times I would, in phantasy, imagine a sex act to be taking place with my sister as I stimulated myself. Sometimes when I had the privacy for it, I would stand nude before a mirror so that I could observe and note with pleasure my physical features before the act and also during it. I would vary my body positions as well as the manual manipulations from time to time, and as for the semen, I would most often dispose of it immediately, but occasionally would accumulate amounts of it in a bottle or jar for a time. At any rate, I firmly established habitual patterns of behavior regarding masturbation which I still use when I engage in this particular diversion. After my sister's marriage, however, I would phantasy other girls as my partner; and, since my own marriage, the object of my phantasies has most often been my wife.* However, sometimes pictures of scantily clad or nude girls have filled this role, and I can recall one period of time when I had accumulated more than two hundred such pictures, each of which provided visual stimulation during a separate self-engagement.

"During the next few years I can remember only five more experiences involving masturbation with another boy. Four of these were again with my uncle Fritz, and mostly were for the purpose of appraising each other's potency and physical attri-

* This is unusual. Only rarely, unless early in the marriage, do men use their wives as the imaginary partner in their masturbation phantasies. The subject of the imaginary sex partner is, by the way an important and fascinating one, and one I will explore in detail in a forthcoming book.

butes. The fifth occasion was when I was seventeen, and was with our minister's son who was then not quite fourteen. This boy, Ned, was spending the day at our house, the family was away somewhere, and I confess I led him on in the suggestive discussion we had. However, it was he who made the proposal that we should seclude ourselves and 'play around' with ourselves. The hayloft in the barn was selected as the site and we proceeded to take off our clothes. I was surprised to find that he was not yet pubescent and thought of calling it quits. But he gave me such assurance he could go the whole way that I decided to continue. Such interest as he expressed in my physical attributes, I have not since found to be surpassed. He wanted to examine every part of my body, and was especially complimentary about my genitals. I rather think that I was filling the same role for him that my cousin had filled for me—a first experience. Having been thus stimulated, I was not long in achieving orgasm after we began to masturbate, but he, though he appeared to be trying, failed to complete the act. This embarrassed me more than it did him, and I felt certain that I had been taken in. The result was that I resolved that I would be more certain of the other's capacity, as well as understanding, if ever I shared this experience again. I was afraid that now he would tell his friends about what I had done. As a consequence, it was not until another whole year had gone by that I shared sex again with another male.

One more important subject, that of dating, should be mentioned here. In my last year of high school a cute little redheaded freshman caught my eye and we started to go steady. We got along well, but sex was the main basis for my interest, and this, I discovered, she was unwilling to give me. She would neck some, but she drew a firm line, and had it not been for my other sex outlets, I surely would have been driven to distraction. Many was the night, upon returning home from a date, that I experienced severe 'stone ache' and would have to promptly masturbate in order to relieve the pain in my testicles. One thing she did for me, however, though I didn't fully appreciate it then: she filled the void which had been left by my first love, and thus by helping me to accept the relationship with my sister as a 'closed chapter in the book of my life,' she contributed to a new freedom of pursuit for me.

"*My Adult Heterosexual Activity:* The sex act itself, as it was consummated in the premarital sex relationships I will describe, was normal and, so far as I know, in no respect unusual. The first of these incidents took place while I was a sophomore in college and was with a girl who had been married and divorced and now was trying to make a fresh start with her life. She was a college classmate. On one occasion, when we had gone for a drive, she sat unduly close to me and was extremely familiar. This prompted me to go ahead and make advances, which were eagerly accepted. By agreement, we stopped the car in a state park, walked until we found a secluded glen, and spread our blanket. We proceeded to have intercourse and she had a lot of fire in her, but was not especially attractive. This turned out to be only a one-time stand, and I doubt she expected it to be more.

"My second experience was with a girl I had dated more than any other during that same year. Sally was an awfully shy girl, but was truly beautiful. Tall, erect, and slim waisted. Her dark brown hair hung well below her shoulders and her complexion was flawless. I think I might have married her, but the fact we had a sexual intimacy seemed to work to deteriorate our relationship. She expressed a good deal of shame about what had happened when it was over. A deeply religious girl, she could not seem to overlook the fact that we had done what she believed to be wrong.

"There was a wooded area a little distance from the campus and it was there that our passions were expressed to one another. I took her in a standing position, after we had kissed and caressed each other for well over an hour. Of special interest, because it sets this experience apart in a distinctive way for me, as we approached our climax and for some minutes afterward, she was trembling uncontrollably. Also she cried for some time after we had been sexually disengaged. (I myself have experienced this uncontrollable trembling as I anticipated a sex act, but never after the act was completed—could it have been that I left her unsatisfied?)

"This was the first time upon conclusion of a sex act with a girl that I hopefully wished a pregnancy would result. Later, when having sex with a whore, I again wished for the same thing. And I always wish for it, too, with my wife, even when definite precautions have been taken to avoid pregnancy. I know that I do, each time, like to regard the act as potentially fertile. I believe that this is the wish of any true heterosexual (or bisexual) male—unless, of course, unwanted responsibility, or consideration of the female's welfare, takes precedence.

"I have mentioned an episode with a prostitute. This did not count for much to my way of thinking, and it occurred in a whorehouse. I suppose I should also include a brief revelation about my relationship with my wife. Here, too, as in the few other experiences, everything was strictly normal. She was a virgin on our wedding night, which was no surprise to me since I had tried very hard to have sex with her before the marriage. My wife is unusually beautiful, and even after bearing children her figure remains outstanding. Sexually, however, she is not as passionate as the other girls were. Her role in sex is strictly the passive one, and to this there have been no exceptions. I cannot recall a single time when she ever approached me for intercourse. Yet she always seems completely willing to have sex when I desire it. If I ask her, she will stimulate my genitals manually, but she never has volunteered to do this. And the farthest departure from the usual caressing I have ever attempted with her is to suck her nipples. She does seem to enjoy this, as well as manual stimulation of her genitals, especially the clitoris, but even in these procedures she will take no kind of initiative. It is gratifying to me that she does achieve orgasm during the sex act, without fail, and for this I should no doubt be grateful. Though perhaps she leaves a few things to be desired as a sex partner, I know that there are those around who must be a lot worse. My desire for her remains strong after all of the years of marriage, and she seems steadfastly anxious to be a good wife to me—as indeed she is in her roles as mother, homemaker, and companion. Perhaps in marriage these last virtues are more important than being passionate in sex. Similarly, I believe that to the best of her knowledge, I am fulfilling adequately the roles of lover, provider, protector, and companion for her. My excesses in sex, and I acknowledge them to be such, have in no way impeded our marital happiness and I cannot see that they ever should need to, unless I should become unforgivably careless.

"*Adult Homosexual Contacts:* Under this heading, not considering experiences where one or the other was immature (those episodes referred to previously), and not considering those contacts which were impersonal to the extent that no exchange of conversation or physical relationship other than visual took place, I have participated in forty-five separate and distinct encounters, to the best of my recollection, involving a total of twenty-eight men, all of them but one being under thirty-five years of age, with the youngest being age seventeen. I met and became acquainted with all of these men in public restrooms in one place or another—adding here that I believe the number of men who have approached me or indicated their interest in homosexual relationship would be at least twice the number with whom relations were had. Some of these other individuals were the ones who, even though no conversation was involved, I observed in the act of self-stimulation, sometimes to the point of ejaculation. Many restroom stalls have walls with holes or cracks in them. The instances which I will enumerate, therefore, are only those during which I shared, in a more personal and intimate way, the sex experience with the other man or men, as the case might be. Some of these encounters turned out to be strictly unsatisfactory, from my point of view, for the reason that the other man wanted only forms of sex which I do not care for; but the most of them served me, at any rate in part, as a very enjoyable outlet. Perhaps I would do best to state at the beginning and clearly those forms of sex which were asked of me, but which I did *not* care for. These were:

"1. Anal intercourse—whether in the active or in the passive role.

"2. Deep kissing or face to face contacts of any kind (when the partner is a male).

"3. To share my excrement, other than semen, with the other person for his ingestion.

"4. To ingest the other's excrement (this was not directly asked for but was implied, and I refused to consider it).

"And then, perhaps, I should also state my preferences in homosexual relations. These are:

"1. Mutual masturbation.

"2. Self-masturbation in the other's presence on a fifty-fifty basis (in other words, masturbation by both parties).

"3. The passive role in fellatio (my penis in the other person's mouth).

"4. The active role in fellatio. (To this activity I have conditioned myself solely for the purpose of retaining the other individual's interest. But I do not particularly care for it and do not do it unless it is specifically required of me. I would much rather be able to visibly appreciate the other man's physical attributes as he is approaching and having his climax. I never ingest the semen if it is at all possible to do otherwise, and yet sometimes one has no alternative.)

"You probably will be wondering why the number of these encounters so far outnumber my extramarital heterosexual encounters (only four of those besides my wife, and all of them before I was married). Well, first of all, I am a person who enjoys variety; and the heterosexual sex I get regularly with my wife. Secondly, these homosexual dates are, as most everyone is aware, much more easily and quickly come by. Thirdly, there is never any implied claim on one's continued participation or fidelity. You can break off with a fellow whenever you feel like it and he is in no position to demand any recourse. Then, too, there is no monetary outlay, such as would be the case if I should go to a prostitute. Also, as compared to relations with a prostitute, one is not desired by the other person simply for money, but rather because that other person wants you for the sake of sex and nothing else. I have never attempted to, nor do I believe I ever will, solicit a homosexual relationship from any male who has not already indicated his interest in a very clearcut way. And lastly, since the other individual is a male, and not a female, he can hardly be considered to have the potential to become a competitor with my wife for my affections. (She has been far too good to me for me to want to put her in the position of competing for my affections.) I could conceivably fall in love with another woman, if I should start playing around with them, but I will not allow myself that opportunity so long as my wife and I both live. I could not possibly, on the other hand, ever fall in love with another man, or with any animal either for that matter, so in this respect the competition between my wife and them could, at the very most, be for my attention.

"Since my wife already has to compete with my children, my work, my church, my friends, my forms of relaxation, and so on, I do not feel that it is entirely unreasonable to expect her to make some allowances for this interest in participating in sexual variety. True, I couldn't consider asking her for this consideration in so many words, for the simple reason that my acts are deviated from what she would be able to think of as normal and desirable. On this point, I'm sure, we could never agree. But I think I can honestly say that if she would want to engage in sexual recreation with other girls or with animals, I would not object. Or, I would not object so long as this did not interfere with our relationship in any way and if I felt certain that she did not have the capacity to fall in love with one of these objects of her sexual interest. But I would certainly object, and in fact wouldn't tolerate it, if she sought sexual recreation with another man! In other words, I don't mind sharing my wife's attention, but I would not consider sharing her primary affection. I feel that love and sex are separate and distinct entities. Now, to simplify the relating of specifics for my homosexual contacts, I will simply list them in order, assigning to each individual a (fictitious) name, giving as best I can a date for the occurrence, indicating the place, and relating in a concise form the basic nature of the sexual contact and also any unusual observations or deductions that I might have made at the time:*

"1. Railroad depot restroom. Each of us masturbated the

* This informant now gives a detailed listing of forty-five homosexual experiences said to have taken place within a period of about fifteen years. Only a few of these will be presented—the others are similar types of experiences.

other, one at a time. One ejaculation each. He was twenty-five, single, white, small, delicate build, brunette, store clerk.

"8. J———. His room at college. Both stripped and he masturbated both of us at the same time. Two ejaculations each. When it was finished, he took the semen and smeared it over his body like a lotion. He was kookie, but OK. Age twenty, average build, blonde.

"12. A———. Age thirty. At his home. We stripped and sixty-nined, both ejaculating. Neither one of us ingested the semen. Genitals were large. Four children.

"15. A———, F———, H———, and R———. At Railroad Dept. A——— fellated me and I fellated him, H——— fellated A——— and F———, and A——— fellated H——— and R———. A regular orgy. That railroad station was a real busy place that day. People coming and going. F——— watched through the door and gave the signal if those approaching were not known and friendly. A——— vouched for me. It was fun to watch the others being sucked.

"24. My car in a railroad yard. Both masturbated ourselves one at a time. Both ejaculated. He was twenty-one, average build, black hair, extremely hairy, beautiful genitals, uncircumcized.

"28. At his hotel room. Both stripped. He hugged and kissed me all over. Copulated with me between my thighs. Then fellated me. Both ejaculated and he ingested semen. His age thirty-four. Brunette. Very, very aggressive. Very large genitals. He wanted me to remain in female role and I didn't care for that. He was so homosexual that he said he wished he could make me pregnant as he found my body very desirable.

"43. K——— and M———. At K———'s home. All stripped. M——— fellated me as K——— caressed my body. I ejaculated. Then both of them masturbated at the same time, wanting me to watch. Finally, K——— fellated me as M——— caressed my body. I ejaculated the second time. Both K——— and M——— ingested semen. Perhaps the best date of all. These two fellows both were really hot for my sex.

"45. N———. A repeat performance. My car. I fellated him and he ejaculated. I did not ingest semen. He wanted to fellate me but I told him that I was planning to have intercourse with a sow when I returned home and wanted to save it for her. Not that I couldn't have satisfied him too, but admittedly I was trying to encourage him to come along with me to the farm. He was almost beside himself because he didn't see how he could explain the time he would be gone to his wife.

"*Bestiality, or Animal Contacts:* To the best of my knowledge what I have just given you completes the list of my homosexual encounters, unless I include the incident that I will relate in a moment. Perhaps this (foregoing) particular part of my biography will give you much insight into the psychological as well as the physical aspects of my sexual makeup. Now I can add to this list one more contact involving a man—a contact which occurred quite recently and which was perhaps not homosexual but involved the sharing of a bestial intimacy.

"The incident referred to happened in the late afternoon and evening of a Thursday when I knew that my wife would be away from home until late at night. This was my opportunity, and I thought of Jack or Danny, or possibly both of them, since I had discussed these activities with them and they had expressed a strong interest. Also, I had two sows which were rutting vigorously that day, a condition which had been enhanced by the injection of 1 cc. V-Estrovarin, Aqueous, an estrogen preparation (more will be said about this later). Well, I drove into town and called up Jack, only to learn that he was tied up for the evening and that Danny was out of town. So I decided to go over to the hotel restroom and see if I could meet and interest anyone else in the proposition. About six P.M. I made such a contact, a fellow in his early twenties who said he was from Chicago and in town on business. He was married, brunette, well-built, and of average height and weight. He gave his name as George. He had been reared on a farm and was anxious to again experience what he told me he had frequently done as a boy. So it was agreed.

"As has been the case in all of my homosexual sex relations, I insisted on anonymity and this would require that he be blindfolded on both the trip to the farm and coming back.

When we arrived, we stripped in the house and both of us were in extreme erection; in fact, his genitals, being somewhat larger than mine, were so visually stimulating to me that I could hardly wait to get a look at them in operation.

"I had confined these two rutting sows in a pen by themselves, so they were both accessible and ready for mating when we made our advances. The conduct of both was very much like that of the sow described earlier, and of which photographs were provided. Before we entered the pen, both of them approached the separating partition and repeatedly gave forth with what I call rutting calls—a hoarse, loud, throaty noise made in a short singular burst by exhaling. When I plan to engage in bestial relations with a sow or gilt, I always answer such a call with my own vocal talents, imitating as nearly as I can the sound and intensity of the animal's evident vocal solicitation. This I then did, and the animals' frenzy was noticeably heightened.

"Temporarily they would attempt mounting one another or would nuzzle each other's bodies, but only briefly, returning their attentions to what was plainly their primary interest—the two sexually tense males who were consuming, with the greatest pleasure, their solicitation. George was somewhat in awe of their conduct, but when I explained that both of them had experienced intimacy with me during their last estrus period and that they now, too, were being influenced by the hormone injection, he could account for their exceptional behavior to his satisfaction.

"We wanted to watch each other during the sex act so it was decided to separate the two sows into pens by themselves, so that the one which was not being served at the moment would be unable to intrude or interfere with the act. This they would most certainly have attempted to do, in order to receive our attentions themselves. I have, at times, been mounted by such an envious individual while sexually engaged with another. And, of course, as noted previously, the interest of that envious individual is always focused on the site of the sexual organs and union—and the nuzzling, if and when it is done a bit too harshly, of the engaged genitals, cannot be tol-

erated. Not that I have ever known a sow or gilt to intentionally inflict any physical injury on a male, either a boar or myself, when she was in estrus. But, owing to the high pitch of her excitement, she may, in her nuzzling, become a little too rough for toleration; however, I am not in the slightest afraid of being bitten.

"As regards noises made by sows, I have mentioned already what I usually refer to as the 'call to the male for his attention.' Another type of vocal expression is the 'communication of intimate reactions given to the male during the familiarities which take place immediately before the female assumes the passive role as she anticipates the likelihood of impending intercourse.' While this is also an exhaling noise made with the throat, the sound is much softer, scarcely louder than a whisper, and instead of being uttered as one singular blast, it is a series of short, one-half-second repeats, made as long as the air of each exhalation lasts. This second sound is always made with the mouth open. The first sound, previously described, is, on the other hand, usually but not always made with the mouth closed. Sometimes, with the sexually excited female, there is a tendency to drool as she is emitting the more intimate communication, but this is definitely not an indication of anger under these circumstances, but instead an indication of an intense desire. I have learned that the using of both sounds by me at the appropriate time conveys to the female at least a suggestion of my interest in being intimate with her. Her responses to my own utterance, in each case, whether by vocal or by physical activity, confirms this conclusion for me and George quite agreed about this.*

---

* With regard to some of the above observations, it may be of interest to note that the pig has been described as the most intelligent of all animals. Its curiosity rivals that of the cat, and it has so many sounds for different occasions that they probably never have been itemized in their entirety. Naturally, intelligence, curiosity, and, as our informant tells us, sex ardor, vary considerably from one individual to the next, just as is the case with humans. Although seldom made pets of in this country, the pig, when so treated, is also noteworthy for the warm affection it develops for its human master, for the fidelity it displays, etc. It would be of

"George was still a little skeptical about whether or not either sow would be as truly gentle during the intimacy as I assured him they would be. So it was agreed that I would mate with one of them first for his visual appreciation and, I hoped, for his sexual enjoyment, as well as to reassure him. I entered the pen with one of the sows and engaged in familiarities like those previously described and also fondled briefly the sow's body and genitals with my hands. She assumed the passive, receptive role almost immediately and stood unmoving for as long as I continued to make the advances.

"Then I mounted and adjusted to the position I always use during the act. Supporting my body on the sow's back by my chest and upper abdomen, grasping her shoulders with both hands for maintaining my position, with legs extended backward and downward in a slightly bent angle and with the balls of my feet and my toes firmly planted on the floor, I was ready to achieve entry and then fuck her with all my strength.

"As a rule I am able to achieve entry with a sow without guiding my penis manually since their vulvas are usually large enough as the result of parturition and as the result of estrus, when this organ becomes swollen and well lubricated by the female's own secretions. Occasionally, I will admit, I have missed the mark and penetrated the anus instead,* but this is

---

interest to learn the effects of bestiality upon the pig's psychology—how its attitude toward the human partner is affected; and whether, as sometimes happens with dogs, sexual intercourse with a human increases its affection and may even cause it to lose interest in sexual congress with members of its own species. That cannot be determined in this case, owing to the informant's practice of disposing of the animals at short intervals.

* The following item of sexological curiosa is not without interest and demonstrates a possible hazard of anal penetration that seems to be but rarely thought of. The famed French surgeon and sex anthropologist, Jacobus X, culled it from the *Paris Médical* of 1883, quoting the following:

"In the tenth century, Jahya-ben-Ishaq, physician to the Emir El-nâcer Lidinillâh, being consulted by a peasant who could no longer support the pain caused to him by swelling and inflammation of the penis, placed the member on a stone and compressed it

readily discernible immediately when it is done. Actually, the
placement of the sow's organ couldn't be better for rear mounting, nor could the size of that organ be more perfect for the
human male's sexual contact with it. Now in the case of the
gilt, however, especially the very young gilt in her first estrus
period, the situation is somewhat different. The placement, of
course, is the same, but the size of the vaginal opening is not
sufficient to make penetration quite so easy. Still, if she is old
enough to be in heat (at age five or six months), she is also
sufficiently developed sexually to participate in intercourse—
enough so, at any rate, that I have never failed to achieve intromission to my greatest extent even with one that was not
only young but also small for her age, and this without excessive pain for the animal. However, I have found that some
manual guidance of my organ is necessary with these younger
individuals.

   "My act of coitus with a young gilt almost invariably results in her being deflowered, at least slightly, and since this
causes momentary pain at the instant when any movement on
her part is the least desirable, I oftentimes will manually de-
flower the gilt some minutes before I intend to proceed with
the act of copulation. This I do by inserting the first finger and
thumb and suddenly spreading them, and by stretching, inflict
a slight tear in the external vaginal orifice. There is usually
only slight bleeding, but even this much can be quite messy
when the deflowering is accomplished during the act of coitus
itself. Furthermore, if the deflowering is accomplished beforehand, the gilt does not then tend to associate the pain with the
sexual act,* and therefore is more receptive during intercourse.

------

so as to cause a mass of pus to flow out of it, in the midst of which
there was a grain of barley. The Arab doctor at once guessed that
the patient had taken liberties with his mare and had thus introduced the grain into the urethral canal, which the culprit was
obliged fully to admit was true."

   * This same reason—to prevent unpleasant associations—is
also advanced sometimes in favor of having human females deflowered by means of instruments in the physician's office, rather
than having them undergo defloration by the bridegroom on the
wedding night (or whenever). The suitability of this measure de-

Sometimes they become a little unsettled and unnerved throughout the rest of the act, if they are aware of pain in association with the act, and deflowering beforehand almost always eliminates this. All in all, I think the size of the female pig's vaginal opening and capacity compares almost exactly, when she is in heat, to that of the human female, ranging from that of the very young girl at menarche or before to that of the mature woman who has given birth to one or more children.

"I have never attempted intercourse with a female pig of any age (or with any other animal either, for that matter) that was not in heat. This is, first of all, because restraint would be needed. But also, in the case of the young gilt, because I am certain that entry would be impossible, or nearly so, so that the act would not be an enjoyable one even for me. The animal's compliance means that much to me.

"With that detailed explanation for your understanding, I shall return to the experience which I was describing before the digression. It was but a matter of a very few thrusts until I had achieved my deepest limit and then began the rhythmic pelvic movements characteristic of a human male's method of copulation. George, meanwhile, proceeded to examine, both manually and visually, the sow's and my genitals as they were connected in this ravishing activity, and his comments were indeed stimulating. Continuing the act typically, I clamped right in on her as ejaculation commenced, and remained in this tense, motionless, muscularly rigid position, thus discharging the entire amount of semen at my limit of penetration. I had begun ejaculating sooner than I would have liked as a result of my sensuous excitement, but then, in truth, this sex act, in this respect, was not perhaps typical of my usual performance. Understandably so, I should say, since the stimulation I derived from having been witnessed so closely by another human being, who evidenced so much pleasure, contributed greatly to my lack of containment.

"George then decided that he would take the same sow,

_____

pends, of course, on the attitudes of the woman—many would prefer to be deflowered by their husbands, painful or not. And certainly many—probably most—husbands would prefer to do their own deflowering.

so immediately upon my withdrawal, he mounted and with no difficulty or uncertainty whatever, indicating to me the fact of his experience, he gained intromission and proceeded to operate in the same manner as I had done before him. It was indeed something to see!—his straining body in such vigorous motion. The muscles of his hairy legs, so taut and well-defined, and his firm buttocks alternating full and then compressed, were testimony in themselves to his masculine capacity. As he neared his climax, I felt of his rock-hard testicles, reaching my hand in from the side. They were wet with perspiration and with sex fluids which had drained from the sow's genitals. In fact, his whole body was dripping with sweat, since it was quite a warm evening anyway. My fingers detected the surging of his vas deferens between his testicles as he began shooting off his load of semen, but then I withdrew my hand as he had plunged forward tightly against the sow in giving her all that he had. He, too, was unsatisfied, however, with his hasty performance and since we had plenty of time yet, we decided to rest for a while and talk a bit and then both of us take on the other sow. I wish I had been prepared to take some pictures, as this would have been an excellent opportunity. I mentioned this possibility to him and he was quite agreeable.* Among other things, we discussed the sow's intense responsiveness during the respective acts of intercourse. I shared with him the substance of the comments—observations and speculations—which I now pass along to you.

"Once complete intromission is achieved, none of the male

* The effect of the Polaroid camera upon a variety of sexual practices in this country will one day have to be assessed. My own files contain much data concerning the importance of photography to persons ranging from wife-swappers and homosexuals to members of teen-age sex clubs and transsexuals. The Polaroid is, of course, the camera of choice for the reason that the pictures are developed on the spot and no professional photographic services need to be utilized. Evidently exhibitionist tendencies, especially where posing for the camera is concerned, are very strong in countless numbers of persons—who thus imprudently expose themselves to the possibility of subsequent blackmail and other unpleasant (or disastrous) consequences.

farm animals with which I am familiar use the characteristic rhythmic thrust–release movements which are commonly used by the copulating human male. In the case of the boar, the action is accomplished more in the corkscrew-ended organ itself by a sort of spasmodic twisting. Very little body movement, on the part of the boar, accompanies the act once he has penetrated in as far as he can go. This fact, therefore, generates a somewhat different response on the part of the copulating female when she is mating with a man than when she is mating with a boar. The tendency is for the female of this (swine) species to respond somewhat, with corresponding movements of her own, when she is being served by a man. This she does not do in sexual intercourse with a male of her own species. Since the boar is not moving his body, neither does she move hers.* The intensity of this movement on the part of the sow or gilt (with a man) is, to me, a good gauge to use in evaluating for any given female pig during any given coital act, the state of arousal, the state of desire or lack of it, and the amount of pleasure or otherwise which exists in and for her.

"By having had intercourse with several such females more than once, even during the same estrus period, I know that there is sometimes quite considerable variation in a female's conduct in this specific activity, especially when the acts are spaced several hours apart, and this is presumably due to the extent to which she is in heat. Between individuals, also, there is a substantial difference. Some never respond in as pro-

* Concerning the boar in the sexual act, Eugene Burns (*The Sex Life of Wild Animals*, Rinehart, New York, 1953) remarks (page 24) that "With others, such as the boar, the penis is corkscrew-like and, when in fairly rapid motion, gives the optical illusion of being twisted into the female . . ." He adds (page 164) that "For the boar, eight minutes may elapse; during that time he makes several ejaculations which increase up to the third minute and are then maintained to five minutes; after that there is a falling off in the rate and a final rise just before withdrawal." Thus, penetration of the sow by the boar lasts much longer than is the case with other farm animals. This fact could be significant when we consider the sow's apparently much greater responsiveness in the sexual act with a human partner.

nounced a manner as others do and this, to me, indicates the receptiveness or frigidity which is inherent in any given female. You can draw your own conclusions, as I do mine. There is another response on the part of the sow or gilt which takes place during the moments that ejaculation is in process, which I have found can also be used as a gauge upon which to base similar comparisons and evaluation. This is that response which can be detected in the vaginal wall as it becomes sensitive to the fact that semen is being received. In most instances this is a definite sucking action; but, in some, it is quite the opposite. The intensity of this action, either way, tells me a great deal. I recognize that it may be true that in cases where the first-mentioned response is lacking and the second-mentioned response is a rejective one, that the motivation implied could be simply that the female objects because her sex partner is not of her own species. But I am inclined to discount this possible conclusion in favor of one or both of the other two considerations—extent to which she is in heat, or inherent frigidity. I do this because the positive reaction in both ways is, by far, the usual one.

"In the case of the two sows which George and I had available to us in this sex experience, the hormone injection served to intensify these two responses during the coital act as well as their precoital eagerness for sexual intimacy. I had secured a ten cc. vial of this hormone from my veterinarian on the pretext that I was considering the possibility of farrowing several litters of fall pigs from these sows which I had just taken away from their last (spring) litters, and would like to get them bred as soon as possible. This hormone is commonly used to bring female farm animals into heat—individuals that, for one reason or another, would otherwise not come in heat at all, or at least not (like these sows of mine) at the most desirable time. I have used this hormone the last several years during the regular breeding season (swine) for its intended purpose. But it should go without need for any further explanation that it also has been a real boon to the pursuit of my bestial interests.

"As George and I explored later these interesting perspectives, I also made mention to him of the opinions I have formed about the intrinsic comparative sexiness of one breed of hogs (or one type of hog) as over against another. It does seem to me that in recent years, when like so many other farmers I have been making a calculated effort to produce a longer, leaner, meatier type of hog, that I have noticed a correspondingly more pronounced intensity of rutting by the females. And the boars of this (generally superior) type also seem to be more active sexually. Some breeds of hog have made greater advances than others in developing this more desirable type. It would follow, then, that females of this type would be more desirable as partners in bestial intimacy. I do know that I find individuals of this type more sexually stimulating than I do the lardy, low-slung, chubby ones. As I contemplate an intimate bestial relationship about to take place with one of several rutting sows or gilts which may be available at any given time, my choice will always, at least in part, be based upon what I regard as comparative attractiveness. I think, though, that the reactions discernible in the female animal during the sex experience are as important to me as the physical desirability of the animal. It is when the both of these factors are favorable that I find the greatest pleasure in the act.

"My elaboration of details concerning my experiences with sows and gilts could not be complete without my mentioning the two postcoital responses in the animal which I have learned to assess as meaningful. One of these has to do with her resumption of rutting activity, and the other has to do with the retention of the semen. When a sow or gilt, even one which has been sexually very active before and during the act, is mated with a boar, and that mating is continued to its completion, the tendency then is for the female to become quiet and unaggressive for at least half an hour before she again resumes her rutting. If, on the other hand, the act, for any reason, is, even after intromission is effected, interrupted before ejaculation begins, then the female will immediately resume rutting. I take this to be a clear indication of the degree of sexual satisfaction which she has received—a satisfaction that has to be seen as in some way bound up with receiving the male's ejaculation. When the responses noted before and during the act

itself are positive indications of desire, I have found, in my
relations with sows and gilts, that the postcoital responses (in
this respect) are exactly the same as if she had been mated with
a male of her own species.

"Regarding the retention of the semen: Due to the fact
that a man's penis is perhaps somewhat inadequate in length
for the sow, there is to be noted quite often the drainage loss
of at least a portion of the ejaculate immediately after the
copulation is discontinued. I have recognized that when this
does not occur, the female is one which has been outstanding
in her performance and response in every other respect as well.
Even then, such an individual will sometimes lose some of the
semen and I believe, in these cases, that the occurrence is certainly not her fault or the result of voluntary action (rejection).
But when it (the semen) is retained completely, one can feel
rather certain that it has been so retained because the female
has made a conscious effort to retain it.* I have found that
when the physical contact is prolonged for as long as possible
after ejaculation, then there is a greater likelihood that the
semen will be retained.

"To return once again to my adventure, after perhaps
twenty-five to thirty minutes, I was ready for sex activity again
and was considerably stimulated, as it happened, by the conversation George and I had had in the interim. This time I repeated, almost exactly, the relationship I had before, but with
the second sow. However, this time I think I stayed with the
animal for close to ten minutes before finally inseminating her.
Before I had finished, my friend George, in his lust, had engaged the first sow again instead, and so for perhaps a minute
or two, both of us were at work in the same all-consuming way
and with the same objective. I will say this, that if interspecies
fertility were a possibility, I'm quite sure that at least that first
sow would have become pregnant—bred, if you please, by both
George and myself.

* We need not agree that the animal makes a "conscious effort" to retain the semen to allow for the possibility that retention,
in fact, may be related to the degree of satisfaction experienced by
the animal during coitus.

"He, not knowing of the scientific conclusions in this matter of breeding, inquired of me on that very subject. I told him what I knew, from my reading, to be the facts, and he actually seemed to be somewhat disappointed and also surprised. I also told him of my own speculations on this subject, before I had availed myself of scholarly information such as I gained, in part, from reading your treatise on human–animal sex contacts. For your information, I will pass along to you those speculations as I related them. It will be quite in detail.

"Back when I was in my teens, and while I still was living with my parents, I used to give a lot of special consideration to whether or not there was a likelihood that my father would decide to save for the farrowing of a spring litter any gilt with which I was interested in having intercourse. Since I firmly believed in the possibility of interspecies monstrous issue at that time, I wanted to be sure that those which I might have impregnated would be marketed before they would have a chance to bear the evidence of my paternity. The exposure of my activity, I thought, would be conclusive if one of these pigs should give birth, and I knew that the punishment would have been extremely severe. Occasionally, though, father's decisions were not in line with my anticipations (his selection of gilts for the breeding herd would sometimes include a gilt or two with which I had had relations), and this always caused me no end of distressing anxiety.

"I remember one spring when one of these gilts, with which I had copulated the preceding December, gave birth to a litter of pigs, the first born of which was a monstrous freak. Believe me, I was seriously afraid that my activities were exposed. As it turned out, though, my father dismissed the occurrence as merely something unusual; freaks are occasionally born to swine, just as well as to other species, he remarked. Though I thought I knew differently at that time, I now recognize that he was right and that this in fact, was the case. Anyway, this individual was living when born, but lived only a few minutes. She (for the creature was a female) was somewhat larger than the ordinary new-born piglet and was completely hairless. The body was similar to that of a pig, but the head resembled more that of a miniature elephant—with a malformed trunk and slightly misplaced eyes. Both the front legs and the hind legs were turned backward.*

"When this individual was born I was so certain that it was actually my offspring that I took it and buried it under a tree, rather than allow it to be disposed of in the usual manner. And always after that, for so long as I was at home on the farm with my folks, I confined my advances to those individual female pigs whose early fate at the market was definitely established. Not that I was dismayed or ashamed for having, as I thought, sired this interspecies offspring. Quite to the contrary, as I recall it, I was rather proud of the accomplishment. But I had the feeling that a second such event would be almost certain to incriminate me.

"After I began farming for myself, this caution no longer was deemed necessary. Mind you, even after having graduated from a good university, and with a degree in animal husbandry, I had not as yet come across any information on this subject that was contrary to my belief. No doubt this was only because I had not thought to look for it. Since I already knew that some interspecies crosses are fertile (the horse and donkey, to give an example), I suppose I simply assumed that others were possible too, and didn't delve any further into the matter.

"I have followed the practice of farrowing just one litter, in the spring of the year, from each gilt saved for that purpose, and then disposing of her, as a sow, on the market sometime in the summer after she has weaned her young. This means that in the fall and early winter, many individual gilts are available to me for sexual relations, and that from weaning time in the late spring and for a month or so thereafter, only sows are available. Early spring and late summer thus are like long, dry spells for me when it comes to bestial sex, except for an occasional contact with a heifer or a cow. Consequently, I have seriously considered changing to a multiple farrowing program so

* Extra appendages, sometimes resembling an elephant's trunk when placed on the face, are not uncommon among pig monstrosities. Neither are misplaced eyes, a single eye (cyclopism), or the absence of eyes. History is replete with accounts of such monsters.

that on almost any given day a bestial relationship would be available with a rutting female of this species which, to me, seems so superior to what I have been able to experience with any other female farm animal, *in every respect.*

"Some years ago, and once again in the spring, one of my own gilts (with which I had also, like the first one, copulated immediately before the boar) produced a freak offspring as one of an otherwise normal litter. This individual was very much like the other one in its size and appearance, with large elephant-like ears and an even more pronounced trunk—indeed, a most grotesque specimen. It, too, lived but briefly. Since, in both cases, these gilts had been served by a boar, I could not, therefore, draw the conclusion to my own satisfaction, which I wanted. I speculated that if this was truly my progeny, why had this sort of specimen not been produced more often? Each year since I had farmed on my own, and this is also true up to the present, I had been intimate with at least fifteen to twenty of the gilts I had saved for farrowing, and with some of them more than once. And many of these matings took place on the same day or in the same estrus period during which they were settled by the boar. I further speculated concerning the anatomical difference between my own penis and that of the boar. Could it be then, I wondered, that the reason that I was not able seemingly to consistently impregnate these animals was the simple fact that whereas the boar with his twenty-inch-long (or more) penis was able to deposit his semen at a depth where impregnation could take place, I with my much shorter human male's organ was really ineffectual?

"Such a speculation gave me the idea to attempt artificially inseminating a sow that spring, after weaning, using my own semen. I prepared a suitable tube for this purpose by cutting off a twenty-inch section of double strand #10 electrical romex wire. Then, by drawing out one wire, I was left with the empty rubber lining of that wire (a tube) alongside of the other wire left in place for rigidity. The whole thing then was wrapped with rubber tape, smeared well with vaseline, and attached to a syringe. I then ejaculated two times within a one-half hour interval and drew the whole amount of both ejaculations

(about 7 cc.) into the syringe. This was sufficient for my purpose and the device worked exceptionally well so that the
project was accomplished without a hitch.

"Needless to say, I was most anxious to ascertain whether or
not this sow would come in heat three weeks later, as she had
not been allowed access to a male of her own species during
the whole estrus period in which this experiment took place.
But once again I was disillusioned, she was regular as a clock,
coming into heat almost to the day when I expected that she
would if she was going to at all.

"I remembered reading somewhere that artificial insemination of female pigs, even with the supervision of a veterinarian trained in this skill, is highly unsatisfactory from the
point of view of obtaining the desired results, so I continued
to suppose that it was the method, and not necessarily the
means, that was faulty in bestial or interspecies sex relations.
It was not until I began to study such books as yours that I
recognized the futility and foolishness of my suppositions and
speculations in this matter. It goes without saying that posses-
sion of this knowledge was long overdue for me!

"Nevertheless, I also can truthfully say that, except for the
anxiety I suffered in my earlier years, and for the reason already
mentioned, the speculating that I did while as yet in ignorance
was fun. I don't believe that my knowledge of the truth in this
case has, or will, dampen my enjoyment of the bestial sex act,
however, since I can and do purposely engage in a good deal of
phantasy on this point. Furthermore, I know that I am going
the whole way in the male role. That is all that can be expected, and conception, after all, is up to the female!

"Now, perhaps, I can return to the record of my bestial
activities as such. My memory has contributed to helping me
determine the exact date of my first bestial experience and
that was, as you may expect, with a gilt. I remember that it took
place on a Saturday afternoon and that on that particular afternoon, my father had gone off to purchase a boar from another
farmer in the community. The sex act was consummated during the time that he was gone from home on this errand. By
going through some of my father's old cancelled checks, I found

the check made out to that farmer, thus establishing the date exactly as November 6, 1943. Checking back, I find that November 6th of that year was, in fact, a Saturday, so I am fully convinced that the date has been accurately established. This gilt was in heat, and to my surprise she would stand when I mounted her. I knew nothing at that time of sexual foreplay or of sex-stimulating gestures which might be conducive to her arousal. So it was simply a matter of effecting intromission and then fucking her to my climax. As I had not even bothered to disrobe, I found, to my dismay, some tell-tale stains on my overall fly whenI was finished.

"Although there are individual exceptions, in general hogs are the cleanest of all farm animals—provided proper sanitary measures are taken by their owners in the maintenance of the housing and lots where they are confined—and will naturally develop habits conducive to their cleanliness. Nevertheless, a certain amount of messiness usually results when a sexual intimacy takes place. From that day just mentioned, up to the present time, and even in winter, I have, therefore, always been completely in the nude while having intercourse with any animal. I don't mind getting slightly soiled on portions of my body as it is a simple matter to cleanse oneself immediately afterward, but dirty clothes would be intolerable and, furthermore, the dirtiness in specific locations might be a little difficult to explain to those who would be laundering them (my wife and, sometimes, my wife's sister).

"I remember, then, that it was about a year later when I again copulated with another gilt. As I considered the impending act, I can remember that I was uncertain whether I could get into her or not as I recognized that my penis had grown in both length and stoutness during the year that had just passed. But I discovered that, with patience, her vulva would stretch to comfortably accommodate me. I also found, upon concluding the act, that my pubic region and genitals were somewhat smeared with blood, for this gilt had been deflowered. I often wondered during the next years, as I was pursuing this diversion more regularly, if my father ever noticed or questioned the resultant engorged condition of a gilt's vulva after I had used her sexually. But if he did, then he must have dismissed it as a bite by another animal. For he never said anything about having noticed such a thing to me.

"I will add here a brief note about my bestial relations with a few other animals. To begin with—cows and heifers.

"I have always maintained a beef herd of fair size, keeping the calves until they are about a year or so old before I sell them off. This means that the heifers among them will have attained their sexual maturity sometime in the spring of the year and therefore are available to my sexual indulgence. I suppose that, since sows and gilts are not available until a little later, that I sort of fill in with these other animals. Heifers are quite suitable as to size, both the body size and the size of their genitals. I don't have to stand up on anything to facilitate the contact with them and if one will jump up on their backs a few times, when they are in heat, they then will stand in recognition of one's purpose and desire. But, unlike hogs (or humans either, for that matter), the sex act in cattle is accomplished in a single plunge by the bull, with the contact itself being maintained only momentarily. Prolonged fucking is, therefore, contrary to the nature of these animals and they tend to become restless as the act continues for a period long enough to satisfy the human partner. Sometimes one will have to achieve intromission several times before one is ready to ejaculate. At times, I have masturbated up to the very point of orgasm and then made a directed leap in bull-fashion—hanging on momentarily as the semen surges in to the heifer, and then releasing. In either case the post-coital response of the cow or heifer is just the same as when she has mated with a bull—she holds her tail in a slightly raised position for several minutes afterwards.

"Cows, because of their larger size, are not desirable as sex partners for humans. I have had intercourse with a few, but found the act in no way worthy of much praise. The cow's genitals are definitely too large to give satisfactory stimulation, and her body size is such that one cannot mate with her without standing on an elevation of some kind. This is too inconvenient and unnatural.

"A Shetland pony would be a somewhat better sex partner

than a cow, I should think. I have never had such a contact, but as a boy I once copulated with a larger mare in much the same fashion that it is necessary when the animal involved is a cow. A mare has one distinctive feature that is superior to all other farm animals, the control of her external genitalia. A voluntary control, it is, and during the act this can be quite pleasant. Also it is evident, perhaps as an indication of sexual satisfaction, after the act has been completed—a repeated puckering of that organ. Ewes and bitches are quite unsatisfactory as sex partners. First of all, because they are not steady enough on their feet to withstand the copulatory action of a human male. Secondly, their genitals are not readily accessible nor are they easily penetrated. Consequently, I have had such relations only once each in the case of these two animals, and that once was enough to convince me that I wasn't going to learn to care for it. Perhaps if I had developed more technique, or become better acquainted with the animal's sexual nature, I would have learned to enjoy it more. As the old saying goes, practice makes perfect! As it is, the undesirable factors involved outweigh far enough any anticipated enjoyment, so that I am not likely to make further experiments along those lines.

"I cannot begin to guess at the number of bestial intimacies I have experienced altogether. But I would suppose that the total number of such acts definitely would run to more than four hundred, considering that I have been practising this diversion with considerable regularity, especially during those times of the year when the animals come into heat, since my early teens, except for the years when I was at the university. Since my marriage, however, the sex acts with my wife have far outnumbered in their frequency any other outlets for the reason, and I want to emphasize this, that I still find her much more desirable than any other partner I could possibly enjoy. It is only, therefore, for the sake of variety, or for an outlet when my wife happens not to be available, or (as has been the case from time to time) for experimentation, that I have availed myself of these other opportunities. And I intend to continue doing so. I simply can't for the life of me see why I should remain continent when I have the desire, since then the sexual urge would only be intensified. This way, once I have achieved the satisfaction, I can go about my business and attend to the other responsibilities and interests which I have without being disturbed by the insistence of my sexual urges. Sex is fun, but to have nothing else on one's mind (as happens when I am frustrated) would be devastating. This is my 'thesis,' and now we will see what you can make of it."

Unfortunately, this case does not end with the foregoing, highly instructive materials. About four months after his writing of the communication just quoted, the informant's wife was struck down by an automobile and her survival was in question. He then wrote me two more letters—one just following the accident, the second about three weeks after the first. These tragic letters very well illustrate how flimsily based was this man's feeling that his sexual activities were, for him, no more than a "diversion"; also, the apparent impossibility of adequately reconciling such sex behavior as his with strong fundamentalist religious beliefs; and the struggle that eventuates when the person attempts abruptly to deny the demands of a very strong sex drive which, over the years, has been given more or less free rein. From his first letter, I will quote only briefly, beginning the quotation as he began his letter to me:

"Hebrews 10, Verses 26 to 31: 'For if we sin willfully after that we have received the knowledge of the truth, there remaineth no more sacrifice for sins. But a certain fearful looking for a judgment and fiery indignation which shall devour the adversaries. He that despiseth Moses' law died without mercy under two or three witnesses, of how much sorer punishment, suppose ye, shall he be thought worthy, who hath trodden under foot the Son of God, and hath counted the blood of the covenant, wherewith he was sanctified, an unholy thing, and hath done despite the Spirit of Grace. For we know him that hath said, "Vengeance belongeth unto me, I will recompense," saith the Lord. And again the Lord shall judge his people. It is a fearful thing to fall into the hands of the living God.'

"These verses express my present position and when I read

them it is as if they were spoken for my personal benefit in
particular.

"Since you last heard from me I have become acutely aware
of the wrath of God in a very special and unmistakable way.
Perhaps, in truth, He had, through His Spirit, been attempting
to confront me with the unacceptable course I had been following in my sexual behavior for so many years. I will acknowledge now that I had from time to time recognized this confron-
tation, but at the same time that I had, as a disobedient child,
continued to turn my back on these repeated warnings. This I
always found myself able to do because the resultant consequences of my willful disobedience had not yet hurt me
enough, if at all. But now I have been brought to my knees at
last."

This informant then went on to tell of his wife's accident
and to expand upon his belief that he was being punished for
his deviant sexual activities and, perhaps especially, for having
provided me with materials intended for publication. These
materials, he now felt, might serve to encourage similar activities on the part of other persons—who then might finally be
punished just as he had been. I responded to his letter by saying that I doubted God would punish him by killing his wife,
who had in no way been involved in what he felt were his
many sins. I also told him that: "Some of the material you
have provided is of considerable potential benefit to others—
to scientists, for example, by contributing to their understanding of the behavior described; and to persons with a variety of
problems, by assuring them that they are not unique or monstrous specimens of their kind. The case history provided by
you is only one of many thousands compiled by me and other
investigators. Together, this material illumines the meaning of
what it is to be human . . ." His response, written several weeks
later, again is of much interest. He writes:

"First of all, let me say that I realize I have done you a
grave injustice by drawing the conclusions I did regarding the
motives behind your work and some of the beneficial effects

that your work may have. This is not to say that I rule out completely the possibility that your contributions to man's storehouse of knowledge may be improperly used and as such may be a means for stimulating abnormal sexual behavior in some people.* But we know that anything however good, if improperly used, can be detrimental, and the burden thereby falls on the user rather than on the producer. If your motives are what you say they are, to contribute to a better understanding of what it is to be human, and to help those with problems of a sexual nature, then your efforts should be commended rather than castigated.

"By now you certainly must be aware that I am just such a person who, having this sort of problem, needs some kind of help in order to be able to realign my sex drive with my religious convictions, or vice versa. This, it seems to me, will have to involve either a complete action of self-denial, something which, despite best intentions and strong determination, I find myself presently incapable of achieving, or else a considerable reevaluation of religious precepts which I believe I can no longer ignore.

"Your letter did very little to alter my views and conviction concerning the possibility that God is punishing me through my wife's accident, which still may result in her death. The Christian believes that through and beyond death lies a

---

* It certainly is true that books on sexual behavior may be "improperly used" by readers. However, I doubt that anyone becomes a sex deviate as a result of such reading—although a deviation may occasionally become overt somewhat sooner than it would have otherwise because of a literary stimulus. "Improper use," however, is much more likely to take the form of a reader's misusing the facts presented in a book to justify his own already aberrant behavior. I know that readers have taken from my own books data out of context and twisted these facts so as to incorporate them into their own tapestry of rationalizations. But no one ever yet suggested to me that he or she became a sex deviate, or even engaged in some new sexual practice of an abnormal or prohibited kind, as a result of reading about it in one of my or some other author's books. Of course it may have happened, but the chances seem slight. These remarks, I might add, are not in the nature of a defense; rather, they only describe the facts as I have encountered them in this area.

blessed reward for those ones who are saved. So, then, it could very well be possible that God is being both good and just to my wife if He chooses to remove her from the 'corruption' which presently surrounds her to place her in such a paradise. Death, his own death, is therefore, to the Christian, not really a punishment at all, but rather a passport to a better life. I'll freely grant you that I am both selfish and egocentric, for no one would have gone to the lengths I have gone to in order to satisfy my selfish desires, if they would be any other kind of person. But I am also realistic enough to recognize that the loss of my wife would be, in more ways than one, a definite punishment by God if this would be His purpose. Even the many problems connected with her injury, not the least of which is the loss of opportunity for this one legitimate form of sex outlet, even if it should be but for a few months, are terribly trying ones. The reader of the *Bible* cannot fail to notice that God does indeed sometimes visit punishment upon the wicked by removing, through death, a loved one. And I can think of few if any ways of punishment which would be harder to take than the permanent loss of a loved one.

"Thinking of loved ones, how truly do I love either the persons close to me or the Lord if I, in my conduct, do those things which would grieve them if they knew of it? I think I once said to you that what they don't know can't hurt them. But the Lord knows—of that I can be absolutely sure. One would think that if this love were genuine, that one would experience a correspondingly noticeable loss of sex interest and sex drive, when in my present predicament. Or that the Lord, if He hopes for my success in my resolve to do His will, would assist me to some extent by slackening my desires or in some other way restricting me sexually. But the fact remains, that instead of this my continence, self-imposed since my wife was injured, has only served to intensify this sex drive within me both physically and emotionally.

"To be specific, for about three weeks I maintained sexual continence in spite of increasing tension. After a few days of this I began to notice an uncomfortable feeling in my genitals and lower abdomen, indicating congestion. My penis was erect

more than it was not, and there was a painful aching in the
testicles. The more intense the physical symptoms became, the
more attention was focused on my condition of frustration and
the more passionate I then was. The more passionate I became,
the more my thoughts kept dwelling upon sex and the result of
this was a much intensified physical discomfort. Finally, I
masturbated rather impulsively. While my physical discomforts
then were relieved, I experienced a feeling of shame or remorse
that I had not had sufficient will power to contain myself.
There was also the tendency to abandon the value of my good
intentions insofar as they might serve the purpose of persuad-
ing God to spare my wife. Further, having failed this once, I
tended to feel the hopelessness of my resistance to the desire to
repeat further acts of masturbation and the desire to have still
other varieties of sex outlets.

"I can see very little if any difference in the degree of sin
involved in masturbation and that involved in bestiality, since
neither one involves another person. But in spite of this weak-
ened resistance, I contained myself with great effort until several days ago. On this day, two heifers in my herd were in heat
and I arranged with a neighbor to bring over his bull to my
place in order to inseminate them. This meant that I had to
confine the heifers in a separate pen from the other cattle to
facilitate the service. But the temptation resulting from that
opportunity was just too strong to resist and again, rather impulsively, I mounted one of them and served her. As a result
of the emotional excitement and stimulating activity, I had
but a fleeting thought of the moral and religious implications
when I had finished. My response was something like 'Oh,
what the Hell, why not?' Thus having disposed of my inhibitions, and apparently not having fully satisfied my desires, I
stripped nude and then began masturbating. When, in a matter
of but a very few minutes, I attained complete erection again,
I mounted the other heifer and served her too.

"As with the instance of masturbation, the remorseful
attitude did not set in until my passions were fully spent. Now
I would like to know, just why do I operate this way? Could it
be that I resemble that one St. Paul describes in the last few
verses of the first chapter of Romans?

"St. Paul impresses me as being someone who had a clear understanding of what it means to be human, for in one place he goes into considerable detail to explain what he finds to be his own personal conflict between his carnal nature and his will power. In his first letter to the Corinthians, he seems to recognize that not all persons have the gift of self-control in sexual matters, for he recommends that those who find they do not have such self-control, should marry. For he says that he thinks it far better for such a person to marry rather than to burn with passion. This advice no doubt offered a good solution in his day, when it was not only expected but generally recognized as an obligation that the sexual desires of one's husband or wife were to be fully satisfied. But it does not solve the dilemma of a husband or wife in our own time who find themselves deprived or restricted in the satisfaction of their sexual needs. What, to raise one objection, is a person like myself to do during this long period of my wife's convalescence, if it turns out to be that, when normal relations within our marriage will be impossible? This is to say nothing of the possibility that, to my dread, I may find myself with no wife at all. Maybe I am being too self-centered in even thinking about my own frustrations, and I do not mean to convey the indication that sex, or the lack of it, is for me the most important consideration involved in my wife's struggle for life.

"If it has to be that my future holds no opportunity for legitimate satisfaction of the overwhelming sex drive which I recognize, then I doubt very much that anything I can do in the way of further resolve would deter or eliminate the physical or emotional aspects involved in that drive. I suppose that the fact that I have failed to resist this drive only these two times in the last several weeks means something. Especially so when I consider the fact that very few days passed, before this time, when I did not avail myself of some form of sex outlet. I think, and in fact I know it to be true, that over the last twenty years and more I have not had a similar experience of going for this long a time with so little sexual activity. So perhaps there is some benefit in making the effort. However, barring an act of Grace, I will, no doubt, 'fall off the wagon' from time to time, knowing the way I respond to the stimulation afforded in the sensation of my physical need. Also recognizing the intense sexual desire which wells up within me when I become aware of the sexually aroused condition of a female animal in heat, and also being aware of the availability and suitability of such an animal as a sexual partner, I doubt that I can always resist the impulse to cast inhibitions aside every time. In the last week most of the gilts in my herd have been in heat and it has taken much resolve to leave them alone sexually. When the time comes around again for mating some of these gilts with the boar, it would really be a miracle if I could resist this temptation, since then they would be not only more or less confined to close quarters and thus more available, but the added stimulation of watching them being bred would be conducive to my own participation in the activity.

"In some ways, I suppose, this all-consuming desire for sex, when it reaches a certain point, can be compared with the very heavy smoker's desire for a cigarette or the alcoholic's desire to have another drink. I guess it is true that these persons will go to a considerable length to satisfy what must be a definite physical craving—and that, the longer they go without satisfaction, the more intense the craving becomes. I know that there are those who have indulged heavily in these habits who nonetheless have been able to break themselves of their desires; but there may be one important difference between these habits and sexual indulgence. I mean that the sex drive would seem to be an intrinsic part of the personal makeup, while alcoholism and smoking would seem to be only acquired tendencies. I am certain that the spontaneous impulse and the corresponding breaking down of the will to resist which the drinker must feel when he fails in his good resolve to quit all drinking (when he takes his first drink after what he had hoped would be a continuing self-imposed abstinence) must be much the same as what I have experienced on these two occasions when I have given in to my natural desire, despite the firm intention not to. Maybe, if the sex drive is, as I am supposing, an intrinsic part of one's makeup, complete abstinence (or continence) is virtually impossible for such a hot-blooded individual as myself. How can one be expected by God or anyone else to reject and overcome what is an intrinsic part of oneself?

"In closing I will say that possibly excessive sex drive, in one way, may be preferable to some of these other extremes of human behavior since it does not seem to be physically damaging or degenerative—at any rate not when it is unaccompanied by inhibitions. I seriously doubt that my own extensive sexual indulgence, before these recent weeks, has in any way impaired my body. And I don't recall any emotional tensions as a result of sex during my adult years, up until this religious conflict and my concern over the connection which my behavior may have had with my wife's accident. There is the possibility I may fail so often in this battle to remain continent that I will decide it is futile to keep on trying. But if I would do this, I would also be giving up in the fight which St. Paul tells us should be the rôle of all Christians."

COMMENTS

In the case just concluded, as regards bestiality, there seems to be no evidence suggesting a sexual deviation; and we may, with some reservations, accept this individual's statement that, for him, the animal contacts are a source of gratification having no greater (or little greater) significance than masturbation. "Personalizing" (making a person, or investing with human qualities and motives) of the animal is minimal. No strong emotional attachments to individual animals are formed and there is no disruption, resulting from the bestiality, of capacity to perform sexually with human partners. The informant appears to have a large physical capacity as well as a powerful psychological drive for sexual satisfaction and release of tensions (which quickly accumulate when there is no outlet). If the animal partners were not available, he probably would compensate by stepping up the range and frequency of some or all of his other possible types of outlets.

He is able to respond and function well, as he describes it, with a variety of sex objects—man, woman, or animal. On the basis of his account, one would say that the earliest overt sex experiences very largely have determined much of the subsequent sexual life. The seduction by the sister seems to have resulted in a certain later passivity with women—reflected in the small number of heterosexual contacts before marriage and in the rigid behavior displayed in sex relations with his wife.

The experience with the uncle appears to have introduced some rather typical homosexual and voyeuristic–exhibitionistic components into this individual's psychosexual pattern—for instance, his interest in the male genitalia and his pleasure in having his own genitals observed, praised, and otherwise appreciated by the male partner in homosexual acts. This emphasis on the visual aspects of the sex experience seems clearly traceable back to the repeated mutual inspections carried out with the uncle. The wish to have his own genitals "appreciated," as well as the emphasis upon genital development, probably derive from his feelings of inadequacy when his still immature sexual apparatus was to his detriment compared with the mature sex organs of the uncle. All of this could be expanded upon at some length, but that will not be done for the reason that there has been no sufficient personal contact that might serve to supplement and make possible analysis of the written statement. It is also this lack of personal contact that accounts for the frequent use of such language as "seems to," "apparently," and "probably" in the paragraphs above.*

* The purpose in this book is not, in any case, to analyze the cases; it is rather to confront the reader with the mentality of the research subject and to provide information concerning his behavior—and to do this to an extent the reader is unlikely to have encountered in any other volume.

"Homosexual" Bestiality

In the case to follow, which also involves a significant measure of bestiality, the animal contacts are mostly "homosexual" (with an animal of the person's same sex) as distinguished from the "heterosexual" bestiality of the preceding case. Here, too, we will meet with a considerable range of sexual activity, but with a primarily homosexual orientation. While both individuals do respond to a variety of stimuli, and so might be regarded as "polymorphous perverse," there exist important differences between them, as should become evident. Apart from the difference in primary tendency—in one case heterosexual, in the other homosexual—there is, in the case to follow, probably a more realistic appraisal of the self as regards the sexual behavior; but also a self-denigration and acceptance of domination by the sexual appetites that is much more pronounced than in the first case. Here, as in the other examples, the person feels himself to have excessive desires with which he is unable to cope—that is, he considers himself sex-driven.

The informant, a white male past seventy, has worked at a number of unskilled occupations, including a rather primitive type of farming. He has had very little formal education, is much less articulate and coherent than the previous writers, and some of the material he presents as factual seems to be, rather, in the nature of wish-fulfilling phantasy.

It also should be mentioned that with this case, as distinguished from the ones preceding it, I have found it essential to impose some organization upon the materials provided. I have also had to delete repetitions, correct some spelling, and do a small amount of other editing. Apart from this, the presentation is the writer's own. His account now follows.

"I am going to do the best I can to tell you about myself and to give you whatever information you will want. I am not a writer and don't pretend to be one, but I will do my best and have tried to keep my language so as it will pass the postal authorities and not be stopped on account of obscenity. I have been as factual as I could be, but of course I can't remember everything over a period of seventy years offhand and will have to keep sending you things as I recall them.

"I particularly want this to be authentic with no inhibitions. That is the big trouble with homosexuals, that you never interview them except when they are in the clutches of the law and they do not have the face to call a spade a spade and tell the truth about the matter. I would like to make a true confession for my own peace of mind.

"I am a confirmed homosexual and have been one since I was four years old. Ever since that time I've been interested in the penis of any male (whether man or animal) and I have also been interested in the female of whatever species. I have lived as a bisexual all my life, and I still do, but a penis does me a whole lot more good than a woman can. I can work around men in the wash room or anywhere else and never pay them any mind, but let a man get turgid and offer it to me and I cannot control myself. I got caught several years ago and got me a lawyer and got off with a fine and probation. So I have had to be careful and watch what I was doing from that time on.

"I fought hard against being a homo for more than forty years and was on the eve of suicide when I met a religious woman in Pennsylvania who changed my whole outlook. She told me not to feel bad about the way I am, and so I gave up to my desires and have been at peace most of the time since then. Then I wasn't frustrated so much any more and felt a whole lot better. I have married seven times and my last wife and I have been married for around nine years. I never had any children for which I am thankful as I have had poor health all my life and just barely been able to look out for myself. I am still sexually potent, but naturally not with the strength and frequency of my younger years. I still want a woman about three times per month, and I have spells at least four or five days a month when I want a man and will take him orally but prefer him anally. And when I can secure an animal (male) I will take him for as long as he wants me.

"I prefer Negros to white men as they do me more good and enjoy me more than whites do. Most of the full blood Negros want a white man as there is something from way in the past that causes a Negro to want to plant his seed in a white man. It gives him an assendency (sic) over him some way. I have had a Negro man to leave a woman to cover me.

"I like nearly all males, but I also like females for cunnilingus. But I like some female animals when they are in heat. Also I don't want a woman except when she is hot. I had a boy fifteen years old who covered me once in a while last winter and there was a big hound dog in the neighborhood who would come when I whistled and cover me when I could not make contact with any man or boy. It is hard to do anything here in this little Georgia town since everybody knows about your business and they would put me in the pen if they found out on me.

"I think and have thought so for a long time that I may have female genes as well as male. I would like it if I could will my body to some medical school if it would be a benefit to science in regards to the homosexual urges that we human beings are beset by. Then maybe they could learn something that might help some poor devil after I am gone, for I know what these homos suffer."

Statements Concerning Background: "I was born in the year 189– at Texarkana, Texas. I was a congenital syphilitic and did not have much health till after I was past puberty. I got to puberty when I was about ten and my sexual organs were full size at eleven years and after I could discharge I masturbated regular when I could not make a contact with a girl or a cow or a calf or any thing else female. I never did want to cover a male of any kind but I would take a male, man or boy old enough to discharge semen, any time one would ask me.

"I lost my hearing at the age of seven and never was able to stay in school for long at a time. After I got to be nine years old my folks moved to the farm and I was able to work outside and be with the stock and from living an outdoors life I started to get better from then on. After I was ten I masturbated every day. I do not remember any so-called phantasies in connection with the masturbation, but I would have so-called wet dreams occasionally and most of the time in the dream I was with some girl, or with a man, and would wake up in time to give it an assist. I dreamed of my mother a number of times and was always having sexual intercourse with her (in the dream). I did not give this dream up till I was a grown man.

"My life was happy enough as to home and surroundings and such. But I always wanted a man and I always did want to have a bull cover me. I had contacts with animals and moved away from the farm and thought I could get away from that kind of life and practices. I joined the church and tried to live a so-called Christian way of life. My father died when I was thirty years old, but I was married by then and I had lived a true Christian life with my wife and did not have any outside contacts with either humans or animals. But I could not manage to get my mind clear of them. After my wife died, a year after my father, I went back to my homosexual ways and to animal contacts when convenient. Truth is, I never did care for women too much, but when a woman made herself desirable I was always potent with them.

"Of course you just about have to live on the farm to have any contacts with animals whether as boy or man. As I told you, I have been married seven times and none of my wives knew of my failing till this last one. We did all right sexually in all of these marriages but we could not agree on other matters, so we always separated as they always wanted more than I could give them. None of them wanted children as they all had one or more already by a previous husband.

"As to guilt, when I was young of course I felt a lot of it and I was always careful to keep well hidden all my actions as my mother and father told me that I would go crazy and catch a venereal disease and would grow hair in the palms of my hands, but they did not tell me how to overcome the continual frustration. And I would go till I had a wet dream almost every night and then I would start masturbating again and I would try for intercourse with every little girl and anything else that came along.

"When we were little the neighbor children played a lot on a vacant block that fronted our house and at dusk some of the older girls would come out and play with us and when it got dark we would play hide and seek and one or the other of these big girls would always manage to be with me when I hid and would pull me down on them for intercourse or cunnilingus.* I sometimes was with as many as three girls in one night's play. Of course it only increased my frustration because I was too young then to discharge, but I would not give it up and I did not get any relief till puberty. But then they would not play with me any more as they were afraid I would impregnate them.

"That was about the time when I started the animal contacts and masturbation and kept it up till I was fifteen years old and had sodomy with my first man. That was around between 1905 and 1910. I was on a railroad camp in Kentucky, and the men down there were all a lecherous bunch and on pay night the women would come to work the camp. This one night a man and I were looking to find a woman and as we did not find one he kept talking about sex and showed me his penis and felt of mine and rubbed it up and down a little. Of course I was on fire and he asked me to take him. That was just what I wanted and I lay down for him and he got some saliva in his hand and put it in my anus and lay down by me and eased it in a little at a time till it was hub deep and then he gave a

* At least as regards the frequency of occurrence, this sounds like wishful thinking.

few short lurches and discharged his seed. He discharged heavy
and when I felt his semen was in me I had a feeling all over
me like I had taken a big drink of whisky. From then on I
knew what I wanted. Of course I had had little kids in there
before, but never got anything like the satisfaction from them
that I got from him. I never had him again as he left there, but
there was two or three more tried it, but they did not know
how to do it like he did and they hurt me.

"As for the guilt problem, from then on I mostly had animal contacts up till I moved to Kansas City when World War
One started and I found some work at a packing plant. I had
some relations with prostitutes but didn't like them much and
married and behaved myself for seven years up to the time my
wife died. Then I went to New York and lived there about ten
years and that was where I got in with the homosexual crowd
and got so disgusted with them that I married again.

"My wife got drunk the day after we married and stayed
drunk for five weeks and made such a nuisance of herself that
I went off and left her. After that I went along single for about
two years and then married a young widow in Brooklyn and
lived with her for six months. She was so passionate that I
could not satisfy her and she could not have an orgasm so I
would give her cunnilingus till I was played out and had to
get some rest as I was working hard every day. She would wake
me up nights by sucking on my penis and if I did not respond
she would bite me hard. After she had bit the blood out of me
the second time I got afraid of her and left her. I was just about
ready for suicide but then I went over to Philadelphia and I
met a religious woman and went with her to the Spiritualist
church and we lived together for over three years and she
finally talked me out of my depression. She told me to live my
life according to my own nature and do whatever I wanted to
do. So I decided to just let nature take its course and I have
been more at ease since then.

"After that I moved all over the country for quite a few
years working at farming and a lot of other kinds of jobs. I
was married a part of the time and a part of the time I was
hanging out with the homos. I went with some prostitutes but

got venereal disease and only very little satisfaction. Eventually I married my last wife and we had pretty good sex for four years but then it got harder to get along with her. During this time I had some male and animal contacts and told my wife about my affliction.

"Now, I can't work any more on account of the insurance laws and all I have got is the Social Security. I have me a little farm and can have some animal contacts as I don't have much luck with the humans any more. With the homos I am always getting venereal disease and also I got caught two years ago by the police and it cost me a thousand dollars to get out of it. I didn't have any money left after that and my wife did not have much more use for me. I don't really need a wife no way as she does not want a man but about one time in every three or four weeks and I can do without a woman but I need my male contacts and I am going to have them some way. Now this is about all I can think of just now that happened over the past seventy years, but there was a thousand and one other things that I will recall and I will make a record of them as they come to me and I will send them on to you.

*   *   *

"Here is a resume on my health from the time of my first memory and with what I can find out about it.

"I was born a congenital syphlitic. Of course, while I was small I did not realize what the score was but when I was just past six years old I got poisoned on a home made Easter egg colored with house paint instead of egg dyes and nearly died. From then on I was sickly and at seven years of age I completely lost my hearing. At about eight years old I had granulated sore eyes and my mother put sugar of lead into them and I was same as blind for two years afterwards. When the eyes got better I tried to go to school but could not stay in school for long at a time as I suffered from raging headaches and also had a weak stomach. I only made the fourth grade in all my schooling so I quit trying to go at about age thirteen. I worked on the farm when we lived in the country and I liked the life. Being deaf I never mixed with people too much and still don't. I was a voracious reader and what I know I picked up from books. I was always fond of medical treatises and would have made a doctor if I could ever have got an education. But I always had to work instead.

"My father was a big husky man and drank very heavy while he was young. He lost his potency entirely at around age forty-five and mother went through the change of life at age thirty-six and Dad did not live but about nine years longer. He had what they all called leakage of the heart, but after I got to reading medical books I realized what had happened. He had an untreated case of syphilis before I was born and died before he could reach fifty-five of paresis.

"My mother is still living today and has every one of her original teeth but lately her eyesight has started to fail. I have worked day in and day out all my life and did a lot of hard labor. But I got a hand and arm damaged in an automobile accident once and now they sometimes give out on me. My eyesight has dimmed pretty bad and I have to wear spectacles out of doors but can read all night without wearing them. I have a cataract and will have to have it removed some day if I don't die first. I am still potent, but I doubt I am fertile any more. But I have always wanted male contacts and while I liked the ladies all right I never missed it too much if I couldn't get hold of one. When my libido would get to bothering me too bad I would always masturbate for relief if nothing else showed up. I never did care for sports or anything where there was crowds, except I liked to dance and loved music. I love to read and that is about all I do these days. If my body can't be turned over to a clinic to benefit generations of homosexuals, I would like to be cremated. But my wife is set against it and I will just have to let nature take its course as to what becomes of my remains. It won't make no difference to me no way.

*   *   *

"I do not know whether the writing I have sent you is satisfactory or not but I am doing the best I can. I am not proud of what I have been and done in my lifetime and what I may do yet. I am homosexual and can't help it, and if I don't get some relief from my cravings I become neurotic and break out in rashes all over my body. When I try hard to repress my feelings and do what the law and society say I have to do, I am in torment all the time. So I have just decided to let nature take its course and take what I can get as I can get it and not worry about it so I can sleep at night if nothing else.

"When I go long enough to begin to crave sex, if the wife does not want it I just masturbate and go on. Anyways, sex with me means penis and I don't care much what kind if I can use it. I do not care for fellatio but will do it if the man does not want sodomy (anal intercourse) for esthetic reasons. But I will take cunnilingus any time if the woman is clean. And you would be very surprised and so would a lot of preachers and parents and other folks if they knew how many preachers was relieving girls and women with cunnilingus where the woman is afraid of pregnancy. And they are supposed to be such good Christians too. There are lots of times when I think like the little boy. If that bunch is going to heaven then I'd rather not go.

"I would rather have an animal if I can get it as they don't look down on me for doing what I do the way some people will. I have seen a lot of hypocrisy in my time, and I think the man who pushes his penis in my mouth or my anus is just as low as I am. Or worse, as he could find a woman and I cannot get complete relief any other way. I prefer taking the penis in sodomy as it seems to give me full relief and ease the tension like nothing else does. I don't care for using female animals any more but I want to get me a bull and maybe a boar to relieve me as it is very hard to find men at my age when you want them and there is always the chance of venereal disease and there is also the law. I was in trouble here before and if I get caught again in this county I don't doubt that they may hang me.

"What I want to do is move into a county where there is plenty of Negros as I can get men and boys easier that way. I do not want a boy before puberty or a girl either. There is one boy around here who got wind of me getting into trouble with the law about sodomy and he came in the outhouse on my place and showed me his penis with an erection on and of course I examined it and performed fellatio on him. After that he would come over every so often and would come in my house and get in the bed with me. He is just after puberty and while he is pretty good he is not old enough yet to take the place of a man. This boy has a good sized penis and it is over six inches long but it is bent up over his stomach and it is kind of hard to keep in me. Also, he needs circumcizing. It is hard to do for him as he can't or won't keep it clean. I think he wants me to give him mine for fellatio and sodomy both, but so far he hasn't been able to get up the nerve for it.*

"This boy had a big hound dog and in my opinion some kids had been fooling around with him, because he come over into my yard one evening and made signs like he wanted to cover me. So I went in a room with him and pulled off my trousers and put some spit in my anus and he got up there and put it right in and got hard and swelled almost as big as my fist and I was tied up with him for over fifteen minutes.** After that he would come over every few days and if it was convenient he would get what he wanted and then go on his way.

* The preference of homosexuals for a circumcized penis, especially when fellatio is to be performed, is virtually universal wherever circumcision is practiced. This predilection is based partly on hygiene, partly on aesthetics, and partly on practical considerations pertaining directly to the performance of the act. In some parts of the world, of course, the uncircumcized penis is rejected also on religious grounds—in this case by females as well as by males.

** The reference here would seem to be to the massive ball or knot that is located near the midpoint of the dog's penis—a structural anomaly this animal shares with the coyote and the wolf. Once the dog's penis has been inserted into the human anus-rectum and the ball has become engorged, painless withdrawal is difficult or impossible until after the dog has ejaculated, when shrinkage and flaccidity of both ball and penis occur. This knot is responsible for the familiar "locking together" of dogs in copulation, since sometimes the sphincter of the bitch will clench around the base of the dog's penis, preventing withdrawal. The knot serves no known useful function.

Now, a year after, when he sees me he wants to know if I will take him. If I can't he just goes about his business.

*   *   *

"I have read everything I could get my hands on in regards to homos and all other sex deviations and I do not find much sense in what I read. The only statement I can accept is that in some homos there may be an inborn genetic inherited condition which makes homosexual orientation a necessary part of the personality. That is the best explanation I have seen yet and fits in with all my own observations and feelings.

"I do know that my early years did not make me the way I was because of broken home or neglect of one parent or drunkenness. I was sickly all my early years and was humored and more or less pampered but of course they did not try to ease my frustration as they did not ever know I had it. But they must have known that I was precocious and that my sex desires were far advanced over the rest of me. I wanted to suck Paw and I wanted my mother from the time I can remember till after puberty when I had female contacts with both humans and animals. I was raised on the bottle and I was always interested in my mother's breasts and also my dad's penis. When I could catch either one of them asleep I would lay there where I could smell their genitals. Just the smell of either one of them would cause me to get excited. My mother went through change of life at age thirty-six and from then on her female organs were not taken care of and developed a very obnoxious odor.

"In regard to the alliances and grand passions of the homos you hear about sometimes, it just ain't so. The lesbians may join up with each other and live together for a long while but even then it does not last. The men are always looking for something they can't find and usually one date is enough. Some times a man will meet up with someone who suits him and gives him the satisfaction he is seeking, but mostly they don't. I have met a thousand men in my life that I never wanted to see again. I prefer animals to Negros and Negros to white men.

"Some queer things happen. I have had things happen to me that I would not repeat to any one but a queer as nobody else would believe it no ways. I had a fellow accost me one night to go with him to his home for a date. When we got there there was a woman who he said was his wife and a big strapping Negro man and a very pretty white girl about eighteen years old. He wanted to take pictures with a movie camera.

"First the girl took the head of the black penis in her mouth and then she laid down and elevated her legs and the Negro played his mouth in her vagina and then I laid down and did the same thing and the Negro inserted his penis in my anus and the man's wife took the picture machine and the man straddled the Negro's back and inserted his penis in my mouth and then moved up and did the same thing with the Negro and then the girl. Then he took the picture machine back and his wife came and did the same thing with me and the Negro and the girl. The girl was getting hot by this time and he had the Negro lay on his back and the girl sat on it and I sucked one of her breasts and the wife sucked the other and I was sure the girl would faint. When she got through the wife sat on me and they did the same with her except that the Negro placed himself where I could reach him and I sucked him and then the girl squatted over my face and I sucked her. Then I covered the girl and the Negro covered me and the man covered his wife and we broke it up until next time. There is a lot of this goes on and those pictures bring big prices for stag parties. I was never in another one but I have made movies of a couple of homos having intercourse and sucking each other. I never saw the Negro again or the man and his wife or the girl and I never did even learn the names of any one of them.

"One more thing I can remember about when I was a child. I think I was about five years old and always had a strong libido and I would visit my mother's sister and we would build us a playhouse out in the barn. My step cousin was seven years older than I was and she would lay down on some straw where she could watch the house from a knot hole and she would pull her dress up and take off her panties and pull me down on her and get me to insert my penis in her. She would make me work her for a long time and of course I could not discharge but would stay turgid in her for as long as she wanted it. Her breasts had started and she would have me play with them and suck them and invariably she would have me wind up with cunnilingus. This went on for nearly a year and then we moved out to the country. I got to see my father perform cunnilingus on my mother and she performed fellatio on him. And I would watch the cattle in the pasture when a cow would be in heat and all the other cows would ride her till the bulls began to smell her and then they would take over and proceed to breed her. I asked my mother why the cows rode each other and she said they were looking for better grass. But I knew what the bulls were doing up there so I did not ask her about that but would stand and watch them for hours at a time when there was a chance for it. When a bull rared up on a cow and I could see several inches of his penis before he put it in her I had the queerest feeling and my body inside would tingle and burn and I would want the bull to do me likewise but was always afraid they would go too deep and do me a bad injury.

"I did not have contact with any animals till after puberty, which I had at a very early age. I slept with my dad now and then and I tried to examine his penis but he always woke up and stopped me. I got it hard several times before he woke up but when I tried to suck it or back up to him to take it he would wake up and raise cain and want to know if I was crazy (which I was, for penis), but of course I did not know what it was all about at that time."

*   *   *

Discussion of Bestiality. "Animals are queer but on the whole are more sensible than most people think. When a cow is not in heat she is no good for intercourse at all. You have to pen her up and sometimes tie her and then she will jump around and mess on you and do anything but take it. But you get one when she is in heat and she will stand and let you put a rock or block of wood behind her and get onto it and insert your penis and ram it up her as long as you want to. She will get a hump in her back and reach and strive with her internal organs to encompass more of it and there is a strong pulsating movement of internal feeling that I have found in very few women in all my life. And she seems to welcome a continuation of intercourse, which she does not get with a bull. A man cannot hold out long as she will force an orgasm almost at once. And if he can maintain his erection he can really have some real enjoyment and pleasure for then he can hold back longer and she seems to really enjoy him then even though his penis does not reach back as far as a bull's does.

"I have had slightly over eight inches of penis all my life and while it is not too large it is slightly larger than the average and when I was young I could maintain an erection till I had the third orgasm. But of course not now. I have had some real enjoyment with young cows and heifers when they were in heat but I can not raise an erection even now with one when she is not in heat. In fact, I don't even want a woman unless she shows herself to be hot for a man. (But let me see a penis, whether man or animal, and if it is erect and I can get to it I will take it every time. I have had a black man in at both ends at the same time. I know this sounds like boasting but it is true and I have seen other men do it although most of them will deny it as they are ashamed to let others know that they are so lax in their morals. I was ashamed too when younger but I have decided that I would just as soon be hung for a goat as a sheep.)

"Speaking of goats and sheep I do not know anything about them except what I have heard and read in books. But I have had homos to tell me that the goat is very lecherous and will mount a man often. I do not know how true that is. I have never been around them enough for close contact and I do not like the odor of either one. But horses are susceptible to any kind of sex play and of course as a horse (male) is too large for a man to have to do with, so is a mare. While a man can cover most mares with ease and get an orgasm he can not do the mare any good. But I have noticed that nearly all female animals like a man when in heat and most mares will take a man most any time at all, while they won't take a horse till they are in heat. I tried to take one little runt of a horse (or gelding rather) but I did not have any lubricating jelly and so it was not very good. He had a small short penis. But they swell so large before they deliver that the glans will likely injure a man.

"I went to the funeral of a woman in Kansas who had a small horse tied up to the back of a wagon and had been bending over him. No one knew anything about it except that he had knocked her down and he kept on trying to mount her and trampled her to death. People said the doctor found he had discharged in her at least one time. But her vagina was almost inside out where the horse had dismounted and in withdrawing the head he had stretched her. But they did not know how he got her down and supposed he had kept on trying to mount her. I never saw the woman alive but she was a big woman and had been a widow for a short time.

"I never had animal contacts with male animals of any kind till I was thirty-five years old. I like the male animal best of all but there are many impediments to having them. I could always be potent with a cow or a mare if she was in heat and a few times I have covered a sow who was in heat and who would stand and take me. I have let a boar to me a few times but they have to have a muzzle on as they are apt to want to bite and a year old boar can do terrific damage to a man.

"What causes a stallion or a bull to get vicious is sexual frustration. I have played with the genitals of a stallion or a bull and then worked around them when other people who didn't give them any satisfaction could not get into the same lot with them. I have had a four year old stallion to present his penis to me for me to fondle and I had one stallion who would let me play with him and suck the head and would discharge his seed in my mouth. It is a hard thing to do as his glans swells up so big. But he was gentle with me and was careful not to hurt me. He wanted to cover me but that thing was too big and long to stick in me.

"I thought they would be too heavy but they are feather light when they mount. The bull calf I raised was light as a feather and after he had surged on me, most of the time he dismounted without ever bearing down on me. He was very playful but never rough except one time when I was leading him to water from where I had been grazing him and he butted me hard, though in play. I hit him over the head with the cow chain I had on him and he never tried to do anything rough again. When I was going to him I would slip off my trousers and go in the stall and play with him and he would stand and lick me just like I was a cow. All of a sudden he would throw up his head and sidle around and I would bend over and brace myself on a manger or a fence rail and he would mount and feel till he had found the entrance and then he would surge up over me and pass twelve or fifteen inches through the rectum into the colon and discharge a half tea cup of semen and dismount and the semen would tingle and simmer in my colon and I would feel like I had drank a big slug of whisky.* He would stand and lick me and rub

* Although I have similar claims of anal penetration by young bulls in my files I am doubtful that this could occur without serious injury to the human participant; therefore, I suspect that the informant is providing us with his phantasy material and not a fact of his experience.

Even should the dimensions of the bull's penis be acceptable, the method of a bull's copulation hardly lends itself to this sort of activity. The penis of the bull is pointed and he drives it to its destination with great force, ejaculating very quickly. Often enough, the vagina of a cow will be torn and bleeding after such an assault.

However, there are records of attempts by farmers to have themselves penetrated anally by bulls, with serious injury or death the result—which does not, of course, prove that injury is inevitable, since the cases where no injury occurred would not come to the attention of authorities unless the person were caught in the act. One case resulting in a fatality was reported by the Nineteenth Century French sexologist Garnier, who wrote:

"A more improbable and incomprehensible fact took place on June 4th, 1865, in the Jura. A farmer, aged 31, who was perfectly well when his wife left him, was found in bed vomiting when she returned at six o'clock in the evening. He gave as a reason that an hour previously, while relieving himself near the stable, he had heard his two-year-old bull bellowing. Fearing that there was some danger, he had run into the stable without giving himself time to button up his breeches. The animal, which had got loose, sprung upon him and trampled him down with his buttocks in the air and his legs caught in his trousers. It had then introduced its penis into his anus, in which he felt very great pain. The doctor, who shortly arrived, found in fact his anus stained with blood and a glutinous around for a few minutes and then he would throw up his head and I would bend over again and he would mount and find the entrance quicker this time and it seemed like he went deeper and discharged more and when he dismounted he would smell around my rectum and if any of the semen was leaking out he would lick it off if I would let him but his tongue was too rough and took the hide off me. Then in a few minutes he would make a false start and four or five minutes after that he would mount the third time and when he dismounted he would let his penis hang free and that was a sign that he was through for a time. But if I went back out there in an hour he would repeat the whole thing over. He was right at two years old when I sold him and moved to California for a while. I wish I could have kept him and seen how long I could have used him.

"I would be afraid to take just any bull for I don't know what they would do. Especially the bigger and older ones as they might bear me down and the big penis might go too deep and rupture my insides. Since I got rid of that last one I have not been situated so as I could have one again. But I have heard tell of a number of other men who take them right along. And I see in the *Bible* where it was common practice in biblical times. And it is one of Moses' laws that if a man should let a bull cover him then the man should be put to death. I want to get me a young bull and raise him and keep him for my use. I am well over seventy years old and while I should have caught up with this thing many years ago, as it is I want them more than ever.

"As to injury sustained from contact with a male dog, I do not know. I have never had any trouble. It may be that

matter escaping from it, proceeding apparently from the bull's ejaculation. The wounded man, a prey to the most atrocious agonies, died during the night at 5 o'clock in the morning, having probably had the rectum opened and perforated."

Jacobus, in his *Crimes of the Genital Sense*, found the farmer's tale grossly improbable and thought the farmer must have aided the bull in effecting penetration. I think we must accept that verdict.

I have a larger pelvis than usual but I have never had one that I could not get loose from if I did not like the way it was. Of course some of them do not know any more about how to go about it than men do and they will hurt you, but usually they will insert it and then hold still and let it swell and then will pump till they discharge. Of course they are discharging all the time, but the way the female is constructed she has to have the sperm deposited in her uterus and she locks on him till he has swelled enough to hold her cervix open to receive the sperm. I have had some that would insert it and then turn tail to me and stand till the final discharge. And I have had others that did not seem to know what to do and this kind may just keep hunching and sometimes they hurt you.

"I always use surgical jelly if I have it, but sometimes have made do with saliva, as the rectum does not lubricate itself. That lubrication makes the penis slide back and forth freely and I get the sensation of the contact on the nerves of the rectum and prostate and as anybody knows you can massage the prostate and bring on an orgasm. I have never had a dog so big I could not get loose but I have had a few I could not hold till he was done as it was hurting me so I would reach around and press one side of the anus and it would slip right out. I think where any one gets hurt or injured is that they are dry and get scared and try to jerk away.*

* Most of the injuries of this type do seem to occur when a hasty and premature separation is attempted, usually because the person hears someone approaching and is fearful of being caught in the act. In one reported case, a sixteen-year-old boy attempted separation before the knot on the dog's penis had become flaccid with the result that he suffered an inch-deep tear through the sphincter ani into the gluteus muscles. Although the danger is less great women, too, may be injured if they attempt a hasty separation from a dog that has penetrated the vagina. In one case, a woman was surprised in Washington while copulating with a large English mastiff and when the terrified couple endeavored to hastily sever the connection the dog's organ was so forcefully removed as to bring about a fatal hemorrhage in the woman. Other cases of less serious injury to women also have been reported.

That big hound dog here that I mentioned before will hurt me sometimes and then I disengage. But when he does not hurt me I stay with him till he discharges and then the swelling goes right out of his penis and I could not hold him if I wanted to. All I have to do when he is around and I want him is to say to him, 'Star, you want to f--k?' and he will follow me where ever I am going and stay till I get ready and then when I get down on my hands and knees he will mount and find the opening and shove it all the way up and he may lick my bare flesh if he can find any while he is doing it to me. Though I haven't ever been hurt bad by a dog, still they are dangerous and children especially shouldn't ever fool with them in such a way. I don't fool with them myself unless I am a long time between drinks.*

* There is no doubt whatever that anal penetration of a human male by a dog is possible—or that it often has occurred. However, in the last century even some noted authorities argued that the connection was anatomically impossible. This same argument was once advanced before the Court of Appeals of Paris in the case of a surveyor of roads who was brought to trial after having been seen in the act of being anally penetrated by a large dog. The opinion of the medico-legal expert in this case is a piece of sexological curiosa well worth the quoting:

"QUESTION: *Can a dog perform anal copulation upon a man?*

"ANSWER: No, I think not, for the following reasons: 1st because the penis of a dog has a very special conformation which is only suitable for generation with his own species. 2nd, because its penis, which is very pointed and slender, has an interior bone covered with a very sensitive erectile tissue which, during accoupling, swells considerably, forms a plug inside the vagina, and prevents the dog from withdrawing immediately afterwards, the ejection of the spermatic secretion being very slow, which explains why one often sees dogs and bitches unable to separate, and remaining joined together as long as the erectile tissue has not shrunk nor becomes soft and flaccid again. In this painful situation, these poor beasts are very frequently the victims of odious brutalities.

When bitches are on heat, that is to say in a state of extreme excitement through venereal desires, the vaginal opening becomes dilated very easily, and the mucous membranes acquire a great elasticity; it is then that the dog is able to introduce his penis into

"Another time I had me a pair of hogs that was a year old before the sow come in heat. I had played with both of them from the time they were small. Usually the sow will not breed to her sibling if they have been raised together. She had fought off the boar all morning. I thought she might want it as she got hotter and in the afternoon I got in the pasture

------

it, which is very difficult for him when the bitch has returned to her normal state. How then could the dog, which cannot cover the bitch when she is quiet, on account of contraction and resistance of the vaginal tissues, succeed in introducing his penis into a man's rectum? This appears to me impossible, for the reasons which I have just given, and also for the following physiological reasons, which I will endeavor to make clear.

1st, on seeing a man's posterior, I do not think that it is in the nature of a dog to feel such ardent venereal desires as on seeing a bitch. 2nd, the anatomical constitution of his penis, which is very flexible at its point, does not give enough stiffness for him to introduce it into a man's anus and to overcome the very great resistance of the sphincter, the circular muscle of the anus, the contractility of which is excessively powerful. 3rd, the man's buttocks also display a surface large enough to put the dog farther away and to prevent the introduction of the penis, the length of which is diminished in proportion as the internal bone which forms a protuberance, is brought nearer to the point. In this case only a rubbing of the penis on the skin is possible. 4th, the man being on his knees with his hands resting on the ground, facilitating by his position the pederasty of the dog, will never attain his object if the animal, not being very tall, cannot encircle his body with its two forepaws so as to have a solid point of support.

I have acquired the certitude of what I have stated by placing the dog upon a man who was willing to lend himself to the experiment. Placed, kept there, and held up as he was by me, the dog (the same one that appeared in the case) if he had been perfectly accustomed to the action, would have been eager to try and satisfy his desires, while, on the contrary, he showed indifference, did not understand what was asked of him, and tried to get away; he has given us the evident proof of unwillingness and innocence.

If, contrary to all physiological estimation, the dog had succeeded in overcoming all the obstacles and in completely introducing his penis into the man's rectum, the effect on the erectile tissue of the bone would immediately have been produced, and caused the enormous natural swelling (as in the bitch's vagina during the process of covering) which would have compelled the two creatures to remain stuck together during the entire period of the energetic with them and played with her when she was not fighting the boar off. I got her scent all over me. She would take me but not the boar, and the boar would crowd in and try to mount her and she would break away and face him and fight him off. In the scuffle he tried to mount me a couple of times. I was afraid to let him smell around me much as they sometimes bite and a year old boar can do terrible damage. But I pulled off my trousers and rubbed her scent all over my hips and rectum and filled my anus full of spit and got back in with them and mounted the sow and the boar smelled over me and started to mount me so I just dropped off the sow and braced myself and let him mount. He could not find the entrance and was rubbing up between my legs with his penis. They very often do that and you have to hold him up where his penis will hit the hole. So I just reached around behind me and held his sheath up till he found the place and started in.

"His penis is not big around and the first five or six inches is shaped like a corkscrew and he has an action so he does not have to hunch like any other animal. It rotates around and back and is going in all the time and he will slide up a little

---

contraction of the sphincter. You see here then this most curious picture: the man compelled to remain in the quadrupedal position, and he on his part, and the dog on his, obliged to pull in order to free themselves from the bond which attaches them; the man unable to get up or to stand upright without lifting the dog from the ground, causing himself extreme pain and exposing himself to being dangerously bitten. In this case the monstrosity would be undeniable.

I conclude therefore that the fact of pederasty of the dog with the man is impossible, owing to the anatomical conformation of the anus of the one and of the penis of the other."

As concerns the outcome of this case, the expert opinion reproduced above may have been instrumental in aiding the defendant's cause. He did not get off altogether, but the court ruled that it had not been established that the dog had penetrated the man. Instead, the court held that the defendant had indulged in "obscene manoeuvres in public" and reduced a lower court's sentence of one year's imprisonment to only three months. A description of the whole case may be found in *The Abuses, Aberrations, and Crimes of the Genital Sense,* by Dr. Jacobus X, published at Paris by the famous Charles Carrington around the turn of the century.

at a time till he has his sheath up against me and then he seems to go to sleep. But the penis was working around and going deeper all the time till it was a way up in me and he began to discharge his semen. He would discharge three or four times and wait a few minutes and then he would push as deep as he could get it and discharge again. After he was done he got off and rubbed me in the sides and took on over me like I was a sow.

"It wasn't long then till the sow who had been watching us come over to me and he tried to mount her again but she refused. So I drove her into a separate pen and mounted her till I had a discharge. The boar was trying to tear the fence down by this time so I got back in with him and he tried to mount me before I got down on my all fours and when I did he mounted me and found the entrance at once and he screwed his way up as deep as he could get and did me like he did before. My nerves were singing and tingling and the feeling was so strong on me when he finished that I masturbated to try to relieve the tension.

"I started to leave the lot and he showed so plainly that he did not want me to go that I stayed there with him. I was around there nearly an hour before he made a move to mount me again, so I got down again on my all fours and he repeated the operation. When he got down I was so tired and wore out from holding him up I wanted to go lay down and rest for a while. So I headed back to the house and the semen was dripping out of me and I laid down and turned over on my stomach so I could hold it and went to sleep and dreamed that he was doing it to me again. The sow never did breed to him but I mounted her again and once or twice a week I would let the boar get to me.*

* Again one must wonder whether some wishful thinking is not involved in the account. I have other reports of "homosexual" intercourse between a human male and a boar in my files, but remain unconvinced that this could occur without injury to the man. On the other hand, after years of sex research, one has encountered so many strange occurrences that only the most preposterous are dismissed outright in the absence of conclusive evidence.

"As regards cattle, they have as many different ways in regards to their sex behavior as humans beings do. One cow will come into heat one evening and be out by next morning. Another one will come in this morning and if she does not get to a bull today she will break out that night and try to find one and if she does not succeed then she will breed the second day before she goes out of heat.

"A cow is very hot when in heat. A man just has to walk up behind her and rub his hand over her genitals and then insert his penis in her. She will lower her hips and invite him to give her all of it and when he does he just has to hold it still for a few seconds and she will close up on it with a sucking motion and he will have his orgasm without a movement of a muscle and his discharge will be heavier than it is with a woman."*

Homosexual Behavior and Miscegenation Mystique. "In Florida about thirty years ago I was out looking for anal contacts and run into two soldiers who wanted to get relief but wanted it orally so I agreed to give it to them. They wanted money but I did not have it to give so I went with them down on the beach and took them one after the other. Then they were not satisfied so I took each one again. Then they demanded money and as I did not have it they beat me half to death and left me unconscious on the beach. I was above the high water mark and a woman found me at day break and notified the police. They took me to the hospital and I had to report a mugging. I have not liked soldiers or sailors since and I would never go anywhere again with more than one man.

"About three years later I was in Los Angeles and the Depression was still on and I had got a few days work out on

* With regard to the intercourse of men with cows and heifers, reports concerning the animal's receptiveness and behavior in intercourse vary greatly. For example, I repeatedly have been told that it is almost always necessary to restrain the animal. The reason for these discrepancies remains undetermined. But probably the relations already existing between man and beast have a very great deal to do with determining how initially receptive the animal will be to the man's maneuvers.

a ranch and come back into town and I was burning up for
a man. So I went to the park and there was always a lot of
men standing around looking for some one to take care of
them. We would gang up and listen to one of the sidewalk
orators spout on any subject in order to be able to push ourselves up as close as we could with our hands behind us and
if a man wanted relief he would shove his genitals into our
hands so we could examine them and see if we could get him
hot enough to go somewheres for a date. I felt of one but he
did not build up just right and he gave me to understand that
he wanted money so I slid around and found another set of
genitals and the man responded at once.

"I did not know right off that this was a Negro. His penis
was larger than usual and his testicles were as large almost as
a hen's egg. It was not too light there in Pershing Square so
he was able to slip his hand up under my shirt and caress my
body and nipples without no one being the wiser. Any ways,
he got me so hot I did not care if I was seen. I let him know
that I wanted it in the anus and he seemed to swell up and I
thought he was about to take me right there which we could
not do. I nodded my head and walked away and he followed
me several blocks to where my old car was. When we got there
I saw he was a Negro. He was about thirty-five years old and
would weigh two hundred pounds and stood at least six feet.
We got in the car and I examined his genitals and then I got
afraid. They were so big I did not know if I could take it or
not without harm to me. But he kept petting me and begging
me to go with him and he said he had some vaseline and
would go easy with me, so I drove to a place I knew where
there was a heavy stand of timber.

"We went off into the woods and stripped and he put some
jelly in my anus and distended it with his finger and then two
fingers and then he had a syringe and he shot some of the
jelly up inside. Since I am so slight I looked like a kid along
side him, it was a good thing he had that jelly. He laid me
down on his clothes and started to insert it and he was gentle
with me as a baby. It was quite a stretch and he was some time
inserting it all. When he got it all the way up he lay still and

let me get used to it so I would relax and accept it and he loved me all over my body and sucked my nipples till I thought I would scream. He began to ease in and out but he would never get far out and as he worked on me I raised myself up to where he could get at me better. He bit into my neck and worked on me slow till I opened up and received him all the way and then he quickened the tempo and when he felt me stiffening up he crushed me to him and planted his seed.

"I started to get up then as I thought he was done but he held me and kept on working and he was still stiff and pretty soon I had an orgasm and I think he had another one too. He rested a while but did not remove it and it was in me for two hours. He did it to me again and he talked to me and wanted me to go with him as his mate and said he would rather have a white man than a woman. He said there was something way back in the past that caused the full blood Negro to want to plant his seed in a white man. He rested some more and kissed me and sucked my tongue and I wanted it and did not care if he was a Negro. In fact I was glad he was for I can not let myself go with a white man that way as the white does not want it and he will hurt you if he can after he is satisfied and he looks down on you as just another dirty queer.

"He had me another time and he slid out and we were done for then. I do not know how many orgasms he had, but I had two. I could not go off with him the way he wanted since I had some people there and I had to be careful for them not to find out about me that I was a homo. I told him I would meet him again but I had to work an extra day and when I got back to town he had come and gone. I looked for that man for as long as I stayed in the State of California. I can hardly write this for thinking about him and my penis has been turgid since I started. So I guess I will masturbate and go to bed and dream of my MAN.

*   *   *

"It was at Dallas, Texas, in the fall of 1961 that I got caught one time by the law for sodomy. I lived in Fort Worth at the time and had gone to Dallas to see some people and had to stop to go to the rest room and went to the bus station where there were some closets and in the partition between stalls was what we call a glory hole and there was a man in the next closet who was drinking and wanted relief. He offered it to me but I did not like the looks of it and I would not do fellatio on it and he kept on cursing and asking me to take it. I got up and backed up to the hole and he tried to get it that way but his penis was too short and while it was not thick it had an extra large head and as I did not help him he could not enter. And while he was cussing and trying to get it in I would not hold close enough for him and was standing there laughing at him when the law come in to the rest room and of course I did not hear the law till he was pounding on the doors for us to open up. The man had never penetrated, but of course the law could not tell about that.

"The law arrested us and took us to jail and charged us with sodomy. I got bail and appeared next morning in municipal court. Pleaded not guilty but was bound over for trial. I got bail again for fifty dollars. My wife was with me and wanted me to fight it as she thought my health was too bad for me to go to the pen. So I got me a lawyer and they set trial. When the trial come up the lawyer pleaded me guilty to disturbing the peace and I got a suspended jail sentence and a one hundred dollar fine and the lawyer charged me seven hundred and fifty dollars and I have not been back to that place since and am not about to go if I can help it.

"Well as to Negros and the Negro prostitutes as compared to white people, I prefer the Negro to the white woman every time as a sexual partner as the Negro woman is more passionate when she is loving a man because she wants him. Of course it is true that some Negro prostitutes are as dirty as can be and will rob you every chance they get, but a dirty white woman can out-nigger a nigger every time. And the white men are usually a vicious lot who will hurt you if they can and maybe beat you up or knife you after they get what they want or maybe if they don't get what they want. But a Negro homosexual will treat you kindly.

"There is two classes of homos as I have observed it. There

is one who wants to cover another man and he is called a Wolf. And the one who wants to take it from another man is called a Fag. I am a Fag and I hardly ever mount a man unless I have to do it to get him to mount me. I do not care much for the penis in my mouth but a lot of men do not want to go in the anus so I will relieve them the way they want it if I can not get it the way I would prefer.

"But with a Negro Wolf he will mount you and be all easy and kind. He will stay with you for half the night if you will let him. They mostly like the contact and do not seem to care about the orgasm as much as the white man does. While a white man will want to get it over with as soon as he can and will hold you and be rough with you a Negro more likely will take it slow and easy. Some of the white men will grab you around the neck when they have it in your mouth and will go as deep as they can and hold it there till they discharge. I have been nearly choked to death several times that way. But as I am so slight a big stout man can take advantage of me if he wants to.

"The Negro penis is usually larger than the white but does not get as hard as the white man's till the time when the Negro is about ready to discharge. I am talking about the black Negro and not about the half-breed. I do not like the yellow Negro or the light colored Negro women. The black Negro woman will try out a white man and if he should suit her she will open up and keep taking him till he is given out and then she will want more. She will be jealous of him and will not want any other Negro woman to have him. She will not care for how many white women he gets hold of for she can always get him back to her. A Negro will go to a white woman but she can not hold him for long as he will always go back to the Negro woman.

"I have lived where there were lots of Mexican people but I never made friends with many of them. They have the name of being hot natured and also are handy with a knife so I did not fool with the women much but have had some contacts with the Mexican homos. But I do not like them too well as they mostly have an acid odor that I can't stand in my mouth.

"I am not a lover of the Negro but I believe in living and letting live. I would not mind the white man saying we are superior if he would be that way. But I have seen so much skullduggery pulled by the whites that I can not but feel a compassion for the underdog Negro. I have seen so many Negros take the blame for crimes and sins of the whites that I have no brief for the so-called superior race. Who appointed them so? All in all, I would rather be a nigger than poor white trash any day.

"Well that is the story of my life and I hope it will do some body some good. I wish I had stayed away from homos and prostitutes as no body can fool around with these and not get venereal disease and get into trouble now and then. I prefer the animal contacts on this account. I have been so full of gonorrhea that even my teeth hurt and they are false and have been since 1933. I do not know why the syphilis I was born with has not had any later effect on me as on my father unless it could be because I have had so much penicillin shot into me.

"That is all that I can tell you except that I have had so much sex in my life because I just could not help myself and I do not see how I could do it different if I had it to do all over again. Sex has tormented me all of my life in one way or another and I might have had a different kind of life if I could ever have controlled it. I just never could help myself and now I am past seventy years of age and I still can't."

Concerning Bestiality

Since the dawn of history and throughout the world human beings have had sexual relations with creatures of many species. They continue to do so today and doubtless the practice will cease to exist only when the time comes, perhaps in the not distant future, that man has crowded all the other animals from the land masses of this planet. And, even then, there will remain the creatures of the rivers and seas—for among the objects used to satisfy human sexual desires can be counted the crocodile and the *dugong* (or sea-cow).

Legislation against animal sex contacts has included the penalty of death for both human and animal participants. Punitive legislation is not found everywhere—for instance, not among the Trobriand Islanders or in our own State of Illinois; but it is common and of varying degrees of severity from place to place and time to time. Like all legislation against the multivarious sexual practices of mankind, it frequently fails to deter and is irregularly enforced. Doubtless this was about as true in the days of the Hittite and Israelite prohibitions as it was in the face of the penalties laid down by Charlemagne in the Eighth Century and the Parliaments of Paris and Aix in the Seventeenth, and as it is in this country today.

Historically, the prevalence of bestiality is attested to not only by laws and court records, but by literature, especially mythology, and by paintings as well as sculptures adorning both Christian and Indian religious architecture—for instance, the temples of Conjeveram and Jaggnath, and the cathedral at Orléans, which offers an ape copulating with a woman. Copulation with subhuman primates, by the way, has for centuries been fairly common practice in parts of Africa and the Middle East—as witness the old Egyptian saying that 'Nothing poketh and stroketh, nor lusteth after a female, more strenuously than does the baboon.'

As regards mythology, the Greek is particularly rich with instances of humans copulating with animals and with gods in animal form. For example, Zeus assumed the forms of a bull, a swan, and a serpent to cohabit with Europa, Leda, and Persephone, respectively. Such bestial amours as these were also acted out on the Greek stage.

Naturally, in our own country rural males are the most frequent practitioners of bestiality—having a greater opportunity rather than a greater tendency. Second to these rural males in frequency of practice, would appear to be city-dwelling females, and after them urban male homosexuals, whose relationships most commonly are with the dog. My evidence strongly suggests that the few investigators, including Kinsey, who have concerned themselves at all with the incidence of animal contacts have failed to uncover the true extent of these female and homosexual male dalliances with dogs, which are more numerous than was thought. It might be added that the heterosexual male, in the city, rarely has an opportunity to engage in bestiality since the orifice of the bitch (or any other available animal) is seldom adequate to his purpose. Also, as one of our farmers has advised us, the bitch is not sufficiently steady on her legs, so that intercourse with that animal in the position natural to it is made still more difficult, if not impossible.

Only very rarely is the animal contact a product of sexual deviation in the sense that the person's desires are exclusively or customarily and preferentially, and for reasons beyond his or her control, directed towards animals rather than towards human partners. Rather, in all but a tiny minority of cases, bestiality is engaged in for other reasons. It may be a substitute or supplemental type of sex outlet, as masturbation is for many persons. Occasionally, it may be performed by persons who are too anxious to have sex relations with another person (although their desire is for a human partner). The male with a small penis has been known to turn to animals on that account. And, in the past (and to some extent presently), superstitious individuals have copulated with animals in the belief that this would cure venereal disease, make the penis grow, or confer supernatural powers on the practitioner. In the ancient world, historians tell us, nymphomaniacs were cured by having them repeatedly copulate with goats.

Havelock Ellis mentioned "three conditions" favorable to the "extreme prevalence" of bestiality. These were: 1) primitive conceptions of life which fail to set up barriers between man and beast; 2) the peasant's "extreme familiarity" with his animals; and 3) the aforementioned folklore beliefs that the animal contacts will cure venereal diseases, etc. The "offense is usually committed," he said, "either by persons who are morbidly abnormal or who are of so low a degree of intelligence that they border on feeblemindedness." Bestiality is, concluded Ellis, a "vice of clodhoppers."

A more contemporary view of human–animal sex intercourse is that of D. O. Cauldwell (*Animal Contacts*) who, influenced primarily by Kinsey, writes that "In former times, sexual experiences between man and animal were regarded as a form of perversion on the part of man. More recent studies indicate that man, in having sexual relations with the lower animals, is merely pursuing basic biological instinct. Psychologists who have given the matter serious study from an unbiased point of view are of the opinion that the sexual urge and an outlet are of far more importance than the nature or form of the outlet. It is, therefore, the opinion of such psychologists that man's sexual experiences with the lower animals represent

a diversion (because a more convenient outlet than the autoe-
rotic is not at hand) rather than a perversion."*

Cauldwell's view is doubtless correct as regards farm youths
and some other individuals having sex relations with the "lower
animals"; but it does not allow for the few persons for whom
bestiality is a true perversion, or for the larger number of
persons whose animal contacts, while not a deviation, do result from some psychosexual disorder such as an anxiety-based
impotence with human partners. There are also a few cases of
bestiality which occur during epileptic attacks and transient
psychotic episodes (when the behavior may be impulsive with
no effort made to avoid discovery).

In the first of the two cases presented in this section, the
informant was especially interested in the possibility of a fertile
union between man and beast that would yield a part-human,
part-animal offspring. This is a subject that always has excited
the human imagination and that continues to do so. Many,
including some reputable scientists, still believe in the possibility of a man–ape hybrid; and many of the writings of the
old historians contain accounts of human–animal contacts alleged to have resulted in the productions of monstrosities of
various sorts. Gould and Pyle noted, in their classic *Anomalies
and Curiosities of Medicine,* a number of such reports.

"According to (Ambroise) Paré," they wrote, "there was
born in 1493, as the result of illicit intercourse between a
woman and a dog, a creature resembling in its upper extremities its mother, while its lower extremities were the exact
counterpart of its canine father. . . . Lycosthenes says that in
the year 1110, in the bourg of Liège, there was found a creature with the head, visage, hands, and feet of a man, the rest

* Lest the reader be misled by Cauldwell's prose, there has
never been an exhaustive, serious *psychological* study, unbiased or
otherwise, of human–animal sex contacts. Since Cauldwell wrote,
there have been two fairly extensive treatments of the subject—my
own, referred to previously, and Prof. Hans von Hentig's *Soziologie
der zoophilen Neigung,* both published in 1962. But Cauldwell,
unless gifted with precognitive powers, could not have been referring to those; and, in any case, neither would qualify as serious,
exhaustive *psychological* studies.

of the body like that of a pig. Paré quotes this case and gives an illustration. Rhodoginus mentions a shepherd of Cybare by the name of Cratain, who had connections with a female goat and impregnated her so that she brought forth a beast with a head resembling that of the father, but with the lower extremities of a goat. He says that the likeness to the father was so marked that the head-goat of the herd recognized it, and accordingly slew the goat-herd who had sinned so un-naturally.

"In the year 1547, at Cracovia, a very strange monster was born, which lived three days. It had a head shaped like that of a man; a nose long and hooked like an elephant's trunk; the hands and feet looking like the webfoot of a goose; and a tail with a hook on it. It was supposed to be a male, and was looked upon as the result of sodomy. Rueff says that the pro-creation of human beings and beasts is brought about (1) by the natural appetite; (2) by the provocation of nature by de-light; (3) by the attractive virtue of the matrix, which in beasts and women is alike.

"Plutarch, in his 'Lesser Parallels,' says that Aristonymus Ephesius, son of Demostratus, being tired of women, had car-nal knowledge with an ass, which in the process of time brought forth a very beautiful child, who became the maid Onoscelin. He also speaks of the origin of the maiden Hippona, or as he calls her, Hippo, as being from the connection of a man with a mare. Aristotle mentions this in his paradoxes, and we know that the patron of horses was Hippona. . . .

"Writing in 1557, Lycosthenes reports the mythical birth of a serpent by a woman. It is quite possible that some known and classified type of monstrosity was indicated here in vague terms. In 1725 Mary Toft, of Godalming, in Surrey, England, achieved considerable notoriety through Surrey and even all over England, by her extensively circulated statements that she bore rabbits. Even at so late a date as this the credulity of the people was so great that many persons believed in her. The woman was closely watched, and being detected in her ma-neuvers confessed her fraud. To show the extent of discussion this case called forth, there are no less than nine pamphlets

and books in the Surgeon-General's library at Washington devoted exclusively to this case of pretended rabbit-breeding.
Hamilton in 1848, and Hard in 1884, both report the births
in this country of fetal monstrosities with heads which show
a marked resemblance to those of dogs. Doubtless many of the
supposed results of bestiality, if seen today, could be readily
classified among some of our known forms of monsters. Modern
investigation has shown us the sterile results of connections
between man and beasts or between beasts of different species,
and we can only wonder at the simple credulity and the imagi-
native minds of our ancestors. . . ."

Presently, there still exists a fairly widespread belief in
the possibility of offspring resulting from human–animal contacts. This is based upon ignorance usually, but also, it seems,
upon a will to believe in this possibility. Folklorist Vance
Randolph, in *The Ozarks*, has written that tales of women
"giving birth to litters of puppies, mares bringing forth colts
with human heads, and a great variety of similar phenomena
are related and very generally believed. I have never been able
to locate a hillman who has actually seen any of the monstrosities—'th' folks allus puts 'em out o' the way,' as one old
man told me." I myself verified that such beliefs still existed in
the Ozarks in the 1950s, although their prevalence was less
widespread than Randolph found them. Nor is the Ozarks
region of this country by any means the only one where such
superstitions exist. Probably all rural areas still have a certain
number of believers; and a fair number of uneducated city-
dwellers too, when they have given thought to the possibility,
suppose that hybrids might result from bestiality. Twice, when
interviewing prostitutes, I heard about women who refused to
perform in exhibitions where intercourse with animals would
be required of them—not on any moral grounds, but because
they feared they might become pregnant.

When we come to the possibility that a hybrid might be
produced by mating the highest type of subhuman primate
with a human on the lowest rung of the evolutionary ladder,
then we may be in an area where flat rejection would be im-

prudent. The idea that human and ape might be mated, to produce a slave race or for some other purpose, is an old one that continues to attract the attention and sometimes stimulate the serious efforts of man. Such an effort is being made presently by a French scientist, and has been made in fairly recent times by Soviet and German ones.

Near the end of the Nineteenth Century Sir Richard Burton, who is always worth listening to in scientific matters, considered the crossing of man with ape and remarked upon it as (in part) follows:

"Modern science which, out of the depths of its self-consciousness, has settled so many disputed questions, speaking by the organs of Messieurs Woodman and Tidy (*Medical Jurisprudence*) has decided that none of the lower animals can bear issue to man. But the voice of the world is against them and, as Voltaire says, one cannot be more clever than everybody.

"To begin with, there is the will: the she-quadruman shows a distinct lust for man by fondling him and displaying her parts as if to entice him. That carnal connection has actually taken place cannot be doubted; my late friend Mirza Ali Akbar, of Bombay, the famous Munshi to Sir Charles Napier during the conquest of Sind, a man perfectly veracious and trustworthy, assured me that in the Gujurat province he had witnessed a case with his own eyes. He had gone out 'to the jungle,' as the phrase is, with another Moslem who, after keeping him waiting for an unconscionable time, was found carnally united to a she-monkey. My friend, indignant as a good Moslem should be, reproved him for his bestiality and then asked him how it had come to pass. The man answered that the she-monkey came regularly to look at him on certain occasions, that he was in the habit of throwing her something to eat, and that her gratitude displayed such sexuality that he was tempted and 'fell.'

"That the male monkey shows an equal desire for the woman is known to every frequenter of the Zoo. I once led a party of English girls to see a collection of mandrils and other anthropoid apes in the ménagerie of a well-known Russian millionaire, near Florence, when the priapism displayed was such that the girls turned back and fled in fright.*

". . . But some will say that the grand test, the existence of the mule between man and monkey, though generally believed in, is characteristically absent, absent as the 'missing link' which goes so far as to invalidate Darwinism in one and perhaps the most important part of its contention. Of course the offspring of such a union would be destroyed, yet the fact of our never having found a trace of it except in legend and idle story, seems to militate against its existence. When, however, man shall finally became *homo sapiens,* he will cast off the prejudices of the cradle and the nursery and will ascertain by actual experiment if human being and monkey can breed together.

"The lowest order of bimana and the highest order of quadrumana may, under most favorable circumstances, bear issue and the mule, who would own half a soul, might prove most serviceable as a hewer of wood and drawer of water, in fact as an agricultural laborer. All we can say is that such miscegenation stands in the category of things not proven and we must object to science declaring them nonexistent."**

Also in the late Nineteenth Century the French army surgeon and sex anthropologist Jacobus Sutor became interested in this problem. Sutor, who as "Dr. Jacobus X" authored many curious and instructive volumes, was inspired to his effort, as

---

* Mandrils, along with chimpanzees, were made drunk by the ancient Romans who then unleashed them to rape and kill young girls in the arena at the Games. It might be added that the practice of having women raped to death by animals as a punishment also has been reported. For example, Sir George MacMunn (*The Underworld of India*) writes, in 1933, that: "It was the common talk of Mandalay in modern times that Theebaw's queen, Su-pi-ya-lat, put her offending court maids to death by having them raped by one of the little Burma pony stallions . . ."

** The above quotation may be found in Burton's edition of the *Arabian Nights*. It might be added that the function of agricultural laborer has been performed in the past by a nonhybrid, the Hamadryas baboon, which once weeded garden plots for the Egyptians.

probably was Burton, by the reports of Du Chaillu on the matings of apes and monkeys with native women. The gorillas of the Gaboon, said Jacobus, rape grown women and carry off young girls, who become their mistresses. He noted a report by Delaborde of a native woman who lived for three years as the "wife" of a gorilla. Jacobus announced his intention to make some efforts of his own toward producing the hybrid; but apparently he did not get around to it, or at any rate did not succeed, since his later writings describe neither experiment nor results.

A little previous to World War One, a Berlin biologist, Dr. Herman Klaatsch, conceived of a plan to hybridize the gorilla with some of the more vigorous tribes of what was then German West Africa. He wanted to produce "on a large scale working-men more powerful of muscle than any now living and who, by reason of their more primitive minds, might be more readily exploited." Apparently the start of the War served to thwart or put an untimely end to the efforts of the German biologist.

At Atlantic City, a few days after Christmas in 1932, the members of the American Association for the Advancement of Science heard an enlightening address by a Dr. H. S. England, who reported on a then-current Soviet attempt to produce a human–chimpanzee hybrid.

The project, Dr. England said, was being financed by the government of the Soviet Union. At its head was a Dr. Eli Ivanoff of Moscow. Dr. Ivanoff, along with his brother and one other scientist, had been, with the help of nine female chimpanzees, laboring for more than a year in some remote region of Turkestan. Although three of the chimpanzees had died, the Soviet team remained undaunted and confident that the first of an intended series of hybrids would be forthcoming at almost any moment.

The stated aim of the Russian project was to provide some evidence substantiating evolutionary theory. The chimpanzees were to be rendered pregnant by means of artificial insemination. I have not been able to obtain information concerning the ultimate outcome of the Ivanoff expedition.

It is worth adding that at the Atlantic City meeting Dr.

England went on to advise his colleagues that for more than a quarter of a century he had taken great interest in encouraging just such a project, but had failed to gain the needed support. He remarked that there now seems to be no other way of demonstrating man's development from what is presumed to be his common ancestry with the subhuman primates.

The most recent account of a hybridization attempt was reported by a newspaper several years ago.* A feature article disclosed that a French anthropologist and biologist, Dr. Gustav Monteil, was currently attempting to crossbreed humans with anthropoid apes. Dr. Monteil, of the Rhodes-Livingstone Medical Centre in Livingstone, Northern Rhodesia, had discussed his work at a meeting of the British Medical Association.

"First of all," Monteil is quoted as saying, "my studies, observations and experiments prove conclusively that the blood of the anthropoid ape is the same type characterizing human blood. Not only are the apes' anatomical formation and structure practically identical with those of men, but that blood which nourishes them is absolutely identical with human blood."

Monteil said he conceived the idea for his experiment after hearing some reports of successful crossbreedings between anthropoids and Bushmen, Hottentots, and Bantus. Additional reports of this nature had been obtained from members of a Portuguese expedition in Angola.

"The Darwinian theory," Monteil told the Britons, "claims a very close relationship between men and the orangoutang, the gibbon, the chimpanzee, and the Rhesus monkey. Darwin held that we are descended from a common ancestor.

"Not only would crossbreeding between an ape and a human help in verifying this conclusion, but there is now a very strong possibility of being able to breed a super-race of apes with intelligence almost equal to man's.

"I have heard reputable reports about offspring of a native woman with an ape. The result, from the conclusions I was able to make, was a male of fair intelligence. However, though there may be hundreds of offspring throughout Africa of a

* Richard Delaney, "Doctor Plans to Mate Apes with Humans," *Midnight,* April 8, 1963, p. 3.

human male and a female ape, because of the sacred image such crossbreeding holds on the natives, I can only draw from my own scientific conclusions.

"Gentlemen, I am on the verge of subjecting myself as the necessary male in this experiment.

"The chances are that the resulting offspring would have more dominantly human physical characteristics than ape-like. Outside of its bearing on the Darwin theory, the results would undoubtedly be a milestone in human biology."

As another factor conducive to the success of his effort, Monteil mentioned that the number of chromosomes per cell is the same in the ape as in man. Biologists and zoologists from several universities are said to have agreed that what he is attemping is at least theoretically possible in the case of the chimpanzee.

Even should Monteil succeed in his experiment, leading to similar endeavors by others, presumably no very large number of hybrids ever would come into being—since the hybrid itself would be sterile, as mules are. In view of the population explosion, that seems all to the good. Also, any numerous new race of this kind would throw jurists and clergymen into confusion, and probably would further swell the already overburdened welfare rolls of New York City.

In conclusion I would say again that, in general, the sexual contact with an animal has importance only if it appears within the context of a psychopathological syndrome, or if it results in excessive feelings of guilt or loss of self-esteem. The great majority of practitioners are not victims of a zoophilic perversion and, if the act inflicts no injury on the animal, there would seem to be little or no reason for society to concern itself with this type of behavior.

There exists no detailed psychology of bestiality and, while I might speculate at some length, the data are as yet too limited and so it seems best to resist the temptation. Meanwhile, the cases presented should have been instructive—as to animal as well as human behavior in a situation outside the experience of most persons and concerning which even few sexologists have much knowledge.

PART THREE

Transsexualism: Men Who Want to Be Women

The Background
and the Problem

The phenomenon of the man who wants to be a woman, and who feels that psychologically he is one, was described by the writers of antiquity and the problem still is with us today.* Such individuals are found in primitive as well as in civilized societies. In our century there is not one single authenticated instance of this condition having been remedied by psychotherapy or any other therapy. Only in recent years has medicine found a way of dealing effectively with the problem; and that way—hormonal and surgical "sex change"—remains extremely controversial. Only gradually is society coming to recognize that there may be a justification for "sex change" in the case of such individuals as the widely publicized Christine Jorgensen.

In many cases the transsexual has no memory of a time when he did not feel himself to be mentally and emotionally female—"a female psyche in a male body"—and parents, siblings, and others may support the individual's claim that even as a small child he seemed much more a girl than a boy. Al-

* There are also, of course, female transsexuals—women who want to be men. However, such complete psychosexual inversion is not so frequent among females as males. Here, the discussion will be of the male transsexuals.

though the fact remains to be established, it is likely that transsexualism, at least in some cases, has a physical, probably
genetic cause and is not always and entirely a product of conditioning. As a part of its program of transsexualism research, a
scientific foundation is presently attempting to find this under-
lying physical cause.

The principal life-goal of the male transsexual is to be
physically female, or as close to physically female as contemporary science can make him—only then will the body be experienced as being in harmony with the mind. His male genitalia
are hateful to him—so much so that phantasies of auto-castra-
tion are the rule, attempts at self-castration are frequent, and
not a few have actually succeeded in removing their own
testicles, penis, or both, sometimes with fatal results.

When he is obliged to live as a man, the transsexual is
always tense and uncomfortable. Only when he dresses as a
female, and is accepted as a female by others, is he able to relax
and experience some degree of emotional comfort. Yet, as
noted, even this does not suffice, and the feminizing hormonal
procedures, castration, and finally creation of an artificial vagina
are required before any lasting peace of mind is possible. Until
all of this occurs, the transsexual is among the most *sex-driven*
of persons—although here the sex-based drive is not primarily
towards intercourse and gratification, but rather towards the
transformation described. As to intercourse and gratification,
the transsexual may be promiscuous or chaste (asexual), or
something in between; this sexual behavior will be discussed
and exemplified later.

Transsexualism is a much more extreme condition than
transvestism, although the two are often confused and the
transsexual is frequently regarded as being a homosexual transvestite. Transvestism, however, in most cases is a condition
wherein the person wants to sometimes wear the clothing of
the opposite sex and may be sexually excited by so doing. The
transvestite may be otherwise normal, often has a satisfactory
marriage, and the last thing he would want would be to have
his male organs removed, or to become a "sex change." The
case of the homosexual transvestite differs somewhat from that

of the heterosexual transvestite; but the former no more than the latter wishes to lose his penis, and this is but one important respect in which he differs from the transsexual.

The transsexual finds himself, in our society, in a thoroughly unfortunate position. If, as is true of so many of his kind, he exhibits from childhood a feminine appearance, mannerisms, and tastes, he begins by being teased and otherwise abused by other children. "Sissy" and "pretty boy" are among the more mild of the early epithets addressed to these persons. As they grow older the terminology becomes increasingly abusive and the ostracism more complete.

The antagonism these individuals fall heir to is ancient and traditionally has been aimed at such, at least superficially, similar phenomena as sex-role and sex-identity confusion, transvestism, homosexuality and eunuchism, and effeminacy. In fact, historically, all of these phenomena appear so intertwined and interrelated that it often is impossible to distinguish hostility toward one category and its representatives from hostility to another or combination of other categories. Nor is it possible always to determine whether the old (and some much more recent) writers are speaking of transsexualism, or of homosexual effeminacy, hermaphroditism, and so on.

To look at some of the historical data, it is clear that among the ancient Greeks, and whatever the tolerance for homosexual acts, the effeminates, the transvestites, and the transsexuals were objects of derision and even detestation. Hans Licht (*Sexual Life in Ancient Greece*) remarks of attitudes prevailing during the Classical Period:

"The word *cinedus* (*kinaidos*) . . . gradually became the nickname for those half-men, who by their feminine behavior and gestures, by painting the face and other tricks of the toilet, incurred general contempt. A satire in the *Anthology* (xi, 272) says of them: 'They do not want to be men and yet were not born as women; they are no men, since they allow themselves to be used as women; they are men to women, and women to men.' "*

* Apparently at least some of the effeminates were "bisexual."

The Greeks had various explanations for "effeminacy," which of course must have ranged from the slight to the extreme. Apart from considering it a punishment of the gods, they saw the behavior of effeminate males and transvestites as resulting from impotence, too much time spent on horseback, homosexual seduction, and eunuchism. Many believed it to be an inborn condition. Some considered it a logical outcome of homosexual behavior, especially anal intercourse; or a mental disorder, "in fact a form of melancholia."

Some of the behavior and attitudes described in the old writings show us how little these have changed over the centuries intervening. For instance, the Roman poet Manilius (*Astronomica*) writes of men who "will ever be giving thought to their bedizenment and becoming appearance; to curl the hair and lay it in waving ripples or else to gather in the locks with circlets and arrange them in a heavy top-knot, and to alter the head by adding false ringlets; to polish the shaggy limbs with hollow pumice stone; yea! and to hate the very sight of a man, and long for arms without growth of hair. Women's robes they wear; the coverings of their feet are less for use than for show; and steps broken in to an effeminate gait are their delight. Nature they scorn; indeed in their heart lies a pride they cannot avow, and they vaunt their disease (vice) under the name of virtue. Ever to love is a little thing in their eyes; their wish will be to be seen to love."

Philo, the Jewish philosopher of Alexandria, who urged that the effeminates be put to death, also offers an interesting portrait:

"They suffer from feminine disease. In fact they are effeminated in body and soul, and not one spark of manliness do they suffer to appear in them. They braid their hair to look like women, they smear and paint their faces with cosmetics, anoint their persons with fragrant ointments . . . Expending every possible care on their outward adornment, they are not ashamed even to employ every device to change artificially their nature as men into women . . . These men–women may be seen constantly strutting in the *agora* at the hour of high market, walking in procession at the sacred festivals . . . Some of them have brought the charm of their youth to such a pass that craving a complete transformation into women, they have amputated their generative members"—as also did the transvestite priests of a number of early goddess cults.

It is possible, scanning the accounts of historians and travelers, to take from many times and places similar descriptions of effeminate males, some of them undoubtedly transsexuals, and of the reactions of individuals and of their society to them. The degree of disapproval and the harshness of the penalties may vary; but, some opportunities in the theatre apart, the societies of the West have never dealt rationally with this problem or found a useful place in their midst for this small but constant segment of the population.

Some primitive societies, on the other hand, do find a place in their midst for men who prefer or feel the need to live as women. Among them such a man, while not always "accepted" or integrated into the society, may be tolerated as a *berdache* (feminized or sex-changed male) and/or feared and reverenced as a shaman (priest and sorcerer).

A *berdache* is a man who wears the clothing of a woman, does a woman's work, and behaves as a woman, insofar as this is possible, in his sexual relations with male partners—as wife, communal concubine, prostitute, participant in sexual rites, or whatever. In some societies, this rôle is assigned to a boy while he still is in infancy and then, with conditioning, he meets the expectations of the group by developing feminine mannerisms and predilections, including erotic ones. In other societies, the choice is made at puberty, when usually the most effeminate among the males will be selected. In still others, the rôle of *berdache* is chosen by the effeminate male himself. In a few societies, a mature and very masculine man is designated and then is feminized by psychological pressures, sometimes by castration, and possibly chemically (by administration of hormones in the form of the urine of animals which are pregnant or in heat). The *berdache* may become a shaman and then he is considered to have been invested by the gods with supernatural powers.

When an apparently normal male is designated for the

berdache rôle and then (without castration or other physical measures) becomes feminized, the psychogenesis of the effemination is fairly clearcut. It is not so clearcut, however, where, as among the Sakalavas of Madagascar, the children selected and then raised as girls are initially picked because of their delicate and girlish appearance, mannerisms, etc. Similarly, in our own society, effeminacy up through its extreme—transsexualism—may or may not be a product of evident conditioning.

In some contemporary cases in our own and similar societies evidence of blatant and forceful conditioning is found. For instance, a boy may have been dressed and treated as a girl for months or even years; or the boy has been made to understand that his parents expected and wanted a girl—motivating him to try to fulfill the expectation and wish. In a few cases the sex was ambiguous at birth and the physician or parents were mistaken as to the child's sex and he was raised accordingly up to such a time as the error became apparent. However, in at least some of these cases, the question arises as to whether, initially, the child did not "condition" the parents—by his obvious girlishness and even by his persistent demands that he be treated as a girl.

In considering the causes of effeminacy, other factors sometimes mentioned are the little boy's desire for the "privileged status" accorded little girls—for example, the more attractive clothing, greater pampering, less harsh discipline, etc.; the absence of a paternal model upon which the child's masculinity could be based; and the assumption, by a delicate child, of female-like behavior in order to escape the necessity of competing unsuccessfully with other boys—a phenomenon that might be roughly compared to that of "presenting" as encountered among the subhuman primates.

As I have remarked elsewhere, "It will be readily recognized that the possible causes mentioned above are also those advanced very often to explain homosexuality, transvestism, and transsexualism. In fact, most cases of effeminacy probably stand on a continuum with transvestism, transsexualism and much if not all homosexuality (when the latter is exclusive, or nearly so). Just as transvestism seems to have the possibility of ripening into transsexualism, so does effeminacy seem to have the possibility of developing through homosexual transvestism to its apparently logical conclusion in transsexualism. Why the effeminacy progresses along the continuum in some cases but not in others, remains a matter for speculation.*

"As noted, efforts to convincingly demonstrate genetic (or possibly endocrine) causes of effeminacy and transsexualism have not been successful to date. Nonetheless a fair number of sexologists are inclined to believe that an unknown constitutional factor underlies some of these cases, especially when the female-rôle identification is as extreme as in transsexualism. Some German psychiatrists have demonstrated that the identification with the opposite sex may be discernible as early as the first year of life . . . The possible etiological significance of brain malfunctioning, resulting from congenital anomaly or later brain damage, also has received consideration and studies are under way. But so far as I know there exists no evidence sufficient to sustain this hypothesis."**

To return now to the life-situation of the male transsexual in our society, from the time he reaches adolescence, and for the rest of his life should he continue as a man, the transsexual impresses almost everyone he meets as being "a queer." This means that he is in economic trouble along with his other difficulties. Almost every kind of employment is closed to him. Living as a woman, he is acceptable and could hold any position for which he is qualified. But the necessity for providing documents, along with some other practical obstacles, make the pretense a difficult (though not impossible) one to carry out.

Professional female impersonation provides a way of earning a livelihood for some transsexuals. However, to earn a

* I would like to stress the word *possibility*. When no such development occurs, effeminacy, transvestism, and homosexuality may be radically distinct from transsexualism in many important respects.

** Masters, R. E. L., "Effeminacy and the Homosexual," in Ellis, A. and Cory, D. W., *Encyclopedia of Homosexual Behavior*, Citadel Press, New York, 1966. This article also contains much additional material of historical and anthropological interest, including discussions of the *berdache* and *berdache-shaman*.

living as a female impersonator (entertainer), the individual in most cases must be exceptionally attractive and be able to sing, dance, or otherwise "perform." Naturally, most do not possess such specialized qualifications.

Some, unable to find other work that they can engage in while living as females, become prostitutes. The transsexual male, posing as a female, and working in some area of prostitution, may earn a good deal of money; of course, there are problems.

Such a prostitute wears a little belt that draws his genitals back between his legs. Over this, he wears a tight corset, which his customer would have to resort to violence to remove. He offers oral contacts to his customer, explaining that he is menstruating, or just that he prefers to "French." Since many transsexuals today, even though they have not had surgery and been equipped with a vagina, have acquired female-like breasts as a result of hormone treatments, the prostitute may offer himself "from the waist up." This is is not only more stimulating to the customer than the oral contact alone would be, but it is helpful in allaying such suspicions as might arise.

It is interesting that, like his female counterpart, the transsexual prostitute typically is not aroused by his relations with his customers. One such prostitute, describing his responses to oral intercourse with a customer, said his own genitals almost always were "dead" during the intercourse and any other pleasurable stimulation was lacking. "When I do it," he said, "I just close my eyes and think about the money." In his case, the money he thinks about is the thirty dollars he usually receives from each customer.*

The whole question of transsexual sex responses is an interesting and little understood one. The transsexual, who has not been operated and has no vagina, in many cases either never experiences ejaculation or does so by masturbation only. He does not consider himself to be homosexual, and may find homosexuals repulsive. In his sex contacts, he must preserve the illusion that he is female. Therefore, he performs only as

* Much of the material in the remainder of this discussion first appeared in my article, "Men Who Want to Be Women," published in *Real Life Guide,* February, 1964.

receptor, experiencing some gratification, but almost always short of orgasm. If he used his own male organ in sexual intercourse, he could not preserve the illusion of being female. In masturbation he uses, of course, his male organ; but in this case his phantasies enable him to overcome the difficulty. (Those transsexuals receiving large doses of female hormone are in any case unable to achieve erection or to ejaculate.)

Still, it would appear that the transsexual masturbator, by means of his phantasies, does not overcome entirely the difficulty of having to make use of the male organ. The transsexual who has been operated, and who then masturbates vaginally or at the vulva, finds in most cases that the orgasmic sensation is much more intense than was the case when he still had a male organ. This suggests that, previous to surgery, considerable inhibition of sensation was being experienced.

The possibility of "sex change" or "sex conversion" surgery is recent. Transsexuals have existed throughout history, and many have managed to have their male organs removed, but only in the last several decades has there been any possibility of replacing the removed male organs with a "functional vagina" (i.e., an orifice suitable for coitus) and female-like external genitalia. This possibility now dominates the thinking of every transsexual who has heard about it, and of those not yet operated many "live only for the day" when they will be able to have the conversion surgery performed.

Unfortunately, since the operation is so desperately desired, and since the results appear to be favorable in the great majority of cases,* there still is much medical resistance to "change of sex." Legally, on the basis of an old statute directed toward quite another purpose, there remains the possibility that the (American) surgeon could be prosecuted for "mayhem." (However, while this possibility often is mentioned,

* See especially Benjamin H., *The Transsexual Phenomenon,* Julian Press, New York, 1966. Dr. Benjamin is this country's, and possibly the world's, leading authority on transsexualism, and the results he cites are extremely impressive. My own numerous interviews with transsexuals have been with Dr. Benjamin's patients in most instances, and his evaluations of the results of treatment and surgery seem to me to be entirely justified.

there seem to have been no such prosecutions.) The result has been that the surgery sometimes has been performed in other countries by quacks and bunglers who have badly mutilated their patients.

At its best, the sex change surgery creates female-like genitalia sufficiently realistic to deceive the male (including, even, the gynecologist). More often, however, as regards appearance, the transsexual has to explain away certain scars and other imperfections on the basis that "she" was involved in an accident, or something of the sort. There remains, too, the problem that the vagina may lack lubrication sufficient for coitus. In most cases, an artificial lubricant has to be employed.

A slight additional problem results from the fact that the newly or recently operated transsexual, at orgasm, ejaculates from the urethral opening prostatic fluid resembling semen. There is, of course, no real semen since the testicles have been removed. (An exception is one surgeon who does not remove the testicles, but conceals them in the abdomen.)

Along with the surgery that creates a vagina, and almost always preliminary to it, the transsexual receives repeated dosages of female hormone. This has the effect of feminizing the body contours, most strikingly the breasts, of helping to change the voice, and of inhibiting body hair growth. Hair is also removed by depilation. Female hormone dosage must be continued for a long while after surgery, and probably for the remainder of the person's life.

Of course, sex conversion surgery, and the other feminizing procedures, cannot transform the patient into a full-fledged female. His chromosomal sex remains male. He can never ovulate, become pregnant, or give birth to a child. What can be given is the external female-like appearance and the vagina that makes a "normal" sex life possible for the new "woman." When, after surgery, a change in the legal status is secured, it then is possible for "her" to work, love, and marry without society's interference. In the following case, it will be seen how "sex change" can result in improved adjustment and even happiness for an individual who otherwise would have been condemned to maladjustment and misery.

Confessions of a "Sex Change"

The autobiographical statement now to be presented necessarily has been pieced together from both written materials and the contents of interviews as reconstructed from my notes. For this reason, the personality of the informant emerges somewhat less clearly and forcefully than in the preceding cases. On the other hand, much instructive and striking information is presented, particularly as concerns the sexual practices and problems of transsexuals both before and after sex change, and also of female impersonators. What is said in this connection appears to be accurate and is supported by my own investigations among both groups.

The informant in this case is a thirty-year-old male who says that, since childhood, he always has felt himself to be female. About two years ago, after both psychiatric counselling and feminization treatment, he underwent a "sex change" operation which seems to have been outstandingly successful. He now is legally a woman, has a good job, and claims to be free of all major mental and emotional problems for the first time in his life. His first statement, made about a year ago, now follows:

"I am presently twenty-nine years of age and up to a year

ago, when I had The Operation, was one of the most unhappy
people on the face of this earth. But that, as you know, is a
normal way to be for us transsexuals who still are looking forward to The Day.

"As far back as I can remember, I always felt 'different,'
but, as my mother clearly remembers, I was eight when I first
announced myself a girl and demanded to play with dolls, dress
in girl's clothes, and let my hair grow long. Before that, I had
had an imaginary playmate named Dolly, and everyone
thought it was a big joke. But gradually, it seems to me now,
I must have come to recognize that the girl Dolly was actually
my true self and that John (my boy's name) was the person who
ought to be regarded as a make-believe. That is why, when I
told my family I was a girl, I also told them I wanted to be
called Dolly from then on.

"When I first started this, nobody took me too seriously.
But they did begin to worry pretty soon, since I started putting
on the dresses of my sister (only sibling, one year older than I),
and began to show all the signs of a 'sissy' or boy who was going to turn out to be very, very effeminate.

"Two other things happened when I was eight. My father,
an alcoholic, woman-chasing lawyer, ran off with a woman and
left us, and I started to masturbate, usually wearing a dress of
my sister's when I did it. I believe, and my psychiatrist agreed
I am right, that it would be a complete mistake to see any connection between my father's departure and my announcement
to my family that I was a girl.

"(By the way, I had to go to several psychiatrists, and to
several other doctors besides, before I found one who didn't
think I was just another nut, and a degenerate in the bargain.
That, too, I now know is the way it usually goes for us transsexuals.)

"As I got older, mother, who I loved very much, tried
every way she knew how to get me to act more like a boy, but
nothing ever did work. I kept putting on my sister's clothes, or
any other feminine apparel I could get hold of that would fit
me, and used to worry a good bit that I was going crazy, maybe,
because of playing with myself. I tried to stop these practices by

my own will-power and used to pray to God to either straighten me out or turn me into a girl or else just let me die, but nothing ever happened to change me.

"Up until I was thirteen things went along fairly well. I stayed away from boys as much as I could, since they didn't like me much and I didn't like them either, and played with the *other* girls, who seemed to like me fine. In gym class, when we had to play games like baseball, I was always about the last one to be picked when the boys chose up sides. You can't blame them for that, since I would usually duck when a ball came my way, and everyone said that I threw like a girl (which secretly pleased me *and* encouraged me to not try to suppress all the feminine mannerisms that naturally were mine). My body was poorly developed for a boy—even now, I am only five-feet-four and thinnish—and really looked more like a young girl's body. So did my face look more like a girl's, and people would comment that this was so.

"When I was thirteen, and the kids started getting sex conscious, my life took a very bad turn for the worse. I didn't have much of an idea till then what 'homosexual' meant, and the other kids evidently didn't either. But when I was thirteen, and after that, everybody decided I was queer. Probably as a result of this rumor—utterly false, since I never had thought about having sex with any person at all—a boy named Jerry, who lived across the street, decided he was going to try me out. He was sixteen or so, and a weight-lifter, a lot bigger and stronger than I was. While his mother was away from home, he got me over to his house, showed me his penis, and told me I had to put it in my mouth or he would beat me up. I refused, he punched me several times, I cried for a while, but then finally I did it. I had no 'instinct' for this act, and he had to tell me how to go about it. I remember I almost vomited and was sick at my stomach all the rest of the day.

"After that, he made me come over to his house about once a week. Then he started bringing in some of his friends, until naturally the word got around. I had had relations with maybe seven or eight boys in this way (mouth–penis contact) and, once, anally, with Jerry, when the world fell in on me. The first thing that happened was that I came out to go to school one morning and right in front of our house, on the sidewalk, somebody had written in chalk: JOHNNY IS A DIRTY QUEER. I was able to erase this before my mother saw it, and probably she wouldn't have believed it anyway, but it did *terrify* me. Even worse, a couple of days later somebody, the same person I suppose, scribbled another sign: JOHNNY SUCKS PETERS. I still can see those words on our sidewalk, and recall how I wept and shook all over while I rubbed them out with the bottom of my shoe.

"My mother saw none of this, but evidently some other people in the neighborhood did. The following Saturday, when Jerry got me over to his house and I was going down on a friend of his, his mother broke in on us and she was perfectly hysterical. She called me everything in the book, then dragged me across the street to my house and told my mother how I was a dirty little cocksucker who was corrupting her boy and all the other boys in the neighborhood. It became plain at this time that she had had her suspicions, possibly awakened by those things on the sidewalk, and had set a trap to catch us.

"When that terrible woman finally went away, my mother was both mad and heart-broken. She said we would have to leave town right away, that I had brought disgrace on the whole family and we would have to make a fresh start. (Today, it seems to me we need not have moved. We lived at the time in Kansas City and it surely would have been sufficient in a place that size to change neighborhoods.) But anyway, within a week my mother was able to arrange for a job in St. Louis, and soon afterwards we moved there. Meanwhile, my sister and I were taken out of school immediately and made to stay at home. I think my mother *did* believe my story that Jerry had forced me to do those things. But she also believed, as she since has told me, that I was headed for a life as a homosexual and it would have happened, sooner or later, anyway.

"Concerning my relations with those boys, I *never* got any pleasure out of it and only did it because I was afraid. Never, at any time in my life, have I *ever* wanted to be homosexual, or heterosexual either for that matter, *except* as a real girl having *normal* relations with a normal boy.

"One strange thing, although I got no pleasure from these experiences—not even an erection while taking care of them!—once I would get over to Jerry's and would be ordered to go down on him or some other boy, I would feel extremely weak and passive, almost like someone who is in a trance. I would seem to have no will to resist, I would just do whatever I was told, and afterwards, looking back on what had happened, it would seem like a dream, or something that had happened to someone else and that I had been told about. Yet I did know that it was all for real, I felt ashamed and guilty, and I was *very* afraid that people would find out.

"One other thing about this, the time that Jerry had me in the anus it was somewhat different. That time there may have been a little pleasure, not sexual pleasure exactly but pleasure that came with my feeling or imagining that I was a girl who was having sex with a boy. On that occasion, I instinctively took command of the situation and insisted that I lie on my back during the intercourse, not on my stomach as Jerry instructed me to do. I have since learned that this is a very common way of doing it for transsexuals, but very unusual practice for homosexuals. After that incident, maybe two or three times, I phantasied myself as a girl having sex with Jerry while I lay on the bed wearing mother's bra and panties and masturbated. I never had masturbation phantasies about any of the other sex experiences of that time.

"We moved to St. Louis, where mother went to work as a legal secretary—the job she had had at the time she met my father—and I was determined to stay far away from all homosexuals. I tried to put on a very masculine front, and my inner life was even more of a secret from everyone than it had been before. I was convinced by now that I was by nature an effeminate male homosexual, which I found it a detestable thing to be. But if that was what I was, at least I could keep my disease to myself, stay out of trouble, and not disgrace the family any further. All the while, of course, I did continue to 'dress' (put on female clothing) when I was alone in the house, and to masturbate. Once in a while, since I now could ejaculate, I would get some semen on my sister's clothing, and I think she knew what it was and what I was doing. But, if she did, she never told on me. She would sometimes, though, when angry, call me a 'dirty little queer' or something like that. At the same time, she seemed to go out of her way to let me see her in the nude, and once or twice, I am pretty sure, she went out of her way to hint that we might have sex together. I thought about it, and wouldn't have felt guilty if we had done something. But I didn't really want to, and besides was afraid I wouldn't be able to. When I would see my sister in the nude there always was one very strong reaction—envy! I'd have damned myself to hell in an instant if, by so doing, I could have traded bodies with her or acquired a body like hers.

"Shortly after moving to St. Louis, not very long after I had turned fourteen, I had my first wet dream. In that dream, I was a very pretty girl and walking down a city street. A boy came up to me and asked me something, probably for a date or something like that, and I think that was all there was to it. I woke up in the middle of the sensation and my pajamas were all wet. Fortunately I had heard about wet dreams and so wasn't frightened. *Always,* all of my life, whenever I have had a wet dream I have dreamed that I was a girl—sometimes having sex with a boy, sometimes just walking down the street, etc. But such dreams never have been very frequent—maybe four each year when I was in my teens, after that only two or three a year.

"In school, I did just well enough to get by. My I.Q., I was told, was quite superior (125), but my teachers, from the very beginning, would complain that I 'daydreamed.' That was unquestionably true, and I would sit and watch the prettiest girls in the class and try to pretend that I was one of them. One day I would pretend to be Elaine, the next day Sylvia, and so on. Once I got in trouble for following around too much a girl who I wanted to be. This was very funny, actually, since everybody thought I was interested, *as a boy,* in this girl. I had to go to the principal's office, the word got around, and it even did me some good with my classmates, who decided maybe I wasn't queer after all.

"All through high school I *never* had a close friend. But how I needed one! I had, by this time, come across the idea of 'a woman's soul in a man's body' and felt certain that that applied to me. I knew I was a freak, somebody who had gotten into the wrong body. I needed someone to discuss this with, but there was never anyone. So I lived most all the time in a make-believe world where I was a girl. I took long walks alone, went to a lot of movies and imagined I was some famous actress, and, the rest of the time, stayed mostly at home reading magazines and books. I also went to the library a lot, where two of the young (male) librarians pretended to take a big interest in me, then showed me pretty soon that their real interest was in making out with me.

"I also had the problem of my mother constantly watching me, suspecting me, whenever I went out, of going with homosexuals, and then accusing me of that although I was entirely innocent. She worked hard at the office and usually she was tired, but it still was hard to take.

"Mother's fondest hope was that both my sister and I would go to college and make something of ourselves. Our performances in high school were not very encouraging, but still she had hopes. Then my sister, when she was seventeen, got herself pregnant and insisted on having the child, although mother had an abortion all arranged. My sister did this so as to force her boyfriend, a stupid but cute-looking young soldier, to marry her. He did, and they have lived unhappily ever after.

"With that, mother's hopes all were centered on me. I felt them just as if they were a physical burden, weighing several tons at least. I had decided I wanted to be either a writer or an artist, and I think I had some real talent for both. But mother, who could see how effeminate I was, and who surely should have known that it was out of the question, wanted me to go to law school. She seems to have had a kind of 'thing' about lawyers.

"My father *never* came to see us, just sent us money every month—the child support payments—and cards and little notes, along with ten or twenty dollar bills at Christmas, for birthdays, and on other such occasions. I had it in my head that he had learned about the scandal in Kansas City, had decided he wanted no part of a queer son, and had written me off. (Later, he told me this was not true. He had just thought it better for me, so he said, if he stayed out of the picture completely. When he *did* write me off was when I started to live as a girl, some years later. Then, when he found out, he wrote me a letter and told me I should change my name, which I'd already done, and that if he ever got his hands on me he'd give me a beating that I'd never forget. Good old Dad!)

"At sixteen or so, I learned about transvestites and decided I must be one of those too! I wondered what other kind of freak I might find out that I was! When my sister married and moved away from home, and my mother was away at work most of the time, I dressed in clothing my sister had left behind, padded a brassiere with some rolled up stockings, put on makeup, wrapped something around my head to hide my hair, and spent hours in front of mirrors. Then I would masturbate once, twice, even three times, with phantasies of being a girl and having female organs which I manipulated, or of having sex with a boy. Or I would tuck my penis and testicles back out of sight between my legs, pull my skirt up to above my pubic hair, and excitedly contemplate my "female" body. After that, I would weep, sometimes for hours on end.

"I decided that my penis was abnormally small (which a doctor later confirmed. It never got to be more than not quite five inches long when erect, and also was slender.) I read lots of popular psychology books and decided, since I had no interest in sex with anyone, and since I liked to look at my own body (provided I first concealed my male organs), that I was a narcissist! I hated my male organs and thought about cutting them off. At that time, I started thinking of this as my 'castration complex.' I used to wish, lots of times, that I was dead, and pretty often I thought about killing myself and all the ways I might do it. So, I was suicidal. I believed that people didn't like me, which they didn't, since I wasn't giving enough to be liked, and then decided that this was all in my head and probably I was paranoid. At eighteen or so, then, I could take stock of myself and find that I was effeminate, homosexual, a transvestite, a narcissist, a masturbator (with an abnormally small penis in the bargain!), a would-be castrate, a potential suicide, and a paranoid. I had no friends and wasn't likely, so I thought, to ever have any. I was a disappointment to my mother and had brought disgrace down on the whole family. I was a real mess and I wondered how such an existence as mine could be justified.

"I wondered what I had done to deserve all of this. It seemed that everything happened *to* me, without my ever doing anything to bring it about. I was very religious, although only by spurts, and would try to figure out just what sins I had committed to have all these things happen to me. I tried going to church, but never was received with much warmth at the churches I would go to. I couldn't blame them for that since I was such an obvious homosexual type, or so I thought.

"At seventeen, my body was not much bigger than that of a boy of thirteen or so. I had no muscles at all! Some body hair —too much for a girl, not enough for a boy. My hips were a little wide for a boy's and my breasts were slightly overdeveloped. My face was very feminine looking and people always were telling me: 'You look more like a girl than a boy.' (Or they remarked to each other about my feminine appearance.) All of this pleased me in a way, but it made my life much more difficult. (Later, I tried male hormone injections to 'masculinize' me. They just made me a nervous wreck and soon had to be discontinued.)

"I was getting more and more of a desire to go outside dressed as a girl so that other people could see me that way, and it was hard to control. I had a (very cheap and not too real looking) wig, also my own cosmetics and a few under things, a girl's swimsuit, etc. I kept these very carefully hidden away, behind a loose panel in my closet. We had a little sun deck and several times I went out on it in the wig, made up, and wearing the girl's swimsuit—looking real enough at a distance. Several times boys and men, standing on balconies, would look my way and I would pose for them, while pretending not to know they were there. Once some kid whistled. Was I ever thrilled! But afterwards I cried for hours and thought about killing myself.

"I was also getting more and more propositions from

homosexuals—and considering them. It was not that I wanted sex, just that I was so damned lonely for companionship. I thought maybe I could make a few friends, somebody I could confide in and who, being queer themselves, would be sympathetic. If I had to put out sexually to them to have their friendship, then—as a last resort—possibly I would do it. But I just thought about these things and never, except for a few conversations on the street, did anything to get myself in with a gay crowd.

"The pressure was really on me to go to college when IT happened! The Christine Jorgensen case appeared in all the newspapers and changed my life, as it changed the lives of so many transsexuals all over the world. Suddenly, like a revelation, I knew WHO and WHAT I was—and that something COULD BE DONE ABOUT IT! Christ only knows how much time I spent poring over every last item about Christine I could lay my hands on. Not Christ but Christ-ine, I thought, was my Savior! Now everything about me made perfect sense, I knew what had to be done, and I had some real HOPE of being able to live a normal life *as a woman!* Talk about your shock of recognition! Man, this was IT!

"I told my mother, 'I am a case like Christine Jorgensen, I am just exactly like her, and I am going to have the same things done to me so I can be a real girl.' I went on for at least half an hour, pouring out everything I had had bottled up inside me, and mother didn't say a word until finally I ran down. Then she said, 'You're not anything of the kind. You're a boy who needs some help from a psychiatrist so he can develop into a real he-man, and you're going to college and be something in this world besides an uneducated fairy! You've hung around home long enough and now you're either going to college like I've always wanted you to do, or else you're going out and get yourself a job. Like it or not, if you don't go to school, you're going to be the man of this house and bring in some money. You'll keep busy enough so you won't have any time to think up all these crazy ideas about being a girl, and we'll use what you earn to pay the psychiatrist. But *please, please* go to school instead. Do that, and somehow I'll raise enough money to pay for the doctor bills and the schooling. You know how much it means to me that you get an education.'

"She was crying and so was I. I asked her, 'Is that your last word on this subject?' She said, 'Yes, that's my last word.' We talked some more, and it was obvious she never would agree to my having the (sex conversion) operation.* That night I decided I would have to leave home, and next day, when mother was at work, I took about seventy-five dollars we had around the house, left her a long note, as kind as I could make it, and moved out, taking with me what I could carry in one suitcase. Naturally this included all my girl's things I had accumulated—such space as was left, I used for men's shirts, trousers, etc.

"I took a bus to Kansas City, possibly because my father still was living there, and checked in at a little downtown hotel where the rent was only nine dollars a week. It was a dingy little room with the toilet out in the hall, a couple of doors away. However, there was a sink in the room—everyone using these sinks, as I learned, for urinals, and visiting the toilet only to defecate (and to write invitations, mostly homosexual, on the walls).

"After putting my few things in the closet—the female things I left in my suitcase—I went downstairs to sit in the lobby, where many of the people staying in the hotel congregated. Mostly, they were old men, but there was one good-looking guy, probably around thirty, who came over and sat next to me and struck up a conversation. His name was Leo and, as I learned later, he was an ex-convict. The day I met Leo was a bad one for me, but I didn't know it at the time.

"Leo did not have much education, but he was very sharp in some ways, he was a smooth talker, and he could seem very warm and friendly. Evidently, he sized me up pretty well from the start. We went out to a nearby nightclub with a small floor show, after he had promised to pay for everything. Now I know the place was just gaudy, but it impressed me as being elegant at the time. I had never had anything much to drink and it

* Among transsexuals, THE OPERATION means only one thing—"sex change."

wasn't long before I was high. All the time he was talking to me more and more the way a man talks to a girl, and I was responding. Next thing I knew, we were in his hotel room, we were drinking some more from a bottle he had bought, and I was telling him all about myself—the very first time I had ever told anyone, the conversation with my mother being the only exception, and even with her I left out some of the things I told Leo.

"When Leo kissed me, what with being drunk, I felt none of the revulsion I always have felt when thinking about homosexual relations. I felt like a girl, and he contributed to this feeling by telling me how feminine I was, how he really thought of me as being a girl instead of a man, and how he was not a homo and couldn't stand homos, and lots of other jazz like that.

"It seems to me that the next thing I knew after that, I was naked, lying on my stomach, and screaming bloody murder. I felt as if I had been ripped wide open, and then Leo had his hand over my mouth and was slapping me and telling me to shut up. It hurt like hell, but he kept moving in and out, taking it easier than before, and after a while it didn't hurt so bad. Again, even through the liquor, I was conscious of that funny trance-like condition I remembered from the episodes with Jerry. It was as if I had no will of my own and was completely submissive to Leo, who could do anything he wanted with me.

"Finally, I guess I went to sleep, or maybe I passed out. Next morning, he woke me up, pointed at his penis, and told me, 'Take care of it, baby doll'—the nickname he had given me. I went down on him without a word of protest. After his ejaculation, I started for the basin, intending to spit it out. 'Come back here,' he ordered. I came back. 'Swallow it,' he commanded. I swallowed it. 'Now,' he said, 'let's go up to your room and see how you look as a girl.' We went.

"After I had dressed and made up, he gave me plenty of compliments. I walked up and down the room, turning around, like a model. 'Well, I'll be goddamned,' Leo said. 'I'd sure never have believed it. You're a real knockout.' That was the beginning of four weeks of pure hell.

"In no time, under Leo's supervision, I was out hustling on the street. I didn't do awfully well at that, so Leo started pimping for me. That was better anyway, for financial purposes, since I could be sold as a female impersonator instead of just as another young male hustler. He brought me perverts of every description, and some of them paid plenty. As will be no surprise, Leo kept almost all the money I took in, using a part of it to pay off the desk clerks, but keeping most of it for himself.

"You will wonder why I didn't leave there, since I honestly *hated* what I was doing, or what was being done to me, but I just *couldn't*. It was kind of like the trance condition had become permanent. Sometimes Leo would have anal intercourse with me. Sometimes I would take care of him orally. Sometimes he beat me up, but always being careful not to leave too many marks. He finally admitted that he was queer and said he had got to be that way in the penitentiary, where he had served several years for armed robbery. I fully believe it was after he told me he was queer, and that he thought of me as a queer and not as his girl, that I began finding the strength and getting up the guts to leave him.

"Really, that month of my life is like an old nightmare, almost forgotten but not quite. Even at the time it was nightmarish. I was doing revolting things—acts involving urine, feces, sadism, the whole works—and now, in my memory, they are very vague and all blurred and run in together. But I do know that once I decided to try to get away my mind cleared a little, so far as making plans. I tried to put on a good act and make Leo feel sure I intended to stay with him. I was also scheming how I was going to get hold of some of the money I had earned.

" 'Leo,' I told him, 'if I had a really good wig, a really good human hair wig, and a few nice clothes, I could go out hustling and make a lot more money than we are making now. You could point me out to the Johns (customers), and that would make it easier to get a good price.' After a while, I sold him on that idea, and we laid out a good bit of money for a really stunning wig, some high heels and stockings, and a couple of very sexy dresses that were still in good taste. Also, of course, some high-priced 'falsies,' since I had no breast development to speak of at that time. So far so good, but I wanted to get hold of enough money so that I could get out of town— far away, where Leo wouldn't be likely to find me. That was hard to do, since Leo gave me very little money, and I didn't dare try to steal it from him until I was ready to make the final break.

"My chance came when I got to be very friendly with a bartender in the neighborhood who I knew hated Leo. I talked this guy into giving me some knockout drops, a 'mickey,' and that night, in the room, I slipped the stuff into Leo's drink. It worked, he was out cold, and I packed my stuff in a hurry. From Leo's wallet I got two hundred dollars, and another hundred and fifty from behind the picture of his mother the bastard kept on his dresser. I really would have liked to kill him—the only time I have ever wanted to kill anyone—both for what he had done to me and because of what he had threatened to do if I ever tried to leave him. But I thought it wasn't worth taking the chance of getting caught. Then I cleared out of there in a hurry, taking a bus down to Dallas. From Dallas, I jumped over to Tucson, then from there to Los Angeles. I figured that way, he would be less likely to be able to follow me. So ended the most hellish period of my life and, believe me, I have known some pretty bad periods in my lifetime.

"In L.A., I lived as a girl almost from the start. I was letting my hair grow and meanwhile I was wearing the wig. I changed my Social Security card and other identification to read Joan (instead of John), but worked around so much, as a car hop, cocktail waitress, cigarette girl, B-girl, etc., that it didn't much matter. I met some female impersonators (professional), and also quite a few 'queens,' or fairies who dress more or less like girls. All of these people were queer in various ways and most of them were prostitutes, part- if not full-time. But we had some common interests, and I was learning a lot.

"I went to several doctors in L.A., looking for someone who would start me on a program of hormones to make my breasts grow, and who would arrange for me to have the sex change operation. I got nothing but abuse from two of these doctors, another one was friendly and understanding but wouldn't touch my case, and a psychiatrist wanted me to sign myself into a mental institution. I told them all to go to hell— funny thing, now that I was living as a girl I lost a lot of my shyness and sometimes was even aggressive. John never would have dared to tell a doctor to go to hell. Joan could do it easily, and effectively.

"Through my impersonator friends I met another transsexual who was getting female hormones. She (or he, if you'd rather) was also getting psychotherapy—but psychotherapy to prepare her for the sex change, and to make her better adjusted while she waited! That was for me! So she arranged for me to have an appointment with her doctor.

"This transsexual's doctor was very nice and friendly, but he told me his hands were tied since I was not yet twenty-one years of age. If my mother would give her approval, and if a psychiatrist examined me and okayed it, then he would treat me. Otherwise, not for the present. I was crushed! I really thought about throwing myself in front of a train or jumping off a building, but didn't do either one. Instead, I went back to my hotel and cried for a long time. Living as a girl, I felt I really was a girl in every way that ought to matter to the world. Why wouldn't they do the few things needed to make it official so that I could live in peace and be happy! I looked at myself naked in the mirror and my eyes fell on my razor—a razor I didn't have to use very often, since my beard was very light. I took hold of my penis with one hand and pulled it out straight. If I'd had a big straight razor, I might have cut it off with a single stroke. But all I had was a razor blade. I made a cut, not really very deep, saw some blood, and then fainted dead away. When I came to, I had bled some, but not enough to do me any serious harm. I washed the wound and used the styptic pencil on it. Then I put on a bandaid—it wasn't any bigger a cut than that. I now knew that, at least for the time being, I didn't have the nerve to cut off my male organs, hate them with a passion though I did!

"I called the transsexual whose doctor had turned me down and told her about what had happened. She came over and, perhaps to keep me going, promised to get enough hormones so that I could have some too. I didn't know then that most persons really need them by injection for them to do the most good, and the thought of getting pills was a great comfort to me. Alas, as it turned out, I never did get any.

"When my twenty-first birthday arrived, I was broke and couldn't afford medical treatment. However, soon after that I got a job as an impersonator. This didn't pay much and was only part-time work, but I liked it and it kept me going emotionally and financially. This was the beginning of a career that lasted for some time. For quite a few years I would be an impersonator, sometimes with a permanent position, sometimes just working for a few days here and there.

"What I liked most about this work, from the start, was the feeling I got when on stage. All the self-consciousness left me after a second or two. Then, in some curious way, I was transformed so that I felt I really had become a woman. There was no play acting, no rôle-playing to it. While on stage, *I was a woman*. Maybe this is the same kind of total identification with the rôle some actors report feeling—the experience of *becoming* the person portrayed. Anyway, that is how I felt, and it was a wonderful feeling.

"I think I can skip over those years without giving too much in the way of details of what I was doing. So long as I could appear before audiences regularly as a woman, life wasn't too difficult to bear. I did have to wear male clothing to enter and leave the clubs where I was working—almost always a house rule in such places—and this meant I couldn't wear my hair as long as I would have liked to. But as soon as I got home I would once again 'dress' and feel at ease. I acquired several lovely wigs of different colors, a wardrobe, and once again I was saving for my 'sex change' that I always kept in mind as an ultimate goal.

"No, you are right, I wasn't making that much money

as an impersonator—a business where only the top attractions make much more than enough to barely survive on. From time to time there was some prostitution, although I never went in for this in the big way some of the other entertainers went in for it. Not that I didn't have plenty of offers! But, as is probably clear by now, I am not and never have been by nature a promiscuous or even very highly sexed person. I would perform as a prostitute, usually, when enough pressure was put on me (by my friends) to do it, or when I would get to thinking that I must add money to my bank account against the day when I would be having medical expenses, culminating in my operation. (I was not under treatment during most of this time because I could never learn of a doctor who would treat me and also, much of the time, I was not settled in any one place.)

"To include some observations I have made, I would say that professional female impersonators are, on the whole, the most sexually active group in the American population—and I understand it is no different in other countries. Perhaps, or rather surely, prostitutes working in houses are more active, but that does not seem to me quite voluntary or, with rare exceptions, for the person's own pleasure, so I do not count it. The impersonators, I believe, would be about equally active even if no one ever paid them for their services. I agree with your theory that this is mostly the result of an imbalance of supply and demand—that the number of impersonators is always much smaller than the number of persons attracted to them, so that they are constantly being tempted both sexually and with offers of money.* In every club where I ever worked the volume of offers was so great you would hardly believe it. And the money offers are not at all meagre, presently fifty dollars being common for a date (short intercourse), and offers of a hundred or even several hundreds of dollars not being rare when longer periods and special performances are wanted.

"Impersonators, at clubs where it's allowed, pick up very

* For a discussion of the female impersonator–prostitute and his activities see Benjamin, H., and Masters, R.E.L., *Prostitution and Morality*, Julian Press, New York, 1964.

nice tips just for sitting with the customers, drinking with them, and answering their questions, in between the shows. As you know, in some clubs there are varieties of prostitution that go on right at the tables—surreptitious masturbation, minor tortures, urination into drinking glasses, and speaking dirty language (or listening to it). I myself have done all of these things. And I even worked at one little club, very dark and with tablecloths down to the floor, where at special tables in the corners of the room the impersonators would get down under the table and perform orally on the customers—usually men, but occasionally women too! I have done this along with the other things, but only on men. I have had a woman ask me, and offer fifty dollars. I confess I needed money at the time, and it wasn't moral considerations that held me back. I just knew I'd be sure to get sick if I tried it.

"These clubs, in some cases, have so sexy an atmosphere you can darned near feel it in the air, like surges of electricity. They may, besides the males, have lesbians working there who are dressed like men. This brings in many additional women customers, who are hot after the lesbians. I have seen perfectly straight (heterosexual) girls come to work as waitresses in these clubs, and in no time the lesbians have seduced them and they are bisexual if not completely gay. It is the sex-charged atmosphere of these places, and I have never seen anybody work in one of them for very long and still resist it.

"I have heard stories about such people, but I have yet to meet a female impersonator who was completely heterosexual. Some, however, are bisexual and definitely enjoy it both ways. And, as far as prostitution goes, I can only agree with your report that practically one hundred per cent of all impersonators are available at least sometimes. This statement will not be appreciated by my former colleagues, but I know that it is true and I feel obliged to say so.

"However, there are great variations between them as to what sexually they are willing to do when it comes to prostitution. I have known a few who would draw a line and only agree to masturbation of a customer, so being able to convince themselves they were not really prostitutes at all. Or this can be a way of 'staying true' to one's lover. Most, however, will be agreeable to the usual range of homosexual practices. And, what I'd say is much more than a simple majority, will go in for most perversions if the price is right and there isn't too much danger involved. Also, they are among the most status-conscious people around and will do almost anything to get to go with a celebrity, especially if he is an actor.

"Many impersonators give courses of instruction in how to dress, how to walk in high heels, and how to use makeup, to transvestites who come to them for this. I once made over five hundred dollars meeting once a week for about two months with a wealthy middle-aged man who had just recently started dressing. A funny thing about transvestism as I have come across it is that, unlike most other perversions, it sometimes comes on fairly late in life and there may have been no signs of it in childhood or even in early adulthood.

"There are a few women who are attracted to impersonators. We always suspected them of being lesbians who didn't want to admit to themselves that that was what they were. They would want you to make love to them while dressed and made up—I, of course, could not engage in that type of activity, being totally ineffective with women. Similarly, some men are attracted to impersonators, but not to queers who look like men. Again, we always said among ourselves that these were men who can't admit to themselves that they are homos. They make a big point of telling you that they just can't think of you as a man, that it's just like going to bed with a girl, or something of the sort. At first, I thought they were saying this for my benefit; but then I learned they were saying it for their own.

"I have been at parties where some rich person would hire a whole group of impersonators to come home with him and his friends when the show was over. These were real orgies. At one of these parties, the host and his friends lined up, men and women alternating, and one very good-looking singer from our show, still in drag (dressed as a girl), went down the whole lineup, almost a dozen persons, and performed orally on them all. It took a long time, and everyone else watched without saying a word. You could have heard a pin drop, except for an occasional giggle. About mid-way through he got very excited, pulled his dress up, and one of the women ran over and went down on him. He was so steamed up it was over with in a second. Her husband was there and egged her on. Then the impersonator finished off the rest of them. After that, there was wholesale carrying on, impersonators with guests, guests with each other, and finally, as a command performance, a lot of impersonators working on each other all at once.

"At one of the biggest clubs in the U.S.—I have heard this from those who worked there, so it is only hearsay—every year or so a millionaire takes over the whole club after the performance. Sometimes he brings friends, sometimes he is alone. Then an orgy and all sorts of sex contests are held on stage, with this man giving prizes. Everyone gets at least a hundred dollars, and the impersonator he likes best gets a thousand —so everyone goes all out to give him a good show. The management must be very well paid for this too, if the story is a true one. It sounds kind of phony, but I have heard it several times, including from persons who have worked at that club.

"A lot of impersonators are drag queens (homosexual transvestites), but not very many are transsexuals. When I first began work as an impersonator, I only very rarely met anyone who wanted to have the sex change operation or who said he felt he was really a girl in a boy's body, as I have always felt myself to be. Most of them, when they understood that I wanted my genitals removed and a vagina constructed, were pretty horrified. A homosexual, no pun intended, is just as attached to his penis as a normal man is. Maybe more so, since homosexuals tend to be real penis worshipers. Some of them can tell you all about the penis of a man they were with, but can't tell you anything else about him. They are interested, first of all, in size, and then in general appearance. His face, they may forget five minutes later, while after ten years they still can tell you what his penis was like, if it was an exceptional one.

"Anyway, it used to be rare that you would find a transsexual among the impersonators. Now, with so many sex changes around, it is more common, but still a long, long way from being the rule. In part, I think, it used to be that the operation was regarded as being a very dangerous and painful one. But by now, almost every impersonator knows someone, or several someones, who have made the change. They know it isn't so bad, they aren't afraid, and they admit to themselves that they would like to have it too. I personally know half a dozen impersonators who, some years back, denied that they had the slightest desire to become women. Now, they are saving for the operation. Of course, it may be that some of these people get progressively more feminine as time goes by. But I think it more likely that they just aren't so afraid any more and so will admit to themselves what it is they really want. Also, they see that the people they know who have had the operation are happier and more normal in most cases than they ever were before. That, too, might be an important inducement.

"The psychology and sex lives of female impersonators is a very fascinating and complicated subject and I am surprised somebody doesn't write a book about it. Maybe I will do that some day. Why not? I always thought that I might become a writer.

"Before I leave this subject I want to try to correct any impression I may have given that female impersonators are bad people. They are not. I have known them to chip in their money to send some transsexual to have an operation, and that can mean several thousand dollars. And I have seen them do many other kind and generous things too. I view almost all the impersonators I have known as falling somewhere between transsexuals and plain homosexuals, who I detest. They are a dirty lot of people, and I would hate them (the homosexuals) if I didn't pity them. They are liars, will stab you in the back every time, and generally have a very bad character. I suppose there are exceptions, but I have rarely met one.*

---

* This extreme dislike of homosexuals is commonplace among transsexuals—because they so often are accused of being homosexual when they feel that they are not, and perhaps as a way of denying to themselves that they are homosexual when they fear that, actually, they are. However, many declared homosexuals also have a very low opinion of their group—deriving from their own self-esteem and/or from objective observation of persons with whom they have been associated.

"Impersonators, in my experience and according to my judgment, are usually very immature, really almost child-like individuals. They are constantly being tempted and, like children, they are not very good at resisting temptation. Perhaps they are also more passive than the average individual. They are confused, don't know quite what or who they are, and this also leads them to behave in ways society disapproves. But they are not bad in any greater percentage than the rest of the people in the world are bad. A few are bad, most aren't. I have no wish to cause them any pain with the revelations I have made. They may not like what I say, but in their hearts they will have to admit that what I have said is the truth.

*   *   *

"About a year or so after I ran away from home, I made a telephone call to my mother. She had been so worried about me that all was forgiven, at any rate for the moment. Later, of course, she began to act like a mother again, urging me to go to college and, sometimes, rebuking me for my 'queer friends' and telling me to try to straighten myself out and be a man. That always hurt me deeply, because I wanted understanding from her and because I could not possibly do what she asked of me. Yet I knew that this was a very difficult thing for anyone else to understand. After all, if most doctors didn't understand it, why should I expect my mother would be able to?

"Over the years, I went home from time to time. I always made an effort to convince my mother that nature had played a very bad trick on me, and that medical treatment would eventually turn me into the girl I should have been from the beginning. I told her—it wasn't true at that time—that psychiatrists had interviewed me and all agreed that I had the mind and emotions of a woman. Also I told her—another 'white lie'— that a doctor had found female genes and a trace of what he thought was an undeveloped ovary in my body. Maybe, at the very least, I argued, I was some kind of hermaphrodite. Gradually, over the years, she began to accept more and more that I could not help being what I was. Still, she didn't like it and would cling to her hope that I would 'straighten out.' The sex change surgery idea, she wouldn't consider rationally at all. One time, I came to see her in girl's clothes, really looking like a pretty young girl. At first she didn't even recognize me, since my voice had been trained to sound more and more feminine. But, when she did recognize me, she threw me right out and told me never to come to see her unless I came looking like a man. That same night I went to a hotel and took a whole bunch of aspirins, trying to kill myself. Obviously, it didn't work. (Later, when I finally did have the operation, mother finally reconciled herself to everything, said she would get used to having a daughter, although that would 'take some doing,' and today our relations are probably as good as those of the average mother and daughter. I have always loved her deeply and I'm sure I always will.)

"Before it all was over, I made two additional unsuccessful attempts at suicide and another at castrating myself. A man, I think, eventually would have succeeded in these endeavors. I, being typically female, always botched the job.

* * *

"Finally, at the age of twenty-six, I found, through another transsexual friend, a doctor who was willing to take my case. A psychiatrist examined me and gave me all sorts of tests. I was terrified. What if these psychological tests wouldn't work for someone like me and the test results showed my mentality to be a male's? If that happened, I told myself, I would jump off a building (though, with my luck, I probably would have caught on a hook, if I didn't float gently down like with a parachute!). However, all was well. 'It's amazing,' this psychiatrist told me, 'your mind is perfectly feminine. I will tell your doctor to start the treatments, although as definitely girlish as you are I can't see that you need very much done. And good luck with your operation.' Needless to say, I was on Cloud Nine!

"After an experimental period with the hormones, so as to see how I was going to react, I began getting an injection of female hormone every week and was taking tablets every day. One of the first noticeable effects was on my mind—I began to experience a tranquility such as I had never known before. It was like a very effective tranquilizer pill—but one that makes you awfully happy as well as at peace with yourself.

"Another fairly early effect was that I stopped having all erections—which was welcome, since I had practically given up masturbating for the reason that the sight and touch of my erect penis were so hateful to me and reminded me that I was still a man, anyhow anatomically.

"After several months the breasts were definitely growing and the nipples were enlarging and taking on the appearance of a woman's nipples. This process, as it continued, thrilled me more than just about anything I had ever known. I spent countless hours admiring myself in the mirror. My transsexual friend, also under treatment, and I made daily and sometimes several times a day comparisons. Through her (or him), I met, for the first time, a very attractive girl (former male) who had had the sex change operation about one year earlier. This girl was extremely knowledgeable about all aspects of sex change and talked to us for hours about it, while we hung onto her every word with bated breath. As the fitting and untoppable climax to the first evening I spent with her, she showed me her new vagina and explained about dilating it and other matters that couldn't have been more important so far as I was concerned. I had seen female sex organs before, and hers looked perfectly real and normal to me. She described all the thrills of having sexual intercourse with a man, while shivers ran up and down my back.

"Another effect of treatment with hormones was that my body hair grew in very sparsely. On the other hand, the hair on my head had never been more luxuriant or looked better. Here, I should explain that I already had had almost all of my body hair and my light beard removed by electrolysis, although this is a continuing chore and I had to keep going back. Electrolysis is just one of the major expenses connected with sex change. A typical rate for this service is around twelve dollars an hour. However, I, and this also has been true of some other transsexuals I have known, received a special low rate. Even with that, however, by the time I had been in medical treatment for six months, my diary showed that I had spent eight hundred dollars having the facial hair removed (during that time and before). The arms cost about two hundred dollars more, and the legs cost almost four hundred dollars. There was also the chest and abdominal hair, although of these I had almost none. Fortunately after the operation, this hair growth practically ceases and my electrolysis expenses would be small. That varies from one individual to the next, but I have met *no* sex change who ever had any problem about a beard. Thus, the nasty stories that used to be circulated about a famous sex change showing a 'five o'clock shadow' when she stayed out too late, were nothing but malicious falsehoods invented by sensational writers.

"Even though I had saved a good bit of money, I became somewhat alarmed at all the expense I was encountering. I no longer could work as an impersonator because of my long hair, and this created problems. However, I found occasional work here and there. By special arrangement with various friends of mine, I did work some more from time to time as a prostitute. But I told myself this was out of absolute necessity and, once I became a true woman, I never would defile my femininity in that way again!

"A whole year dragged by, a year in which I saw myself, before my very own eyes, become more and more of a woman all the time. This of course gave me great pleasure and satisfaction, but, even with that, I was getting more and more impatient all the time to take the final step. My doctor, who I loved as if he were my own father, nonetheless bore the brunt of my impatience from time to time. I began to feel that he was stalling for some reason, that he didn't want me to stop paying him for the treatments, and so on. Actually, I knew that he must have a good, scientific reason for keeping me in this state of almost unbearable anticipation and suspense. But that didn't help any. I wanted to be a woman NOW!

"At this point, however, some extremely interesting things happened to me and made the waiting a little easier. Through some long-time friends, I met a highly intelligent graduate student in psychology who was experimenting with hypnosis and various drugs, and who wanted to use me as a subject. (I am sure you are right that this is a very stupid thing for someone in my position to do—to play around with drugs and hypnosis, since what if, at this stage of the proceedings, I had suddenly been brainwashed into considering myself to be basically a man after all! But I went ahead with it and for once, I guess, I was lucky.)

"I might explain here that I have always felt—not believed absolutely, maybe, but felt—that reincarnation has something to do with cases like mine. My theory is that, if reincarnation is true, then maybe once in a great while a female spirit or soul accidentally incarnates in a male body (of a fetus), instead of in a female one as it ought to do. How such an accident might happen I don't know, but if it did it would explain how there happen to be transsexuals in this world. I told my story to the hypnotist and he said, 'All right, let's try and take you back to one of your former lives and see if you were a woman then.' He gave me the Bridie Murphy book to read, and some similar stuff, and I was sold on the idea that it is possible, with hypnosis, to go back to one or more previous existences. I was aware that most doctors think this sort of thing is pure nonsense. But, then, most doctors don't believe in such a thing as transsexualism either—and just think that people like me are queers who are crazy and want to have their male organs cut off for no good reason. But the few *experts,* the ones who have worked with a large number of people like me, know it isn't so. So, God knows, doctors can be way off base too!

"Maybe luckily for me, I turned out to be unhypnotizable. I regretted this very much at the time, since I really felt I would discover that I had been a woman, or several different women, in a past incarnation or incarnations. We tried many times, and he was a good hypnotist, but with me it just wouldn't take. He said I was resisting the hypnosis, but if so I wasn't conscious of it. In fact, I wanted desperately to go under.

"However, with one of the impersonators, who is not a transsexual so far as I know, he did get a very good, deep trance and this person went back to 'other lives' in four different times. Now listen to this, in two of those lives he was a woman, in two he was a man. When he was a woman, the voice was a woman's voice, the gestures were feminine, and so on. When he was a man, he had a man's voice—and in fact, a deeper and more manly voice than he ordinarily has. Superstitious or not, this struck me as being very significant. Maybe these effeminate men, such as this impersonator and most other impersonators are, are sexual types not very well defined, who can turn up as complete women, complete men, or as something in between— as I take this particular fellow to be in his present incarnation.

"This same subject was told by the hypnotist to go ahead in time a hundred years and be whoever he wanted to be, or was destined to be at that time. On this occasion, he again was a woman—a little girl at first, until he was instructed to 'grow up.' Make of it what you will, it was extremely fascinating to me and suggested many possibilities.*

"One more series of interesting experiments was made with this same impersonator. Various sexual situations were described to him and he was supposed to act them out. Told he was a woman being made love to by a man, he acted just like a woman with a man on top of her. But told he was a man making love to a woman, he became very agitated and had to be brought out of the trance. When it was tried again, he performed very well as a man with a man, and as a woman with another woman. But when the hypnotist tried a second

* Possibly a better experiment would be to hypnotize, if possible, a transsexual previous to his surgery, then suggest to him that the surgery has been accomplished, that he is as much of a woman as the operation can make him, and then determine whether he is satisfied with the results. I have proposed this and similar projects to physicians and psychiatrists working with transsexuals, but so far as I know it never has been attempted. A somewhat similar procedure has been profitably used in the case of plastic surgery of the face—the operation and its likely results are described to the subject, he is told that he has had the operation, is instructed to examine his face in a mirror, and his favorable or unfavorable reactions are then taken into account in deciding whether to proceed with the surgery.

time to get him to be a man with a woman, he again got very excited and upset and had to be brought out of it.

"The experiments with drugs included several kinds, but the only one I was given was hashish (although one experienced 'pot' smoker told me later it was not hashish, but marijuana. I don't know about that, or what the difference is, if any.) Anyhow, I was given hashish, and if it was marijuana it was much better and stronger marijuana than any I had had before, and I have had it maybe seven or eight times.

"After I was really stoned, I was told to feel that my body was completely a woman's body, with a natural vagina, and of course with no male organs. Absolutely, that is what I felt! The hypnotist kept talking to me, using the same voice he used when talking to the people in trance, and maybe I really was hypnotized then, because whatever he told me to feel, that is what I would feel. He told me I would become aware of a penis moving inside the vagina, as if a man were making love to me. I definitely did feel something of that sort, but couldn't reach an orgasm as he suggested, possibly because of the hormones I was taking that had practically eliminated every last trace of sensation in my penis or desire to have any.

"That was the high point of my own experiences with this group. I tried, under the influence of hashish, to envision my past incarnation, and I also tried looking in a mirror to see my past incarnation, but that was a dud. Some of the others reported better luck, but nothing happened that seems to me to have any bearing on the problem of transsexualism. Some of the people in this group went on to take psilocybin, LSD-25, and some other very strong mind-affecting drugs, but they thought I shouldn't have any. (As you commented, at least they showed some good sense in that!)

*   *   *

"As I waited for my own operation, I heard a lot of gossip about various sex changes, some of it not too encouraging. I was told that this person or that one regretted the operation and wished that she had her penis back. I have never heard any transsexual I have talked to personally say a thing like that.

But you do hear stories once in a while and, if you are waiting for your own operation, they can be a little disturbing.

"I also heard what is one of the classic tales, about a French sex change who dilated her vagina so often and so enthusiastically that it got to be so big it would have taken at least two good-sized men to fill it. I told my doctor this story and he said such a thing would not be quite so calamitous as it sounded to me. Probably it could be rather easily repaired.

"Other sex changes, including one I knew, complained about the vagina being too small to be of any use. She meant too narrow—the length (or depth) of the vagina has never been any problem in any case that I have heard about.

"Some transsexuals were having all sort of additional operations—they were almost like surgical addicts, or so it seemed to me. The most common operation, and one that actually is needed in many cases, is plastic surgery to give the nose a more feminine appearance. Probably most sex changes have this one. Some—a couple—were having the adam's apple trimmed down, and others were talking about having it done. (In my case this is not necessary.) Injections into the breast to increase size is also common. In at least one case, an operation was performed to make the person shorter—of course, many transsexuals are rather tall as women. This consists of removing some of the bone from the leg, so shortening it. Apparently it works all right, but I am certainly glad I don't have to have anything like that done. Then, there are measures fairly often used on all women, like 'peeling' the face to give a fresh and youthful appearance to the skin. When you calculate the cost of some of these operations, on top of electrolysis, hormones, and sex change surgery, it gets to cost a small fortune to have it all done. In a great many cases, these people have been lucky enough to have rich patrons (meaning male lovers) who have put out the money for everything.

"One sex change told me a funny story about how a boyfriend was performing cunnilingus on her and she ejaculated, out of the urethral opening which, of course, remains, and there was this white stuff, the prostate fluid, all over his shoulder. The boyfriend, who thinks she has always been a girl, was very impressed by this and now says that she is about the sexiest girl around to be able to shoot out her juices like that. (Eventually, after surgery, the prostate gland will atrophy and then there are no more such embarrassing ejaculations.)

"In one case, the vagina grew back together after the operation—because the person had not understood when it was being explained to her how to dilate the opening to prevent this growing back together of the vaginal walls. I made up my mind that nothing like that—a real catastrophe!—was ever going to happen to me.

"I also heard about tragic cases where the doctor did not finish the job and left the person with a stump of a penis and no vagina at all. There were also stories about serious infections, resulting from the doctor being careless or not knowing what he was doing. Most of such stories seem to involve people who went to Mexico for their operation. It seems to me that anyone, having so all-important an operation, would want to check up very carefully on the surgeon and have a look at some of his work, before putting themselves into the hands of the doctor. But some, evidently, went to Mexico in desperation, because the rates were cheaper, because they just couldn't get it done any place else, or for some reason like that. Of course, it is no saving when you have to go ahead and have a second operation—always assuming that you live through the first one!

*   *   *

"When my sister learned I was planning to have the sex change she practically flipped! She wrote me two *very* abusive letters, and then she finally came to see me—the first time I had seen her in almost five years. She had never, since what happened in Kansas City, liked me too much, but we had seen each other once in a while. Now, she was living just a couple of hundred miles away and her husband, who had made first lieutenant, was serving overseas. They had been getting along so badly that my sister, Gwen, had stayed at home. They figured that maybe a couple of years separation was what they needed at this point.

"I had always made a better looking girl than Gwen and

now, at my most feminine, I was prettier than I had ever been. That, I guess, was the first thing she thought about when I met her at the station. She made several nasty cracks about my being a 'glamour girl, or maybe a glamor *it*,' and then, when I wouldn't fight with her, she just stopped talking. We hailed a taxicab and rode all the way to my place in a very tense silence. I was trying to imagine why she had come to see me if she was going to behave in such an antagonistic manner.

"No sooner did we get to my apartment than Gwen took two fifths of whisky out of her suitcase and placed them on the table. We sat down and started drinking and pretty soon she was high and started asking me all about my plans. As we drank, she *did* get mellower and finally became, so I thought, very friendly. She asked if she could have a look at my breasts and, when I showed her, made some very complimentary remarks. She even asked if she could feel them and when I, not knowing how to get out of it, said 'yes,' she played with them for at least a minute. I was uncomfortable when she did this and wondered what she could be up to. I half expected her to give them a hard yank, I guess, but she caressed them just like a man would.

" 'Rey, honey,' she said—calling me by the name I had started using and still use—'I have never really understood all this business about you wanting to be a girl. But it is very hard any more, when you look like this, to think of you as a brother. So I guess, from here on out, I will do my damndest to regard you as my sister. Okay?'

"I was pretty taken aback by all this, and suspicious, too, but I said, 'Okay, and Gwen, I hope you really mean it.'

" 'Sure I mean it,' she told me, 'What else would I be here for but to get a look at my new baby sister? Don't you mind what I said to you when I first got here, or what I put in those letters. All this has been pretty upsetting to me, and to Mom, too, I would suppose.'

"After that, we talked for several hours, Gwen getting drunker, and she told me she had been doing a lot of drinking and thought that maybe she was an alcoholic. I had a strong

feeling, though, that all along she was building up to something else, and finally she said to me:

" 'Rey, baby, you know that Charlie (her husband) has
been overseas for almost six months now. Well, I am about
two months pregnant, and I don't know what I am going to do.
If it weren't for the kids (they already had three children) it
wouldn't be so bad, but as it is I am really in a spot.'

"So that's it, I thought, actually feeling a bit relieved, she
wants me to help her arrange for an abortion. I would have
liked to help, but in the circles I have moved in, pregnancy
isn't very often a problem. 'Gosh, Gwen,' I said, 'I wish I could
tell you I know somebody. I don't, but I can always ask around
for you.'

"She talked a little more about what a spot she was in, and
then she really started getting things off her chest. 'You and
Mom always thought that I was the normal one, didn't you?
Well, baby doll, I am a long way from being all that normal.
Maybe I'm not a full-fledged nymphomaniac, but I don't miss
it by too far. If Charlie wasn't damned near as queer as you
are, he'd never have put up with all the running around I've
done since we've been married.'

"I said I hadn't known that Charlie was bisexual, and in
fact I was surprised to hear about it.

" 'I'll bet you didn't know, honey,' Gwen said to me.
'Listen, how dumb do you think I am? Are you going to sit
there and tell me that Charlie never got into you? Come on,
now.'

"She was quite drunk by this time. I controlled my temper
as best I could and told her to believe whatever she wanted
to. But no, Charlie had never showed even the slightest sign of
being interested in me. I couldn't tell if she believed what I
was saying, but it was true.

" 'Rey,' she went on, 'I have gotten lots worse since I
started drinking so much, and especially since Charlie went
overseas. Now that he's an officer I'm not supposed to have anything to do socially with enlisted men or their wives any more.
But, baby, believe me, since Charlie went away, I've been
fucked from one end of Fort ———— to the other, by just about

every GI who is man enough to get a hard-on. Who is the father of this kid I am carrying? Honey, you could put the post roster in a hat, draw out a name, and you'd have a good chance of getting somebody who might have done it.'

"After that, the conversation, or rather Gwen's speech, got very specific and obscene, with her giving me a blow by blow account of her affairs and everything that had happened, which was plenty. I was *very* uncomfortable during all of this, but Gwen didn't notice or care about that, and she also appeared to be sexually very excited. Finally, she sprung what she evidently thought would be the real blockbuster.

"'And that isn't all, honey,' she said, 'I've had some women too.' Then she went on to describe in very graphic detail her relationships with about a dozen women, including a 'fourteen-year-old lesbian' who, according to Gwen, seduced her, and who was 'the hottest of the whole damn lot.' 'So, kid,' she said finally, 'I'm just as queer as you are. What do you think about that?'

"I have never quite decided whether or not I am sorry for what I did then.

"'Gwen,' I said very firmly, '*I* am not a queer. I have had a medical problem that was no fault of mine and that I lived with the best way I could. Now, before very much longer, that problem will be taken care of and I will be able to lead a perfectly normal life. My problem is called transsexualism and it very well may have something to do with a mixup of my chromosomes and body chemistry or something like that, and not be a mental condition at all. It is *not* the same thing as homosexuality and I have never been homosexual. If what you tell me is true, then *you* are more of a queer than I am since you have no good excuse for what you did. I don't condemn you for what you have done because it's always possible that you can't help yourself. I do feel sorry for you and I think you ought to go see a psychiatrist before you get any worse.' It was quite a speech, for me, and much longer than I am giving it here.

"Gwen slowly stood up and, for the moment anyhow, she seemed to have sobered up considerably. She looked me straight in the eye and said, '*You? You* feel sorry for *me?* Why you filthy little cocksucker!' She came over to me and slapped me across the face so hard my eyes watered. 'I have hated you all my life,' she said. 'Your father hates you, and if Mom doesn't, then she ought to. *You,* with your freak breasts and makeup and dresses! Go ahead and get your prick and balls cut off, they never were used for what God intended them to be used for anyhow. You have never been a real man, and you won't be a real woman either. You'll just be a sideshow freak and the filthiest kind of pervert there is in the whole world. I hate you and I never want to see you again!'

"She grabbed her suitcase and staggered out, and that is the last I have seen of her. She did not have another child seven months later, so I guess she either miscarried, as she had done twice before, or managed to find an abortionist. I do not relate this incident out of animosity towards my sister, but because I think it may be of significance that she, too, turned out to be sexually abnormal or abnormal in ways that affected her sexual behavior.

*   *   *

"Finally, on an unforgettable day, I was told by my doctor that there was no longer any reason to delay my having the sex change operation. I of course broke down and cried hysterically —that curious feminine response to wonderful news, which men seem not to make or to be able to understand. I was told that preliminary correspondence had already been undertaken and that now it only remained for me to confirm when I would arrive in the European city where this operation to transform me into a full-fledged woman would be performed. (I will not name this city, or the doctor who did my operation. They are very touchy about publicity, and I would *never* want to be the one responsible for making it more difficult than it already is for persons like myself to have an operation that is desired more than anything else in the world. Even the publicity about Christine Jorgensen, which did so much good by offering hope to so many, nonetheless had the effect that the Danish doctors refused to do any more operations on Americans—a kind of discrimination that seems to me unfair and that I have never been able to understand the reasons for.)

"I told my doctor, 'Tell them I'll be there on the first plane I can catch. There are no other preparations to make. I've had my bags packed since the day I first walked into your office'—which was only a *slight* exaggeration.

"I felt badly that, because of passport problems, I had to leave and even return to this country, after my 'transformation,' as a man—which not only hurt my pride, but also required that I cut off some of my hair and hide the rest under a hat, as best I was able. But that, in view of what the future now held for me, was a minor thing at most. Once on the plane, it is easy to imagine that my first plane crossing of the ocean did not interest me as it would have done under other circumstances. The magnificent view from the window went almost unnoticed, so absorbed was I in coming to terms with the fact that the culmination of all my fondest dreams was at hand, and that the Rey who came back from this journey would be a woman in body as well as in spirit—and, although I was scared, I never doubted for an instant that all would go well and that I would come back with 'mission accomplished' to my own complete satisfaction. I just couldn't conceive that, after all I had been through, a God of Mercy and Love would let anything go wrong now.

"I arrived at the Clinic, an attractive private hospital, spotlessly clean and extremely efficient, in the early evening. My doctor was not on hand that night, but I was expected and shown to my room—after first making a cash payment of three thousand dollars. I couldn't blame them for wanting their money in advance. As desperately as transsexuals want the operation, many, even of normally good character, would feel justified in trying to have the sex change for nothing if they didn't have the price demanded. Still, this seemed to me a very high fee, to which must be added the cost of crossing the ocean, and it is regrettable that so much money is demanded of those for whom it is very hard just to earn enough to survive, much

less save up such a sizable sum.* Those who condemn this type
of person for sometimes being a prostitute should try to understand how intense is the desire for the operation and how hard
it is for an effeminate man to get a decent job. In my own case,
I had youth, good looks, some talent as an entertainer, a fairly
stable personality, and a lot of will power all working for me.
Plenty of transsexuals have few of these assets, are unable to
save enough money, and live in utter wretchedness if they do
not commit suicide or go crazy.**

"Less than forty-eight hours after checking into the Clinic,
I was on the operating table, having first been made unconscious, of course. The last thing I remember, before the anesthetic took effect, was wanting to go through with it but still,
because of so many stories I had heard, being frightened about
the pain I would probably experience when I came back to
consciousness. This was supposed to be excruciating. I also remember taking my male organs in my hand one last time and
bidding them a not very fond farewell. How hateful those
appendages had been to me for so many years, and now I was

* The cost of a "sex change" operation varies greatly, from
place to place, time to time, and surgeon to surgeon. This operation, to my knowledge, has been performed in most countries of
Western Europe, in the Soviet Union, North Africa, Mexico, the
United States, Japan, and elsewhere. In instances with which I am
familiar, fees have ranged from one thousand to ten thousand dollars, exclusive of certain cases where no charge has been made.
Unfortunately, the fee very often seems to go up substantially and
at regular intervals once the reputation of the surgeon is established.

** In fact, it would seem that very few transsexuals require
hospitalization for mental or emotional disturbances. This is surprising, considering the stresses to which they are subjected. Some
psychiatrists, often without ever having seen such a patient, consider *all* transsexuals to be psychotic—i.e., the transsexualism *is* the
psychosis—but psychiatrists who have studied a number of such
individuals do not agree. It seems significant that once the body has
been brought into harmony with the psychology—once the "sex
change" operation has been performed—many or most of the previously existing symptoms (anxiety, depression, "dual personality,"
etc.) disappear.

seeing them for the last time. If nature could only have spared me these, I thought, and made a few other changes when I was being put together, I might have had a totally different kind of life than I had had.

"I had expected, when I awakened, that however bad the pain was I would feel a great sense of triumph and fulfillment. But when I *did* come to, I felt very little but befuddlement and could not, at first, figure out where I was. The nurse came in, my mind began to clear, and I started asking if anything had gone wrong. Then I noticed that I didn't feel a thing, and got the crazy idea that they had decided not to operate after all. To make matters worse, the nurse didn't speak English, but I guess my behavior made her think I must be in great pain, because she left and at once returned with another, English-speaking woman. They soon reassured me, showed me my bandages—which was all there was to see at that point—and informed me my operation had come off perfectly. I am not sure, but it seems to me they gave me a sleeping pill or something, because the next thing I knew it was daylight outside and I must have slept quite a few hours.

"It was almost a week before I saw the results of the surgery—not too pretty a sight, actually, since, as I had been warned it would be, it was inflamed and resembled a chunk of raw meat. While I couldn't bring myself to see it as beautiful, I did experience a happiness so great as to be almost like a state of ecstacy. This, as I think about it, will probably sound peculiar, if not comical, to some people who read it. I think only another person like myself could fully understand.

"While, in the period after surgery, there was pain, it at no time was nearly as bad as the pain I had expected and heard about. Neither was the vagina's dilation, which came later, as painful as expected although it definitely was worse than any pain associated with the surgery. Actually, especially at the beginning, some of the worst pain came when I had to urinate.

"Now, I wonder if many sex changes have not greatly exaggerated the pain connected with this operation, to get more sympathy for themselves and, in some cases, to scare off other people, since you will find quite a few transsexuals who resent it whenever anyone else has The Operation and who will go to some lengths to try to discourage others from having it.*

"I naturally cannot describe in a scientific way the details of my surgery. However, I do know that the interior of the vagina was lined with skin taken from my penis, while the labia (lips of the vagina) were made from the skin of my scrotum. I have since been examined by a doctor (gynecologist) who found nothing unusual about my genitalia, and who expressed himself as completely amazed when I told him that I had once been a man and that my female organs were wholly the product of surgery.

*   *   *

"I left the Clinic slightly less than three weeks after completion of my operation. I was *very* eager to leave there as soon as possible and take up life as a *real woman,* but stayed the full time recommended since I knew that some serious problems have arisen among those who left too soon and then developed infections, hemorrhages, etc. Having waited almost thirty years to be a woman, I felt I could certainly wait a few more days if that would reduce the chances of anything going wrong. When I did leave, I spent another full week in Germany, in a city where there was a doctor prepared to treat me in event of any emergency. There was none, and my visits to him were routine and as a precaution.

"Then—home at last! And no sooner did I reach my apartment than, one by one, I dropped every last item of men's apparel down the incinerator. When it was all gone, I felt that there remained no trace of that poor, unhappy, no-sexed being I had been for so long. Now, there was only Rey, and the rest of *her* life would consist only of those problems that are normal for normal human beings! (A feeling that was a bit premature as it turned out. There still remained the matter of *legally* changing my sex, but that, too, has now been accomplished.)

* It would seem that the amount of pain experienced varies greatly from one case to the next, some persons having little or no pain at all, others experiencing real agony. These variations may occur among patients who have been operated on by the same surgeon using the same techniques and method.

"It is true that it has been necessary to continue with the female hormones, but that no longer seems to me to signify any link with the past. Many women have to take medicines of all sorts, and that is the way I look at it.

"After the operation these hormones continue to work to make the body increasingly more feminine, giving some 'padding' to the hips, helping the breasts to grow, and so on. In fact, some transsexuals take 'the pill'—Enovid, or some similar preparation, which other women take to avoid becoming pregnant. So, we are only part of a great army of females who may be receiving the very same chemical concoctions.

"About my sex life, like probably everyone who has had such an operation, I naturally wanted to have sexual intercourse, not only in a normal male–female relationship, but to satisfy myself that I would be able to have such relations and that I would be able to reach an orgasm. First of all, and as soon as my vagina was ready for such activities, I tried bringing on the orgasm by masturbation. This included stimulating both the inside of the vagina and the area around the entrance, and stimulating both simultaneously. No luck. I asked some other sex changes about this and they said that sometimes you have to wait six months or so for the first orgasm in coitus and a somewhat lesser time usually for the first orgasm by masturbation. So I wasn't too alarmed. As it happened, it was several months before I could masturbate to orgasm, and almost nine months before I could have one, and then only once in each four or five times, in normal sex relations. The orgasm still is quicker and more frequent in my case when the man performs cunnilingus, bringing me to my climax by that means or bringing me close to it and then penetrating my vagina to finish the process. I think this is probably pretty average, except that most sex changes I know claim to have an orgasm once for every two or three acts of sexual intercourse, which probably is more often than the average woman-from-birth has a climax. As for my reaching orgasm more quickly and frequently when the man performs cunnilingus, I think this would also be true of most women and is due to the physical stimulation provided by that means.

"I 'lost my cherry' to a fellow I met at a party and to whom I was very, very much attracted, as he was to me. It hurt like hell and he was thoroughly convinced I was a virgin, so much did I carry on about the way it was hurting. I had sex with him regularly for about a month after that and it got progressively less painful. However, there was not much physical pleasure, although mentally and emotionally it meant an awful lot to me to be having relations with a normal man who was convinced that I was a real woman. Unfortunately, a 'friend' of mine told him the facts about me and that was that. I was sorry, but didn't take it too hard, since I was convinced that after so many failures I had an emotional block that would keep me from ever having an orgasm with this particular man.

"Although I had promised myself I would not, I wasn't back in the city very long before I was seeing several other sex changes and also some other transsexuals who were planning to have the operation. I also, being somewhat lonely, visited various impersonators with whom I had been friendly in the past. I had planned to completely break away from the old life, which meant from everyone who knew about my past, but that wasn't so easy as I had expected. I found a fairly good job as a kind of girl-of-all-trades in an office, but there was no one there with whom I wanted to be really friendly. And, as I got more lonely, I called up people I knew and soon was seeing quite a bit of the old crowd.

"This was a mistake, and the sex change should definitely try to make a new life away from all former associations. Especially, she should do this if she plans to try to get married and lead a normal life. I say this because there always will be someone to tell about your past, and there will be others who, in one way or another, are going to try to get you into trouble or exploit you. I have learned these things to my sorrow and I know some other transsexuals who have learned it to theirs.

"I don't want to try to alibi my own weakness, but I think I would not have become involved again in prostitution if I hadn't had old friends to talk me into it. But I did work as a call girl for a while, about six months in all, and made a lot of money which afterwards did not give me much satisfaction, just a little in knowing that men were willing to pay me *as a woman* for the pleasure of getting into bed with me. Perhaps if I had been able to reach orgasm, I would not have done this. But I was feeling desperate and wanted to keep on trying out new men until I was sure that the fault was with me and not with my lovers. I had some real doubts about this, since so many of the men turned out to be deviates, or finished almost before they got started, or in some other way were pretty lousy lovers. At my office I heard talk among the other women that convinced me that my sad experiences along this line were by no means unusual. I can't of course say how it has been in the past, yet I find it hard to believe that ever before have there been so many men who are impotent or almost so.

"So far as I know, no man with whom I have had intercourse has ever doubted that he was having it with a genuine woman. Some sex changes have a problem where vaginal lubrication is concerned, but I have had little difficulty of this type. Some saliva at the opening is usually quite sufficient. However, I am always a little uneasy that a man will notice some difference. Because of this, at the time of penetration, I see to it that his attention is partly distracted, urging him to kiss me, fondle my breasts, etc. An extremely large (in circumference) penis gives trouble, and twice it has been impossible to work it into me without the pain being excessive. But a penis of ordinary size gives no trouble.

"I know, and know of, sex changes who only can handle rather small male organs—and others who claim to be able to take care of one of any size. I also know, or know of, sex changes who claim to have orgasms every time they have intercourse, and some who claim to have two or three, or even five or six orgasms, one right after the other—and some who have never had an orgasm, except by masturbation. As stated, I believe my own case is more typical, although my frequency may be a little low, and I am suspicious about the honesty of those who say they have all those orgasms or who say that they have them every time. Maybe so, but I do know for certain that some of these people are inclined to do a lot of boasting.

"I, and others like me, have had the unhappy experience

that those who know about our past, and who still find us sexually attractive, are likely to turn out to have some sexual problem of their own, most likely homosexuality or transvestism or
both, although it may take weeks or even months for this to
come out. Since every sex change I know dislikes perverts (a
few old friends possibly excepted), and wants above all to have
a normal man for a husband or lover, this can be tragic. The
only good marriages of sex-changed persons I know about are
ones where the husband has no knowledge that his wife was
ever anything else than the woman she now is. I have heard of
exceptions—cases where a couple were long-time lovers before
the one had the operation—but I am familiar wtih no cases of
this personally.

"As my vagina became more sensitive, so I was able to have
strong pleasure sensations and reach the orgasm, intercourse
with men I cared nothing about became more and more repulsive to me, until I gave up all activities as a call girl. It now
has been almost a year since I have been involved in any form
of prostitution and it is my intention not to become involved
in it again. I would like to say that it is out of the question that
I would ever do it again. That is what I believe to be the truth,
but my past performances would not make this believable and
I will have to earn the right to make such a statement.

"Since giving up all work as a call girl, I have not been
without sex, but neither have I been promiscuous or carried on
relationships with more than one man at a time. I have had, in
the last year, six lovers, one for four months, one for three
months, and the others for shorter periods. All of them have
been men I liked and found physically attractive and would
have considered marrying, at least at the start of the relationship. One of these men I fell head over heels in love with, so
much so that I evidently frightened him away. It takes time to
learn how to play the man–woman courtship game according
to the accepted rules as the average girl learns them as she goes
along. I am having to take the short, condensed course.

"My greatest desire now is to find a strong, normal man
who will love me and whom I will be able to love in return,
and to marry him. I am very positive I then will be able to re-

main completely faithful. If it is possible for us to adopt a child, as one or two sex changes have done, then that would be perfect and I'm sure I would make an excellent mother. Some persons will shudder at the idea of someone like me adopting a child—but I doubt that there are very many women around for whom motherhood would be more of a fulfillment as a woman than it would be for me. I know I would make a good job of it.

"Sex changes believe, and I think it is probably true, that they are able to give more sexual pleasure to a man than other women are able to give. This is because, having been men themselves, at least anatomically, they know just what to do to give a man the most stimulation. Probably this is not an absolute rule, but I know that men have marveled at my skill in doing just the right thing at the right time and have said that I give them more sensation than any woman ever gave them before.

"My own orgasms, while not getting more numerous, are definitely getting more intense as time goes by. I think that, as has been suggested to me, my body is continually 'learning' to respond in this new way. If it gets much better I don't know how I'll stand it—but I am willing to try.

"The foregoing is the story of my sex change, at your request emphasizing the sexual activities of myself and other transsexuals both before and ofter the operation. I don't think anyone has written about these things before. As with what I told about female impersonators, some of those involved may not like it. But I know how interested I would have been in years gone by to have exactly this kind of information and how important it would have been to me both as an encouragement and as a means of avoiding some of the pitfalls I have fallen into. So far as I know, I have read every autobiography that has been written by a sex change, and by now there are quite a few of them. But, not one has answered these paramount questions about the actual sex relations and behavior and some of the problems that can be encountered. And, if transsexuals themselves are ignorant in many of these matters, how much more ignorant is the average doctor when a case of this kind comes to him and he has no place to turn for information to help him understand his patient. Thus what I have revealed should be useful to professional persons as well as to those of my own kind.

"I am always asked, by persons who plan to have a sex change operation, or who are weighing the possibilities, 'What does it feel like to have relations as a normal woman?' This is the question they most want to hear answered—and I don't suppose there *is* any way to answer it to their satisfaction. All I can say is that, so far as I am concerned, I feel exactly what any other woman would feel. I have talked with other women about their feelings, and what they say does not lead me to believe that their minds, their emotions, or their bodies respond any differently in sexual intercourse than mine. Of course, every individual is different and has her own different responses. But I don't think that mine are any different from those of other women generally, though of course differing in an individual way from the ones of particular women. The best thing I can say about this is what I have said before, that no man has *ever* when with me, doubted that he was with a normal woman.

"Only one thing more. Everyone wants to know if I have ever regretted having this operation. The answer is 'no.' Some of those who are considering sex change for themselves especially want to know, 'Do you ever wish you had your penis back?' For me, the answer to that one, too, is definitely 'no.' And I wonder if anyone, considering the operation, who has to seriously ask such a question, is really the proper person to part with that organ? The step is a very, very final one.

"So now I will end this sometimes painful reliving of portions of my old life—a life that often seems to me, when I look back on it, as if it belonged to someone else. As you know, if left to tell it myself, without those frequent reminders—'Be factual, be objective, don't tell it like you were creating a soap opera'—I would have come up with something a lot more sentimental and flowery, more pleasant to read, a nicer image of myself, but certainly less honest than this has been.

"In trying to achieve a high degree of objectivity, and not

to avoid the more unpleasant facts, I hope that I have not been *too* harsh on anyone, including myself, since that would be equally a distortion. I suppose I wish that this could have been a beautiful story, a lovely fairy tale, a kind of offbeat, but never ugly, version of *Cinderella*. But facts are facts, and it can never have been quite that. Yet, for me, in a sense it is that, and someday it may be that I can tell it that way, recreating all the beauty and wonder I do feel when I think about my new life and of the most important—the Supreme—fact of all: That now *I am a woman!*"

COMMENTS

That transsexuals, after "sex change" surgery, tend not to be chaste while awaiting marriage, and sometimes pursue careers as prostitutes, distresses some persons. However, that distress is not so well-founded as it might at first appear to be, even to the most rigorous moralists.

For one thing, the same transsexual individual will rarely have been chaste, and quite likely was a prostitute, before the operation. His morals, then, can hardly be supposed to have deteriorated; and, what is important is the fact that after the operation the sexual activity is much less damaging to the person than before because it is felt to be more "normal." Or it is not damaging at all. Also, subsequent to the "sex conversion," the high level of sex contact frequency is likely to decline after a few months or a year or two.

Just after operation, the person is strongly motivated to seek frequent repetition of an experience that has been for so long desired with great intensity. Novelty is a significant factor, and as this wears away with experience the frequency of the sex contacts tends to diminish. Further, just after operation, prostitution *as a woman* appears to satisfy profound psychological cravings. That the male customer is willing to pay money for the sexual experience indicates that he places value on the transsexual's femaleness and accepts it as authentic—for the transsexual a quite different experience from the preoperation prostitution when either the client was a deviate or the transsexual was "sailing under false colors." In most cases, prostitution is a phase that is passed through and then abandoned unless economic necessity should require that it be continued.

In general, then, and possibly excepting the immediate postoperative period, it can be said that the transsexual is likely to have sexual intercourse with fewer persons after than before the surgery. He is less likely to be promiscuous and is better able to enter into and sustain relationships of some duration. This is one aspect of an overall improvement of the subjective state and social adjustment that usually follows "change of sex" in the case of the true transsexual.

Statement from a
Syrian Transsexual

Finally, and to complete this gallery of sex-driven people, it should be of interest to consider the autobiographical statement of a self-diagnosed transsexual who is a product of a quite different and more permissive culture than our own—the Syrian.

Throughout much of the Middle and Far East the homosexual transvestite and the (presumed) transsexual have, since time immemorial, enjoyed a degree of tolerance and even acceptance rarely ever accorded their counterparts in the West. With occasional exceptions—Pakistan, for instance, has prohibited transvestism—this remains the case today. Thus, such individuals not only may escape in large measure the disapproval of a hostile society, they may even be esteemed and granted special privileges, as still happens in various localities in India.

The autobiographical narrative to follow is that of a Syrian male, twenty-one years of age, who is almost certainly a transsexual. So far as may be determined from his statement, he has minimal guilt and inferiority feelings because of his unusual condition. However, that he is a "sex-driven" person should be evident from the information he supplies.

"Since my birth," this individual writes, "I suffer from a defect in my genitals. My right testicle remained undescended while my left one is missing. On reaching the puberty, a treatment failed to have it descended. Due to this mentioned defect, my penis, which is too small, is atrophied and never erects. Contact with women is impossible. After masturbation, without erection, my semen showed upon analysis a complete absence of living sperms and considerable quantity of estrogenic substances, this also being found in my specimen of urine.

"As a result of the above facts, at age fifteen, regular female breasts started to grow on my chest and continued growing until they had a very well developed size as normal as in any young girl.* Erectible nipples completed the feminine form of my breasts. All the characteristics of my body turned towards the female. Now, when I am age twenty-one, I am still beardless and with a high pitched voice and feeble constructions. I am a false man in a woman's body by all means.

"I am considered too pretty and attractive, however with a feminine kind of beautifulness, and I am long obliged to use breast supports and double breasted jackets. I am constantly pursued by active homosexuals who offer their advances against my submitting to sexual contacts by anus. This has been true since as long as I remember.**

"As I live alone in my apartment and from the money I inherited from my dead parents, since five years ago I acquired the habit of submitting to sexual contacts by anus with part-

* Enlarged breasts in a male—gynecomastia—most often results from glandular imbalance, but sometimes may be symptomatic of cancer, liver disease, and other disorders. Enlargement of the breasts is fairly common among eunuchs. It may be produced artificially, as was done in the preceding case, by means of estrogen (female hormone) administration.

** Unfortunately, the medical findings with regard to this individual are not obtainable and we have only what he tells us. However, there seems to be no chance at all that this is a female who has been mistaken for a male because of genital deformities. Evidently such endocrine and other disorders as exist have feminized the body and, as a consequence, the psyche. About the childhood, nothing is available.

ners who come to my apartment. I derive great pleasure from such contacts, which are the only kind possible to me, and I submit as any woman submits to her husband.

"Some of my active partners suggested to me that I dress as a woman for them in my apartment, and I did and it succeeded when I put a wig on my head after applying all kinds of cosmetics. Nobody could believe it that he is in front of a man. I appeared as a perfect girl, attractive and pretty with perfect feminine lines and body. On such occasions I pose as a woman in the bed, the only difference being that the contact is made through the anus, instead of through a vagina, while the sensation of pleasure derived is the same sensation any woman derives.

"My name is Madiha. The men who profit of my services call me Miss Madiha, during the private meetings.

"There is something strange in me to all my partners. They are surprised, and sometimes they cannot believe it that such perfect female delineations might be present in a man, and most of all they admire my so fully developed breasts and nipples in a wonderful way.

"By previous appointments I submit every night to three to four partners and I am usually paid from ten to twenty Syrian pounds for an intercourse.* Some of those who come to me are permanent clients, some occasionals.

"Penetration of the penises were painful only at the beginning. But afterward, since my anus became wide enough to contain the biggest organ, it became easy and delicious at the same time. I may even say that I derive greater pleasure with bigger organs.

"In the five past years up till now I submitted to more

* This would be around $2.50 to $5.00—and the sum received is probably not so high. However, it is true that an attractive young prostitute of this type may command a higher fee than the majority of female prostitutes. Similarly, in the United States, female impersonator prostitutes often receive higher fees than do their female counterparts, certain high-priced call girls excepted. In the case of impersonators, demand exceeds supply—and fees go up accordingly.

than two hundred different men who performed more than five thousand intercourses on me. I saw all kinds of penises, small, big, wide, narrow, etc., but I never saw a penis like mine, thin as the small finger and 6 cms. (about two and one-half inches) large and never erect.

"The biggest organ I saw, though unusual, reached 25 cms. (almost ten inches) large and it was thick and hard when erect like the iron. It is so giant as the penis of a donkey.

"The owner of this penis is an electrician contractor. He is thirty-two years old, tall, brown, athletic, and muscular. He is very strong and very powerful sexually. He is rejected by most of the women because of his so big organ. He turned out to be active homosexual and made my acquaintance since eighteen months past. Since then he is a permanent client to me and visits me twice a week. In a month he performs usually about ten times intercourse with me, and I am paid monthly one hundred and twenty-five Syrian pounds (about $32.00) for my services. I accepted this reduced price from him because I derive big pleasure with his warm intercourses. He is my favorite client, and in eighteen months he performed more than two hundred sex intercourses on me.

"Since the time I knew him I became fond of his penis. Also, he is a good lover. Even rude and firm. When he undresses and I hear his deep voice giving me an order to submit, I feel completely dominated by his power, and as I dress as a female during our meetings, compared with him I see myself as a miniature, or as a doll in his big hands. My feminine body so delicate and smooth with pure feminine lines, makes a contrast with his rough hairy body, strong and muscular, and when he kisses me in foreplays I feel his beard like pins pricking my smooth face and lips.

"Before erection his penis might measure 13 cms. (slightly over five inches) and the big testicles are prominent. Then, during foreplays, his penis erects gradually and extends like a snake. The same sight of this scene always excites me so much. The first time he came to me I could not believe it that a human may own a so big organ. I thought I was dreaming. The first sexual contact with him was so painful, and in spite of my long experience my anus was left torn and bleeding. I needed some four or five meetings until I could submit to his intercourses without pain. Later on it became the most delicious, meetings with him.

"The first introduction of his glans in my anus is still somewhat painful, but after a short moment, with the slipping of his large organ into my rectum, the pain is replaced by a so great pleasure. Then, on getting full penetration, I reach the extasis. And also he is so powerful sexually that he needs some ten minutes to ejaculate. Sometimes he leaves his penis inside my rectum half an hour after ejaculation.

"The best pleasure is derived during the movements up and down before ejaculation. I feel his ejaculations like a shower inside my column. After a full penetration when his both big testicles touch my anus, I feel his glans deep in my abdomen. With the movements up and down, with my legs over his shoulders, all my entrails are affected and I feel as in a strange world full of pleasure and delightness. Even in such an exstasis my penis remains soft and flexible and is never a problem in such poses. My ejaculation consists of two or three drops of prostate liquid, after which I feel relaxed.

"Sometimes, after his erection, I take his organ with my both hands and introduce the upper part of his penis in my mouth for sucking. Even so a part of the length of his penis remains free, and once he ejaculated in my throat and I could not help without inhaling (ingesting?) part of his semen. As he plays with my breasts my nipples erect, and when he sucks them I become terribly excited and with him I use all poses and all kind imaginable of intercourses. Sometimes during my exstasis I bite his forearms or his shoulders while I am without conscience.

"Well I confess that the pleasure derived from his intercourses is impossible to describe by anyone. Oily ointments are used before penetration to make it easier.

"One year ago I went in the summer time to spend a one week vacation in a lonely retired small village in the mountains. I rented a small apartment for my sleeping, and I took enough provision with me.

"The second or third day, it happened by occasion, that a division of the Syrian Army composed of about two hundred young soldiers came to camp in a place nearby my apartment for some days. They were realizing exercises and they were commanded by one officer for training them. In a small river passing along, they were bathing and cleaning themselves in the nude.

"From the window of my apartment I was observing them and appreciating their athletic and virile bodies and organs. In that neighborhood, there were no other apartments than mine.

"The next day I went out to walk a bit after my lunch, some of the soldiers were surprised to see me alone, in such an apartment, a pretty face of the female type, and I noted they were contemplating my lines as appearing from under my dresses. Some of them whispered, admiring my features. I did not show I paid attention to them, and after a while I returned to rest in my apartment.

"On sunset, the same day, one of them came to my lighted up apartment and knocked on my door. I opened, and he was a young soldier who came to make a proposal in behalf of the men of the division. I objected at the first, but upon his insistence I agreed with one condition that all things be done quite in order and with calm. He went to report the news to his companions, and they started the play at eight P.M.

"We organized the contacts to be made by turn, one by one each will remain for ten minutes with me. Payment of five Syrian Pounds by intercourse has to be paid me by advance.

"I put on my wig, cosmetics and female garments, and we started the job. From eight P.M. to the next day eleven P.M., more than one hundred soldiers realized intercourses on me, representing half of them all. Resting was granted only for intermittent hours, after which new knockings on my door were repeated. I was exhausted and obliged to leave the place and return to my city the next day. However, the profit was over five hundred Syrian Pounds and this was, I am sure, the most exciting day of my whole life.

"From the above information I give you, you will see that I may be called homosexual, transvestite, and prostitute, all at the same time. However, all the three deviations have been acquired obligatory and for these reasons:

"First, I became a passive homosexual, because I was pursued by the active homosexuals since so far back as I remember. The reasons for this are always my female-like face and features and my body.

"Second, I became a transvestite, because some of my active partners suggested this idea to me, and it resulted a wonderful success.

"Third, I became a prostitute, since apart from the pleasure derived from doing so, I could obtain considerable profits from this job.

"By all means, I can not be otherwise, since my sexual organs are defective, and I have the overdeveloped female breasts. My so small penis never erects and is atrophied definitely.

"Also, from the constant use of my anus in intercourse, it became quite an easy habit without pain, and after the first contacts, continuous contacts during many hours with several men are possible to realize normally and without any pain. As much as one hundred different men realized on me the sexual intercourses in twenty-seven hours. Those who stayed away were only the soldiers who can not realize quick intercourses or who for special reasons did not want to perform.*

"As to my features, I have said that my age is twenty-one years. I have a weight of 136 pounds and am tall 5 feet and 6 inches. Bust is 38 inches, waist is 24 inches, and the hips 36 inches. Legs are of feminine form, round, and converging toward the knees. Small hands and feet. Muscleless smooth skin of white colour, hairless and beardless. Long neck and perfect nipples, erectible, and firm overdeveloped breasts,

---

* If we accept this story in all its details, it surely is worthy of remark that out of a group of two hundred soldiers about half would pay to have assembly line anal intercourse with an effeminate homosexual—as "Miss Madiha" would be regarded by them. True, the standards and customs of the Middle East tend to be comparatively "liberal" in such matters; but, even so, I think some suspicion of exaggeration is in order.

steady and attractive. My face is of the female type with large front, very big black eyes, smooth pretty face, nice-lined nose, white teeth, and voluptuous lips. Dressed as a man, with double-breasted jackets, I appear as a young girl who is dressed in male dresses. But in my apartment, when dressed as a female, I appear quite attractive in the dress that seems normal to my nature.

"In the two last years, as my income increased, I could buy a considerable quantity of the best luxurious female garments imported from abroad to fit my sizes. I have actually a wardrobe containing sets of the best female garments and cosmetics, including several wigs of different kinds and colours. Even nipples taps like the ones used by the dancing girls when in nude. Among the garments are bath suits, bikinis, petticoats, female trousers, blouses, nylon stockings, and the high heeled shoes. Among cosmetics are expensive perfumes, rouges, creams, remelles, manicures, pedicures and everythings.

"Also I furnished my apartment with the best quality of furnitures, and in the operation room in which I welcome my partners, there are romantic feeble lights of several colours to add attractiveness to my treasures and also to give much pleasure to my clients.

"Now, I describe for you the pictures I am sending to give you better ideas of me:*

"Picture No. 1: Dressed in nude with female trousers, high heeled pantoufle, white blouse opened on front. My breasts are prominently seen without brassieres.

---

* These six photos, which the informant next describes, are not, I suspect, authentic—although anyone who has seen photos of such transsexuals as Coccinelle (a famous "sex change") will know how difficult it can be, from a photo, to distinguish a feminized male body from a female one. However, in this case, the photos disclose a degree of breast development exceeding any I have observed even in individuals who have had both extensive hormone treatment and plastic surgery (mammaplasty). Quite possibly "Miss Madiha" is just as feminine-looking as she describes herself; but I think her wish for very large breasts—such persons are never satisfied with their breast development—may have led her to send me a set of pinup photos of some Middle Eastern actress or model.

"Picture No. 2: I am sit in the hammock completely in nude except for black gloves and nipple taps such as used by the dancing girls.

"Picture No. 3: This transparent silk blouse with supports, opened in the front, give more attraction to my breasts. It is preferred by most of my clients during the foreplays before intercourses. According to the declaration of some of them, this pose excites the most shy men and provokes passional responses in them. They say it is sexy.

"Picture No. 4: Needless to explain, it is a bikini. By pressing the breast support, all the volume of the breasts is pushed upwards, contributing so to form the best imaginable picture of my prominent breasts and to the opening between breasts. This brassiere permits an easy penetration of an erected penis between my breasts with followed ejaculation.

"Picture No. 5: This is white blouse put on my nude body. Instead of being opened in the front, it is opened on both sides. It has a waist-ribbon when tied up, and it gives to the side sight of the breast an attractive and exciting form appreciated by most of my partners.

"Picture No. 6: Now this is a complete picture of mine, to show you all of me. Here I used a wig of free (hanging) black woman hair, with elegant brassiere and petticoat of white nylon colour. My eyebrows were aligned and heavy remelles applied on my eyes. Cream and powder with rouge lipsticks were not omitted. The transformation is complete, and you may note the rubber string fixing the wig on my front. Please contemplate this figure and the breasts—not false breasts, true ones—and think a while, is it possible to have in mind the smallest doubt that the one in this picture is otherwise than an attractive girl?

"Well this is myself, in bones and flesh, Mr. ———, the prostitute, or may be the passive homosexual transvestite. At the first look is there any man in the world who does not desire such a girl to be his wife? *Wooooeee!* What a shame! May be for sexual contacts only!

"Coming back to the soldiers, one of the men, who had my address, came to visit me in my city and convinced me to

realize his suggestion. He said that his batallion is then established in J———, a place situated not many miles outside from
the city, and his regiment is composed of about five hundred
soldiers. Most of them are active homosexuals* and he relayed
to me that they sometimes pick boys from the streets for the
sexual services. Those military men have one day off in the
week, the Friday. In this day, as all are longing for sexual contacts, they seek partners anyhow. He continued, it would be a
profitable business for me if I find a small apartment in this
place near where they are and I come only one day a week, on
the Friday. He guaranteed that more than fifty men (ten per
cent) of the batallion may require my services in quick intercourses. He added he may secure ten Syrian Pounds per the
intercourse in my case, which make not less than five hundred
S.P., from eight A.M. to eight P.M. Then I am free to come
back to the city.

"I agreed and found an apartment in this lonely village
near the Camp. The apartment, though poor in its furnitures,
has the necessary bath and the furnitures are enough for what
is needed. I rented it for fifty Syrian Pounds per month, not
very expensive. By the time the soldier was telling his companions of the news, I already prepared myself to go for the
first Friday. I took with myself only the needed garments of
the feminine kind. This first Friday has been a true success.
More than sixty soldiers performed intercourses on me with a
revenue of six hundred and twenty S.P., and I returned back at
nine P.M. to the city. Since more than five months, I go every
Friday and I return with a profitable income which reaches at
this time a total of ten thousand Syrian Pounds net profit from
only what I do in this one place this one day each week. This
mean I have had by now with these soldiers more than one
thousand intercourses. The ten S.P. fee is paid by advance.

"Always Friday, by day, I have only time to clean myself
between intercourses, and I arrive home in the city by night
much exhausted and I sleep as a dead body all the night, but
the good income is the compensation.

"The fee in my city is higher, from fifteen to twenty S.P.

* Presumably: "bisexuals," not exclusive or predominant homosexuals.

according to the case, and long timed meetings are realized, while with the soldiers the quick intercourses system is followed with a decreased fee.

"Among my clients in the city, they are of all kinds and all positions in life. Professionals, commerciants, contractors, employees, owners of the private business, Cheikhs (Mahometan priests), and others.

"Among the Mahometan peoples is prevailing the active homosexuality in a way what is truly fantastic. Because they live in restriction sexually and they are not allowed to mix with women in meetings, they have to seek an outlet and find it in the active homosexuality. So the ground is favorable for those who accept to submit as passive partners. However, when the case is like mine, it is different. Not only the ground is favorable, but also it is considered as a big success, since, not only they appease their sexual appetites on me, but they find it a so big pleasure to have such a feminine body, full of perfection and without the big genitalia.

"Add to that the good character I am endowed with. I speak only occasionally, and I present the best services to my partners so they are fond of me sexually and morally.

"Also, all in my apartment is clean, organized, perfumed, and romantic. The place is quite proper, no botherings of any kind, and the contacts are made in perfect understandings.

"Though the neighborhood around may whisper from time to time something about me, the police can never do anything, since I am an adult person free to do what I like in my private apartment. Nobody can claim about I am doing harm to him in any way. The clients who come to me are always coming by their proper wish and desire and nothing seems abnormal.

"I may, if I want, leave my hair to grow long and dress as a woman, and I am sure I would appear in the streets as looking better than eighty per cent of the existing women in the city. But I do not wish to do so, because in such case there would be many pursuers who would ask for my hand in marriage, and I would be perplexed. While in my case, as things now are, since I have a female face but wear the man's dress, I am only pursued by the active homosexuals, who are always surprised when they see me in nude for the first time. It is something unusual and exciting for these partners, and it is so for me too.

"When I go on Friday to the apartment near the batallion of the Army, the soldiers arrange it to come by groups varying in number from eight to twelve, and they wait in the waiting room which is situated next to the operation room, and they enter to my bedroom by turn one after the other. A group of ten soldiers would finish the job in a couple of hours.

"I am usually receiving from five to six of these groups on Friday and I request any partner in advance of the intercourse to clean his organ well in my bathroom, as I clean myself too. By all means the question of cleaning my rectum before such meetings is technically done and with the benefit of experience. Also, I clean in the morning all the tracts with an enema and I apply special ointments inside to prevent against infections. Also, vaseline on my anus before penetration.

"For the clients who suffer from too quick ejaculation, I have on the table always available an anesthetic ointment which would be applied on the glans of the partner a few minutes before he will begin. This ointment permits a considerable delay in his ejaculation.

"In order to conserve myself in a good state, I reach the orgasm only one or two times during the night except when the clients are many, like on Friday, and when I can not control myself and in spite of my will I reach extra orgasms. However, I play the role of reaching the orgasm with every client so that I leave him fully satisfied.

"The above true story of mine I relate in order to give you better idea of the feelings of the fellows like me, enabling you to better understand the inside sensations any passive homosexual feel, or any transvestite prostitute may be feeling.

"If you have any interest in my life and story, please do not fail to write a report about my case, and thanking you for your attention,

"Yours most sincerely,
"Madiha"

COMMENTS

This individual's sexual expression is limited exclusively to prostitution contacts, so that there is no way of knowing what the frequency of outlet would be if he were not a prostitute. But probably, given an abundance of willing partners, the frequency still would be extraordinarily high.

Very rarely, among American transsexuals, does one encounter an individual whose appetite for sexual contacts approaches that of "Miss Madiha." I do know of several such persons, including one in his mid-twenties who claims to have had, over a six year period, approximately 250 prostitutional contacts and 1,750 nonprostitutional ones, with possibly 1,800 different males. I spent well over one hundred hours interviewing this particular transsexual, observed him in various situations, including his making pickups on the street, and do not doubt that the figures might be as he states them. The six year period was one in which he lived exclusively as a girl—dressing as a girl, working as a girl, etc.

This person—Leslie, as I will call him—was a seriously disturbed individual who was, however, recommended for "sex change" after psychiatric interviews. It was felt that much of the existing disturbance was very largely the product of tensions resulting from the desire to "be a woman," and that "sex conversion" would greatly improve the patient's adjustment.

Leslie has a strong sense of being sex-driven. He repeatedly emphasizes that he has extraordinarily intense sexual desires which often "completely control" his behavior. He is "ruled by" erotic desires. This, he says, has been true since his late teens.

Leslie sometimes has had relations with five or six, even nine or ten men in a single day. For a time he owned his own automobile and, dressed as a female, would cruise around the city, often in Negro and Puerto Rican districts, "looking for sex." He would pull up to a curb in a likely looking neighborhood and flirt with passing males. When a man would come over to the car and strike up a conversation, he would be told to get into the back seat of the car. Then Leslie would ask him: "Have you got something big for me?" This would be followed, if necessary, by a demand that the man show his penis. If it was not erect, he would be instructed to play with it until it became so. If the penis was small, Leslie would persuade the man to get out of the car—telling him to go around the corner and wait to be picked up, or something of the sort, giving Leslie a chance to go look for an organ more to his liking. If, however, the penis was suitably large, Leslie would get into the back seat with the man and "finish him off," or else drive to some location where the contact could take place without too much danger of interruption.

Leslie, it should be added, gives, when dressed, the appearance of being a strikingly attractive and "sexy" young woman. A brief excerpt from Leslie's case history describes a not too atypical evening in his life. He relates that:

"I was sitting in a restaurant and there was a colored man in a booth nearby. He had an erection and I could see it sticking up in his pants. I made him notice that I could see it, and I motioned for him to come over and sit by me. When he did, I played with his prick through the trousers.

"Another colored man saw me doing this and he came over and sat down on the other side of me. He had an erection, too, and it was much bigger than the first man's. He unzipped his fly and I put my hand inside and played with him. His joint was so much the bigger of the two that I lost all interest in the guy who was sitting with me first.

"I got up and motioned for this second colored man to follow me. We went into a doorway and I had him take it out. It was huge and I was terribly excited. I couldn't wait so I copped his joint (American jail slang for fellatio) right there. He wanted me to stay till he was ready to go again, but I told him I had some business to take care of.

"I'm nuts about studs with big joints, the bigger the better. And especially black ones. A big, stiff, black joint, that's what I like best of all.* I lose control when I see one. Let some guy show me a big joint, and I'm ready to go down on him.

"So, anyway, I was walking down the street, wondering if I should have stayed with the guy I just left, when I noticed another colored stud giving me the eye. I walked slow and he caught up and asked me where I was going. I told him, 'That's up to you. Have you got something big for me?' Then we went into a building and up a couple of flights of stairs. He took his joint out and it was a big one and I took care of him.**

"In these poor neighborhoods I usually take guys into buildings, and if there's a community toilet out in the hall, we go in there. If not, we get off in some fairly private place. I have done this hundreds of times and never got into any real trouble yet. I'll tell you, with somebody like me it's safer. I've got a good excuse for going down on them and not taking off my clothes, so there's not so much chance that they'll find out about me, that I'm a boy. Sometimes they want to fuck anyway, but I tell them: 'Look, friend. You're the one who's getting taken care of, not me. Either we do it my way, or not at all.' It's damned seldom they're not willing to do it my way.

"On the steps, see, its convenient. I'm standing a little

* Leslie regards Negroes as being very inferior to whites (like himself). He also dislikes Latins, Orientals, and Jews (he is half-Jewish). He consciously degrades himself by having sex relations with members of these groups, preferring Negroes because he regards the contacts with them as the most degrading of all. He also says, however, that the penis of the Negro is bigger than that of the white, and he prefers Negroes on that basis too. He phantasies going to Africa and sucking hundreds of native penises; or, after his operation, copulating with hundreds of black Africans. The psychology is further complicated by the fact that he considers Negroes to have larger penises while, for him, the larger the penis, the more masculine the man; and, the more masculine the man, the more attractive he is to Leslie.

** As is often true of the transsexual, and unlike "Miss Madiha," Leslie rarely ever reaches orgasm as a result of taking the passive role with his sex partners. In general, of course, the receptor is more likely to reach orgasm when he is penetrated anally than when penetrated orally, this apparently for strictly physiological reasons.

below the guy, you know? I don't have to bend over so far, or get down on my knees, to cop his joint.

"What do I get out of copping all these joints? You mean because I don't come when I do it, and maybe I don't get a chance to finish myself off by hand?

"Mainly, it is a sense of conquest. I prove to myself that I can get them. That I can dress as a girl, and pass as a girl, and get a man as a girl."

As concerns his self-image, Leslie remarks—in striking contrast to "Miss Madiha"—that he is "no goddamned good." He describes himself as "a lousy queer" and "a lowdown whore." He has "no personality" and is "sick, sick, sick." He cannot imagine that anyone would want to be his friend. He has "nothing to offer except sex." He is "obsessed with sex." He "can think of nothing else." He hates his mother for bringing him into the world and, when he has his operation, thinks he might "gift-wrap" his amputated genitals and "mail them to her with a sticker on the package reading, "DO NOT OPEN UNTIL CHRISTMAS!"

A Summing-up

Neither Leslie's bitterness, his hateful self-image, nor his extreme promiscuity is characteristic of the transsexual. Rather, standing in the full glare of desperation, he serves to appropriately punctuate the conclusion of this collection of mutilated lives.

When sex comes to dominate his or her life, a man or a woman is sex-driven. This ascendancy of the person's sexuality may result from an abnormal biological sex drive, from psychological craving, or from other factors. In the case of the transsexual, as noted, the life becomes sex-dominated as a consequence of the individual's feeling that his psychology and emotions are at fundamental odds with his anatomical sex. And all effeminate males and "masculine" females are likely to move in a climate of magnified sexuality for the reason that owing to their physical appearance and mannerisms other persons react to them primarily as sexual objects. The exceptionally beautiful woman also may be assigned the role of sexual object by most persons, at least of the opposite sex, so that she, too, becomes in her own mind primarily a "sexual being" and the sexuality then is magnified to the extent that in some way it comes to dominate her life.

All of these individuals live in a "world of sex" that is a constricted world, smaller and much more oppressive than the world that would be available to them were it not for the suffocating, crippling sex-drivenness.

To some extent, almost everyone is periodically sex-driven. Almost everyone knows some sexual frustration, and experiences a certain constriction or narrowing of the horizons of his or her world as the sexual goal for a time assumes paramount importance and distracts from other objectives and, very often, results in behavior detrimental to the overall aims of the person. To some extent do we all continue to be creatures of nature serving the survival and procreative instincts of the race. But if the drives (biological and/or psychological) are not too abnormal in terms of intensity, nature of fulfillment, or both, the sexual objective is achieved or temporarily put aside and the life does not come to be dominated by it. Sex-drivenness, as exemplified in this book, is thus a matter of degree and the problems of the sex-driven person differ more quantitatively than qualitatively from those of most other persons.

Because of disapproval based upon many factors—historical, religious, political, and economic, among others—and the climate of guilt and frustration this creates, sex-drivenness is more common among the sexually deviant than among those whose appetites as to object and act fall within the range of the socially sanctioned, or are much less profoundly opposed. However, as history demonstrates and as we may observe, not every deviate is powerfully sex-driven, and not every "normal" person (in the sense of object and act desired) escapes this unfortunate condition.

The sex-driven person, as portrayed in these pages, is a mental and emotional cripple and so merits our sympathy and attempts to understand his or her behavior. He or she should be helped if possible and prevented from fulfilling his or her desires if that is clearly necessary for the safety of other individuals. The criteria for such official preventive and sometimes punitive action by society should, however, be rational, soberly considered, and scientific—not emotional, or based solely on tradition, superstition, or arbitrary whim of those in authority, whether past or present.

What this book should demonstrate is that the "world of sex" wherein dwell the sex-driven people is not one to be envied and it is not one that any responsible individual would wish to glamorize or make to seem desirable. The sex-driven person's communion with the other residents of the "world of sex" is at best nothing more than a temporary vehicle for his emergence from a dark and painful singularity.

La commedia è finita.